ICES

The Penny-Ice Man

IN summer when the sun is high,
  And children's lips are parched and dry,
An ice is just the thing to try.
So this young man who comes, 'tis plain,
  From Saffron Hill or Leather Lane,
A store of pence will quickly gain.
"A lemon ice for me," says Fred;
  Cries Sue, "No, have a cream instead."
"A raspberry!" shouts Newsboy Ned.
"What fun! Although we're now in June,
  It feels"—says Ned—"this afternoon,
Like eating winter with a spoon!"

ICES

THE DEFINITIVE GUIDE

Caroline Liddell and Robin Weir

Grub Street · London

EGG WARNING

The Department of Health issued a warning that "although the risk of harm to any healthy individual is small, it is advisable for vulnerable people such as the elderly, the sick, babies and pregnant women to consume eggs which have been cooked until the white and yolk are solid."

Since *all* our custard based recipes require heating to 85°C/185°F and rapid cooling, you will be well within the limits of safety.

However, we would advise that these groups of individuals should avoid raw egg whites in sorbets. Pasteurised egg whites are a useful alternative for anyone who is concerned.

ICE CREAM FOR RE-SALE

PLEASE NOTE! If you intend to make ices wholesale or for re-sale, for consumption *off* the premises, you become a food manufacturer and there are strict regulations that control all food manufacturing premises. It is therefore essential that you register with the local Environmental Health Department.

If you are a restaurant or café and intend to make your own ices, you should discuss this with your local Environmental Health Officer, so that he is aware of this and can advise you on storage, serving etc.

Illustration on page 1: Glaces, Le Bon Genre, Paris 1827. Drawn by J. B. Isabey and engraved by Georges Jacques Gatin (1773–1831).

Published by Grub Street, The Basement
10 Chivalry Road, London SW11 1HT

First published in hardback by Hodder & Stoughton 1993

British Library Cataloguing in Publication Data
Liddell, Caroline
Ices: Definitive Guide
I. Title II. Weir, Robin
641.8

ISBN 1 898697 26 4

Designed by Behram Kapadia

Printed and bound by Biddles Ltd, Guildford and King's Lynn

Contents

For Elizabeth, Charlotte and Matthew,

and for Ed and Phil Marks, who have worked tirelessly to
promote interest in the history and origins of ice cream in
the United States.

ACKNOWLEDGEMENTS

We would particularly like to thank the following for their help in the preparation of this book.

Peter Adams, Bruce Alexander of Boult, Wade and Tennant, Gerald Aylmer (Master of St Peters Oxford), Michelle Berridale-Johnson, Adrian and Howard Binsted of Food Trade Press, Pierette Boissier of Fondation Auguste Escoffier, Dorothy Boraston, Richard Callebaut of Callebaut N.V., Judith Cheek, Trevor Chriss, Janet Clarke, Sophie Coe, Anna del Conte, Ian Cooke, A.C. Cooper Ltd., Derek Cooper, Alan Crowe, Jane and Alan Davidson, John Deith, Clarissa Dixon-Wright from Books for Cooks in London, Herb Engel, San Firlej, Lord Charles Forte, Elizabeth Gabay for helping with the history, Mary and Lee Garfield, Lisa Grief of the Ice Cream Alliance, Tom Hemming, the International Ice Cream Association (Washington D.C.), Norman Hollands, Kate and Tom Jackson, Clare Jenkins of The Milk Marketing Board, Casey Jones, Phil Keeney of Hershey Ice Cream, Heidi and Roger Lascelles for help, advice and tasting, Jacky Laugenie (Vice President Trader Vic's European Division), Leandro Leopardi, Tony Lesi from Askeys, London University and the Staff of the Science Museum Library London, Tess and Mike McKirdy of Cooks Books, Lord John Manners, Philip Marcantonio, Alan Mellis, Grace Mulligan, Professor Robert Multuf, Tony Mycock of Callibaut, Carol Norman for help in San Francisco, Brian and Pam O'Keefe, Jim Phillips, Dr George Prentice, Kay Randall from Mars Confectionery, Alan Robinson of the North West Museums Service (Blackburn), Harvey Roop, Joel Schiff, Michael Schnieder of *Chocolatier* magazine, Michael Selcott for kulfi tasting, Margaret Shaida, David Sharp from British Sugar plc., Timothy Shaw, Professor Michael Smith, Wayne Smith, Emma Stops of the Milk Marketing Board, Angela Tandy of the National Pelargonium Collection (Stratford on Avon), Peter Leoandro Tedeschi, Peter Traynor of the Prudential Corporation, Gilly and Angus Urquhart for translating Italian, Jim Valenti, Hilary and Michael Walter who let us raid their quince tree year after year, Dick Warren, Nach Waxman from Cooks Books (New York), Elizabeth, Charlotte, Matthew and Susan Weir for endless tasting, Frances Whitaker for unfailing support, Professor Roderick Whitfield of the Percival David Foundation for considerable help with Chinese translations and advice, Andrew Wilbey of Reading University for help on alcohol in ice cream and general advice, C. Anne Wilson of the Brotherton Library Leeds, Frances Wood from The British Library, Chinese Section, Delia and Michael Wynn-Jones.

We would also like to thank Jane Judd our agent, as well as all the staff at Hodder and Stoughton, particularly Eric Major, Clare Bristow, Celia Levett, Simone Mauger, Christine Medcalfe, our editor, and Behram Kapadia, the designer, for help and encouragement throughout the writing of this book.

ILLUSTRATION CREDITS

Her Majesty the Queen, The Royal Collection Windsor page 22; Brian Aldridge for the illustrations of equipment pages 38–45 and the diagrams of how to assemble ice-cream desserts page 185; Archiv fur Kunst und Geschichte page 1; Burlington Gallery, London page 101; Judith Cheek page 79; Herb Engel page 37; Mary Evans Picture Library page 2; Tom Hemming page 91; Hulton Picture Library page 134; Illustrated London News page 25; Letang page 166; Lo Ch'ing for the Yang Wanli poem on page 11; New York Historical Society pages 15–16; Punch Publications page 138; Prudential Insurance Company page 15; Schlesinger Library Harvard University page 133; The Trustees of the Wallace Collection page 23; Wayne Smith page 56; and finally the anonymous person page 181. All the other illustrations and artefacts are in the authors' collection.

RECIPE CREDITS

Chocolatier magazine page 78
Anna del Conte page 110, 147
Estate of the late Jane Grigson page 155
Natalie Hambro page 89, 163
Delia Wynn-Jones page 157

Wissenschaftliche Verlagsgruppe MBH Stuttgart, for the information on the composition of fruits page 178–179.

Preface

As a veteran cookbook reviewer and cook I have amassed, mostly by accident, a dozen books on ice cream. They nearly all serve their primary purpose of providing ingredient quantities and instructions for making ice cream but up till now the only one to have risen above the mundane is Mrs Marshall's *Fancy Ices*, published exactly ninety-nine years ago.

Mrs Marshall's book was an elegant refinement of an earlier, more down-to-earth ice cream book, and was meant to instruct the ambitious young wife made suddenly affluent by the industrial revolution. But since Mrs Marshall dealt in quarts, and used patent ice-cream churns requiring the layering of salt and ice to achieve a "sharp frost" and hours of patient hand-churning, the book is not much good for those of us with a pint-capacity electric sorbetière and half an hour to do it in.

So I picked up a proof copy of Caroline Liddell and Robin Weir's *Ices, The Definitive Guide* with hope, but not much hope, of it living up to its name. But it does. The plates of Victorian moulds and sundae cups, the reprints of early American recipes and the brief history of ice-cream production make it interesting and curious. The explanations of the chemistry and physics of ice-making are clear as a bell. But the recipes are the thing. They are written for today's cook with all mod-cons, but they are classic recipes. From parfaits as they once were in the grand hotels of 1900, to the fat-free frozen yoghurts of today, they are as they should be. No mixes, no cheating, no junk. If you want to understand the difference between a spoom, a granita or a sherbert, if you want to amaze your friends with a stunning Christmas Cake Ice Cream and Brandy Parfait Bombe, or you just want to treat the children, then this book is for you. It certainly is for me.

PRUE LEITH

A BUSY TIME FOR THE ICE CREAM MAN.

Title page from *L'Art de Bien Faire les Glaces d'Office*, Paris 1768. The first book published on water ices and ice cream.

L'Art de bien faire les Glaces

L'ART
DE BIEN FAIRE
LES GLACES D'OFFICE;
O U
LES VRAIS PRINCIPES
Pour congeler tous les Rafraîchissemens.

La maniere de préparer toutes sortes de Compositions, la façon de les faire prendre, d'en former des Fruits, Cannelons, & toutes sortes de Fromages.

Le tout expliqué avec précision selon l'usage actuel.

A V E C

UN TRAITÉ SUR LES MOUSSES,
Ouvrage très-utile à ceux qui font des Glaces ou Fromages glacés.
Orné de Gravures en taille-douce.
Par M. EMY, Officier.

Prix, 2 liv. 10 sols *broché*; 3 liv. *relié.*

A PARIS,
Chez LE CLERC, Libraire, quai des Augustins, à la Toison d'or.

M. DCC. LXVIII.
Avec Approbation & Privilege du Roi.

8

Introduction

I doubt whether the world holds for anyone a more soul-stirring surprise than the first venture into ice cream.

HEYWOOD BROWN, "Holding the Baby"
from *Seeing Things in the Night*, 1921

And so it has been for us.

It all started eight years ago when the children sneaked a very large container of ice cream into our supermarket trolley. The ingredients listed on the lid of the container were: – Skimmed milk; sugar; vegetable fat; dextrose; glucose syrup; whey solids; emulsifier (E471); stabilisers (E412, E415, E407, E410); flavour; colours (E102; E110).

Not recognising many of these ingredients, and concerned by the amount of ice cream the children were eating, we considered taking a course in food technology and chemistry. But instead, we took the soft option and bought an ice-cream machine. The accompanying leaflet gave instructions with a few recipes, but no explanations.

Unable to resist the temptation to improve on these recipes we produced our own ices; some would not freeze, some were rock-hard and other ices remained so hard that all you could do was wait for them to melt, then drink them! What were we doing wrong? Were there certain rules or limits to be observed when making ice cream? If so, where could we find out about them?

The more books we read and recipes we tried, the more it became apparent that most other writers either had little idea of what was going on or seemed content with recipes that produced what was, to us, a poor product. What was also confusing was the diversity of recipes; every book we picked up had a different version of "basic ice cream" and nothing by way of explanation. Some of the resulting ices had to be better than others, but how did you identify a good recipe? Was it possible to read an ice-cream recipe like a musical score and "know" that it was going to be an ice cream to your taste?

Antiquarian books provided a fascinating background, but no answers. Then we tried the trade textbooks, which were difficult to find and expensive to buy. Several were not in English and all required that degree in food technology and chemistry that we had baulked at some years previously. Sorting out and interpreting what was useful in these books and then bringing the theory to bear on home-made ices took a considerable amount of hard work. But, by this stage, some four years later, with an extraordinary collection of books on ices, a weird and wonderful collection of ice-cream memorabilia and nine ice-cream machines, we were completely hooked. And the quality of our ices was a revelation. The people who tasted them pressed for recipes and information and almost without noticing it we were writing a book; the sort of book we had been looking for when we started.

We have tried hard to make the physics and chemistry of ices comprehensible to the layman. This aspect of ice-cream making isn't easy but fortunately it isn't absolutely necessary because over 200 excellent and totally reliable recipes are laid out dictionary-style in this book. However, if you want to experiment with different types and combinations of ingredients, and have an average working knowledge of chemistry and maths, Chapter 9 will enable you to make any ice of your choice.

London, 1993

CHAPTER 1

The Origins and History of Ice Cream

Most books are full of myths about the history of ice cream. According to popular accounts, Marco Polo (1254–1324) saw ice creams being made during his trip to China and, on his return, introduced them to Italy. The myth continues with the Italian chefs of the young Catherine de' Medici taking this magical dish to France when she went there in 1533 to marry the Duc d'Orléans, later Henri II. The royal association continues in England with Charles I rewarding his own ice-cream maker with a lifetime pension, on condition that he did not divulge his secret recipe to anyone, thereby keeping ice cream as a royal prerogative.

That is how the story runs and runs, over and over again, and it makes interesting, entertaining reading and seems thoroughly plausible.

Unfortunately, there is no historical evidence to support any of these stories. They would appear to be purely the creation of imaginative nineteenth-century ice-cream makers and vendors. Indeed, we have found no mention of any of these stories before the nineteenth century.

More startling to us was the news that the foremost Sinologists now seriously doubt that Marco Polo got any further than Persia in his travels. Here, imprisoned, he plagiarised the diaries and notes of merchants and traders to fabricate his journeying. There are very curious omissions from his accounts that as a traveller and merchant he would have been expected to note, such as bound feet, tea-drinking and paper money. Furthermore, the arrival of such a man in China at that time must have excited considerable curiosity and yet our academic colleagues tell us they know of no written material relating to this man in any contemporary Chinese documents.

And sadly, Catherine de' Medici would have been unable to introduce ices to France, as the method of artificial freezing of water was unknown to chefs in 1533

and the principle was only just being discovered by scientists.

In a further effort to validate some small part of this history we contacted Professor Gerald Aylmer, Master of St Peter's College in Oxford and the authority on the servants of King Charles I. No trace can be found of this elusive ice-cream maker in the Public Records Office, who was known by at least ten different names during the time this myth has been in circulation.

So, having demolished the popularly held History of Ice Cream, we embarked on an odyssey to track down the real origins.

From our research the first piece of real evidence *does* originate in China. During the T'ang period (A.D. 618–907) various dairy products were made using mare's milk as well as the milk from water buffalo, cow and goat. A refreshingly cool dish, made during the hot summer months, is possibly one of the earliest iced-milk products recorded. For this dish "kumiss" (milk heated and allowed to ferment) was used, which was mixed with flour and camphor and then "refrigerated" before being served. King Tang of Shang, founder of the Dynasty, had a staff of 2,271 people attending to food and wine in his palace, among them 94 ice men.

One of the earliest pieces of documentary evidence concerning an iced dairy product (as opposed to just iced water) also comes from China, in a description of frozen milk by the Sung poet Yang Wanli (1127–1206).

> It looks so greasy but still has a crisp texture,
> It appears congealed and yet it seems to float,
> Like jade, it breaks at the bottom of the dish;
> As with snow, it melts in the light of the sun. ★

★ Translation by Roderick Whitfield, Professor of East Asian Art at the University of London and Head of the Percival David Foundation.

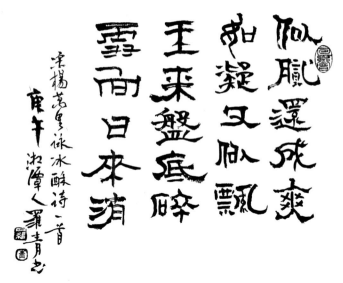

Lo Ch'ing transcription of Yang Wanli poem.

There is further evidence of an ice cream being served at the Mogul Court during the Yuan period in the fourteenth century.

Living in the age of refrigerators and freezers, we take ice and ice cream for granted, but in early times man relied on harvesting and storing natural ice during the winter months.

The place and date for the crucial discovery of the endothermic effect of salt on ice is unknown. Joseph Needham in his monumental work *Science and Civilisation in China* thinks it is unlikely that the refrigeration effect of salt solutions was a European discovery but that it reached Europe from the East via the Arabs and Moors during their time in Spain (A.D. 711–1492).

The endothermic effect appears to have been first written about in the fourth-century Indian poem *Pancatantra*: a verse says water can only become really cold if it contains salt. The evaporation of water at night in flat porous vessels set in layers of straw in shallow pits, an ancient custom in India and in Egypt, may have facilitated the discovery. However, the first known technical description of making ice comes from the great Arab historian of medicine, Ibn Abu Usaybi'a (A.D. 1230–1270) in his *Kitab Uyan al-Anba fi Tabaqat al-Atibba* (Book

of Sources of Information on the Classes of Physicians) in which he mentions making artificial snow and ice from cold water and saltpetre. Ibn Abu Usaybi'a attributes the process to an even older author, Ibn Bakhtawayhi, of whom nothing is known.

The making of ice caused great interest and many scientists and scholars, especially in Italy, continued to study the subject. The first European record of the endothermic effect was about 1530 when the Italian physician Zimara wrote his *Problemata*. In 1550, the Spanish physician in Rome, Blasius Villafranca, in his treatise, *Methodus refrigerandi ex Vocato Salenitro Vinum ac potus quovadis aliud Genus*, describes the cooling of water by the addition of saltpetre. Battista della Porta in 1589 in his *Magnus Naturalis* noted that various salts, if added to snow, could produce very low temperatures. Francis Bacon (1561–1626) gave several formulae for salt mixtures. In 1644 the Jesuit Cabeus stated that 35 parts of saltpetre added to 100 parts of water, agitated vigorously, would cause freezing. (An adequate mixture of ammonium nitrate and water gives a temperature drop from 4°C to −15°C.) Various scholars continued to investigate the making of ice following the same principles and a more scientific approach was possible after the invention of the thermometer in the eighteenth century. In *The Ice Book* (1844) by Thomas Masters details of the various mixtures of ice, acids and salts required to produce varying degrees of cold are listed in great scientific detail.

Despite knowing how to make ice artificially it was still prohibitively expensive to produce on a commercial basis, so a large amount of natural ice was still harvested every year, and stored in ice houses, carefully constructed for this precious commodity. Some were pits with a brick or stone structure at ground level, others were on the surface (see page 12). In October 1660, Walford records in *London Old and New* that an ice house was built in Upper St James's Park (now known as Green Park), for the Royal Family. Ice storage is well recorded and Robert Boyle in 1683 quotes a description given him by John Evelyn the diarist, of snow pits in Italy where beaten snow was stored.

Water ices first appeared in the early 1660s in Paris, Naples, Florence and Spain, thus putting another nail in the coffin of the mythology of Catherine de' Medici as this was over a century after her marriage. These were known as eaux glacées, acque gelate or eaux d'Italie.

In France the earliest recipe for a water ice was in Nicholas Lemery's *Recueil de Curiosité Rares et Nouvelles des Plus Admirables Effets de la Nature* published in Paris in 1674. An English translation was published in London in

---

Endothermic Effect: putting various salts on ice depresses the freezing point of the ice mixture and makes it possible to transfer the cold by conduction from the ice to elsewhere. This is the original basis of the freezing of ice cream. Putting salt on the roads in winter follows the same principle of depressing the freezing point and causing the ice to melt. For us this is where the history of ice cream truly started.

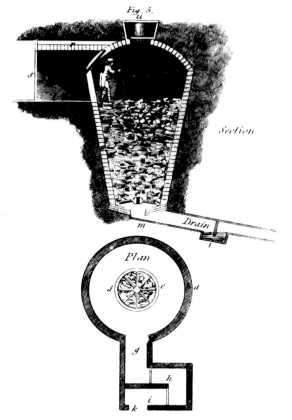

An engraving showing the construction of a 19th-century ice house. The pit could be filled either through the roof or through the double-doored lobby. Reproduced from the *Cyclopedia or Universal Dictionary of Arts, Science and Literature*, Rees, 1819.

1685 with the title *Modern Curiosities of Art and Nature*, though it was not until 1694 that a Neapolitan recipe for sorbetti appeared in Antonio Latini's *Lo Scalco alla Moderna*. Around this time moulds for ices first appeared in Naples as did ices made with a scalded and sweetened milk base. These specialities were partially frozen then transferred to fancy metal moulds for their final freezing.

The first documented reference so far discovered to ices being served in England is in a description by Elias Ashmole in *The Institution, Laws and Ceremonies of the Most Noble Order of the Garter*, published in 1672, during the reign of Charles II. Here there is a list of the food served at the Feast of St George at Windsor on 28 and 29 May 1671. The only table to be favoured with the serving of ices was the king's with "One plate of white strawberries and one plate of Ice Cream" on both the eve of the feast day and at the feast day dinner.

The next reference appears in *The London Gazette* of 20 September 1688, and tells of a banquet in Stockholm to celebrate the birth of James Francis Edward, Prince of Wales, son of James II and Queen Mary, at which iced creams were served.

The first English cookery book to appear containing a recipe for ice cream was one entitled *Mrs Mary Eales Receipts* (1718). Mrs Eales had been Confectioner to her late Majesty Queen Anne. This was written some fifty years after the first recorded serving of ice cream. Her book was reprinted in 1733 and 1744. It is worthwhile pausing to consider what these ices were like. As they had not been churned or beaten, they would have contained larger ice crystals and would have been coarser than today's ices. They were made with cream and fruit or flavourings, but no eggs.

In 1733, Vincent La Chapelle, chief cook to the Duke of Chesterfield, published *The Modern Cook* and had the strange distinction of being the only French chef of the period to publish first in England and then in France. (His book was later published in French in 1735, 1736 and, with lengthy additions, in 1742.) *The Modern Cook* is significant in the history of ice cream for its descriptions of the elegant uses of ices and decorative moulds. However, La Chapelle had plagiarised large parts of the book from François Massialot's *Le Cuisinier Royal et Bourgeois* published in 1691. In the 1742 edition of his book La Chapelle advises stirring the ice cream during freezing to reduce the size of the ice crystals and regards the omission of this in the earlier editions as a serious deficiency. He includes traditional recipes for ice cream without eggs and also, for the first time, with eggs.

The use of eggs in ice cream influences both the texture and taste. Early ice creams were literally frozen "iced cream" mixed with sugar, flavours and fruits. When eggs were added, the mixture became smoother and had a richer taste, more like a frozen custard. One of the advantages of adding eggs was that the amount of cream (a relatively expensive ingredient) could be reduced.

English ice creams of the eighteenth century followed the traditional cream method and remained basic "iced cream".

French recipes of the early eighteenth century did not call for eggs or egg yolks, but when they started to appear in France around the middle of the eighteenth century they were called "fromages glacés" and egg yolks appeared as ingredients.

Egg yolks in ice cream did not appear in England until the middle part of the eighteenth century, probably influenced by the French. La Chapelle, in the appendix on confectionery in the 1742 edition of his book, mentions "Cream-Cheese in Ice" called "fromage glacé". It contains two quarts of cream, sugar and two egg yolks

After the Meat was taken off, there was served up a very fine Defert, with many great Piramids of dry Sweet-Meats, between which were placed all fuch Fruits, Iced Creams, and fuch other Varieties as the Seafon afforded : At Dinner there were Twelve forts of Wines, and all extraordinary good in their kind. The Senators having continued at Table till near Seven a Clock, about an hour after they took their leaves, and then removed to fee the Fireworks, which were prepared upon the Water before the great Bridge, amidft the Ships, which lay there; and for a Signal at the beginning of the Firework, there were fired One and twenty great Guns. The reafon why the Fireworks could not be near his Houfe, was, that moft of the Houfes of the Town being both built of, and covered with Wood, there would have been great danger of Fire, in fo hot a Seafon of the Year; And the fame

(above) *The London Gazette* September 17 to 20, 1688.
(below) The earliest known recipe in English "To ice Cream" from Mrs Mary Eales's *Receipts*, 1718. Reproduced from the 1733 edition.

While water ices continued to remain more popular among the French and Italians, the English clearly preferred ice creams.

Hannah Glasse's *The Art of Cookery Made Plain and Easy*, first published in 1747, does not mention ice cream until the 1751 edition. The late Bill Stallings (in *Petits Propos Culinaires No 3*, Prospect Books) questioned if she ever made ice cream herself when she wrote this or was just reporting what she had either seen or been told, due to the cursory nature of her description of the process. Despite being frequently quoted as an authority by future writers, her recipe is so brief and not entirely accurate that the resulting ice cream would have turned out unevenly frozen and icy, if made according to her instructions.

To make SEGO-CREAM.

TAKE two Spoonfuls of Sego, boil it in two Waters, ftraining the Water from it; then put to it half a Pint of Milk, boil it 'till 'tis very tender, and the Milk wafted; then put to it a Pint of Cream, a Blade of Mace, a little Piece of Lemmon-Peel, and two Eggs, (the White of but one) fweeten and boil it 'till it is thick.

To ice CREAM.

TAKE Tin Ice-Pots, fill them with any Sort of Cream you like, either plain or fweeten'd, or Fruit in it; fhut your Pots very clofe; to fix Pots you muft allow eighteen or twenty Pound of Ice, breaking the Ice very fmall; there will be fome great Pieces, which lay at the Bottom and Top: You muft have a Pail, and lay fome Straw at the Bottom; then lay in your Ice, and put in amongft it a Pound of Bay-Salt; fet in your Pots of Cream, and lay Ice and Salt between every Pot, that they may not touch; but the Ice muft lie round them on every Side; lay a good deal of Ice on the Top, cover the Pail with Straw, fet it in a Cellar where no Sun or Light comes, it will be froze in four Hours, but it may ftand longer; than take it out juft as you ufe it; hold it in your Hand and it will flip out. When you wou'd freeze any Sort of Fruit, either Cherries, Rafberries, Currants, or Strawberries, fill your Tin-Pots with the Fruit, but as hollow as you can; put to them Lemmonade, made with Spring-Water and Lemmon-Juice fweeten'd; put enough in the Pots to make the Fruit hang together, and put them in Ice as you do Cream.

To make HARTSHORN-FLUMMERY.

TAKE half a Pound of Hartfhorn, boil it in four Quarts of Water till it comes to one, or lefs; let it ftand all Night; then beat and blanch a Quarter of a Pound of Almonds,

with added flavours. In the cookbook proper a recipe for "Cream with ice for Custards" (Tourte à la glace) contains a spoonful of flour, six egg yolks, *some* cream or milk, salt and sugar. Beaten egg whites are added later, making this a more sophisticated recipe.

Moulds for fromage glacé are shown in Gillieres' book of 1751 and Emy (1768). The name could have originated from these cheese-wedge shapes, alternatively it could have been used because of the cream-cheese-like appearance of the ice cream, in contrast with water ices.

Filippo Baldini's *De' Sorbetti*, published in Naples in 1784, was probably the first book dedicated to water ices (see page 48).

Due to both the cost and availability of ice and ingredients, ices remained restricted to wealthy households until the second half of the nineteenth century. In England in 1843, Thomas Masters invented a machine that not only froze the ice cream mixture but also whipped it at the same time and which he describes in *The Ice Book* (1844), the first English book devoted entirely to ice creams and water ices. This book promoted the sales of his machines which were then being produced in a range of sizes and were suitable for manufacturers and large households.

During the second half of the nineteenth century Italy went through tremendous political turmoil as Garibaldi

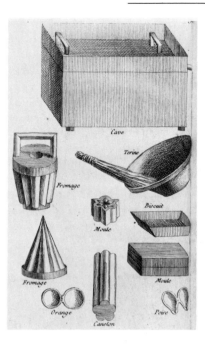

(above) Ice-making equipment.

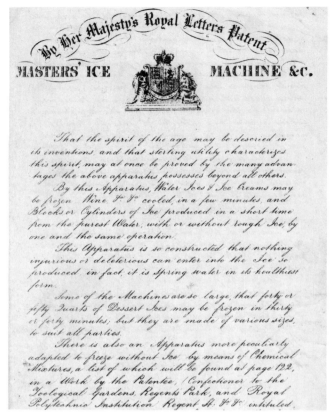

(right) A leaflet describing the machines Masters made. Note that they could achieve freezing conditions either with ice and salt or with chemicals alone which was a considerable advantage in hot climates or when ice was not available.

fought for unification, and the subsequent economic upheaval added uncertainty to poverty. Young Italian immigrants, mainly from Lombardia, Emilia, Toscana and Campania, with their traditions of ice-cream making, made their way from Italy to England, usually on foot, in search of work. Their long march must have taken several months before they arrived at an English port where they wasted no time in setting up in business as ice-cream makers or vendors. When the saturation point for sales was reached in the ports, they moved to other major cities and formed communities in Birmingham, Manchester and Leeds, where even today third and fourth generation Italians work in the ice-cream business. P. Michaels in his book, *Ices and Soda Fountain Drinks* (Maclaren, c. 1910), describes the plight of the "Hokey Pokey" sellers who were mainly unfortunate children who had been persuaded to leave Italy in search of work.

Huddled together, mostly in the poorer quarters of town, where lodgings were cheap and sanitary conditions overlooked, they led a life of a miserly motley variety, overcrowded in sleep and work, more than ill-treated, and forced to make long

journeys to get ice and salt cheap in the early hours of the morning. Then made to freeze the ice cream under revolting sanitary conditions, either in badly ventilated sheds or, as in the Italian quarter in London, on the pavements themselves and then drag their heavy barrows, on a semi-empty stomach, to distant pitches in the town where the boys and hooligans of the neighbourhood annoyed them, broke their glasses, threw dirty matter in their freezers and sent them home in tears without money. Was there any sympathy when they reached "home"? Nothing except curses and blows for the small takings. But one day a maddened "garzone" stabbed his bullying "padrone" with his ice pick and left him dead, lying across a tub.

This episode gained widespread publicity and fortunately started an improvement in the system of making and selling ice cream, but it took a very long time to lose its reputation not only for exploiting young Italian children but also for poor sanitary conditions.

At that stage America also followed the English taste for iced creams as opposed to the water ices. So much ice cream is consumed today in America that it has become

one of the national dishes along with apple pie and hamburgers. Many Americans even consider ice cream to be an American invention.

The first record of ice cream in America we have found is in a letter written in 1700 by William Black, a guest of Thomas Bladen, governor of Maryland, and his French wife. Black describes the dessert as being ". . . no less curious; among the Rarities of which it is composed, was some fine Ice Cream which, with the Strawberries and milk, eat most Deliciously."

By the time of the Revolution, various confectionery shops in New York offered ice cream. The first advertisement appeared on 12 May 1777 in *The New York Gazette and Weekly Mercury* for Philip Lenzi. Lenzi reputedly came from London and set up in business in Dock Street and later in Hanover Square, now renamed Stuyvesant Square.

Contact between America and France increased, following the American and French revolutions, and by the end of the eighteenth century French émigré confectioners were providing a further boost to this already

(above) Carlo Gatti, an Italian immigrant, is reputed to be the first person to sell ice cream from a shop in London. Gatti, a chocolate maker and an ice merchant, occupied this shop on the corner of Leather Lane and Holborn in 1850. The site is now owned by the Prudential Insurance Company.

(below) Earliest advertisement for ice cream featured in *New York Gazette* and *Weekly Mercury* 12 May 1777.

PHILIP LENZI.
Confectioner from London,
Having removed from Dock-street to Hanover-Square, No. 517.

TAKES this method to return his sincere thanks to all his friends and customers for their past favours, and hopes for a continuance; and will have in this present season, a very great variety of the best sweetmeats; preserves marmalades, jellies, &c. in brandy, at very reasonable rate as the times will permit, for ready money only; and every thing of the said branch will be executed to all perfection as in the first shops in London.

Said Lenzi will, in the ensuing season, give a very good price for the very best sort of fruit, such as strawberries, gooseberries, cherries, rasberries, peaches, pine apples, green gages, apricots, &c. &c.

May be had almost every day, ice cream; likewise ice for refreshing wine, &c.

N. B. Wanted to the said business, an apprentice.— Premium is expected.

popular confection by selling ice cream in Philadelphia and New York. Their ice-cream houses sold ice cream by the quart or by the glass to be eaten on the spot. In 1795 Joseph Corre had an ice-cream house at 8th and Market, in Philadelphia, where he sold ice cream "at the modest price of eleven pennies per glass", which despite such proclamations, was in reality not cheap. A certain M. Bosse ran two houses – one in Philadelphia and one in Germantown in Pennsylvania – where he served ice cream in quarts along with syrups, French cordials, cakes, clarets, and jellies. M. Collot sold ice creams and iced cheeses "in all the perfection of the true Italian mode", which M. Moreau de St Méry, a French traveller, declared "would bear comparison with that of the cellar of the Palais Royal in Paris". These French confectioners did not just serve ice cream to be consumed on the premises, they also catered for social occasions.

Pleasure parks, similar to the Vauxhall and Ranelagh Gardens in London, were also created at the end of the eighteenth century. Grays Ferry in Philadelphia and Columbia Gardens in New York were just two amongst several pleasure gardens. Genteel ladies would stroll down on a summer evening to eat ices; as Eliza Boune, who was visiting New York in 1803, wrote to her friend Octavia Southgate: "In the cool of the evening we walk down to the Battery and go into the garden, sit half an hour, eat ice cream, drink lemonade, hear fine music, see a variety of people, and return happy and refreshed."

In the early 1800s ice farming and the distribution of ice

Street ice-cream seller from *The Cries of New York*, by Frances Osgood. Published by John Doggett, 1846. Note the freezer pot in the wooden bucket.

(previously only available from local sources) became important. Ice was cut and stored in ice houses for use during the summer. It was shipped down the eastern seaboard from Boston as far south as Miami, which made possible the spread of ice cream to states which had no natural ice. Until this time ice cream was made in pot freezers (see below); the mixture was beaten in a pewter pot whilst being shaken up and down in a mixture of salt water and ice in a wooden bucket. In 1846, Nancy Johnson, the wife of a U.S. naval officer, revolutionised ice-cream making by inventing a small hand-cranked ice-cream freezer, which agitated the ice cream by means of a slowly turning dasher. Her machine was similar to the hand-cranked ice-cream makers still in production today. Her invention was patented by W. G. Young on 30 May 1848.

In the 1840s ice cream became more popular and street selling increased. Sadly, the usual cycle became apparent; mechanised production introduced to meet the increasing demand certainly reduced the price but inevitably affected the quality.

In 1851, Jacob Fussell Jr, an enterprising milk dealer, established, at 180 Exeter Street, Baltimore, the first commercial ice-cream factory in America. Realising that there was an annual surfeit of cream in his dairy business during the summer months, Fussell hit on the idea of making ice cream. As a milk dealer, he had a great advantage over the confectioners in the making of ice cream and was able to undercut them by selling outside their price-fixing cartel, at about 25 cents as opposed to the confectioners' 60 cents per quart. Quickly finding ice cream more profitable than dealing in milk, he opened a series of factories in Washington D.C. (1856), Boston (1862) and New York (1864). However, he fell foul of the Associated Confectioners of New York who demanded that he sold ice cream at the exorbitant price of $1.25 per quart which he refused to do. Fussell was a hard-headed businessman with good contacts (he was a friend of Lincoln's), a fanatical abolitionist and a frugal, hard-working Quaker. Undaunted by the antagonism he aroused, he moved his business to Boston after being almost lynched in Baltimore by rival ice-cream makers. New Yorkers loved Fussell's ices which he sold at a price that the masses could afford. Fussell, more than anyone else, was responsible for starting the Americans' love affair with ice cream. In 1869 he took in partners, one of whom, James Horton, ultimately took over the business in 1874. Renamed the Horton Company, it continued as such until 1928 when it became a subsidiary of the Borden Company which is still in existence.

After Fussell's success, others tried to follow in his

Jacob Fussell Junior, father of the American wholesale ice-cream industry.

footsteps. Such a man was an adventurer called Risley who in 1864, only eleven years after Japan was opened to the West, shipped ice in from China to Japan. In 1865 he shipped cows from California to Japan. The first recording of ice cream in Japan was in 1869, though it was not until 1921 that ice cream was manufactured there commercially.

In 1888, the first refrigerated railway truck increased internal distribution around the States and helped to continue the spread of ice cream. Mechanical refrigeration took over from ice and salts in the ice-cream industry in 1902. This meant that companies were no longer controlled by fluctuations in the price of salt, or ice famines following warm winters.

By the early 1900s the Soda Fountain, first introduced in the 1820s and popularised in the late 1800s, had become an integral part of the ice-cream business. The soda fountain found a home in the drug store as the making of carbonated water required a chemical process and the local pharmacist was the chemist, the alchemist and the druggist. The acids and gases in drug stores made explosions in these premises a common feature. Increased availability of ice cream unfortunately went hand in hand with a decline in standards. Ice cream sold on the streets, made by unscrupulous wholesalers, often had a butterfat content as low as 2 per cent and was described by the confectioners as "cheap trash". Of doubtful origin and hygiene standards, nevertheless these ices sold in huge quantities in the summer months.

Prohibition had been slowly, but steadily, gathering momentum since the mid-nineteenth century. Ice creams were selling well in bars in hot weather and by 1919,

when the Prohibition Act came into force, major beer manufacturers, such as Anheuser-Busch, had already changed to become important ice-cream manufacturers. The Prohibition Act did more for the ice-cream industry than any other single event since the invention of the hand-cranked ice-cream maker, as all over America bars were converted into ice-cream parlours.

Up until the early 1920s ice cream was a summertime business and September/October marked the end of the season. Home freezers had not been invented and ice cream made at home was consumed within a few hours. If purchased and brought home ice cream had to be eaten before it melted. During this period, due to the competition, ice-cream makers became creative and started to produce ice cream in a variety of colours, shapes and combinations including "Eskimo Pie", "Good Humor Bar" and "Popsicle". The factory-filled paper cup was introduced by H. P. Hood of Boston in 1923 at the National Ice Cream Convention in Cleveland, and was called the "Hoodsie". It was renamed the "Dixie Cup" in 1924 (see page 27).

Increased mechanisation contained the price and increased the production between the two World Wars. It was at this time that the salt and ice era came to an end in commercial production, although they were still used for making ice cream at home. Improvements in domestic

The Kewpie doll was used to promote the ice-cream industry in the 1920s.

and commercial refrigeration made ice cream available all the year round and enabled Americans to become the largest per capita ice-cream consumers in the world. In 1923 the A&P chain of supermarkets introduced ice-cream cabinets throughout their 1,200 stores, and other grocery chains quickly followed suit.

The depression of the 1930s and the ending of Prohibition in December 1933 brought a sudden stop to the seemingly endless growth of the ice-cream industry. Which of these two factors was the worse no one will ever know, but together they were a disaster for this flourishing business. Street sellers reappeared and so did the resentment of the shopkeepers who demanded the licensing of the street peddlers. Cheap products made from inferior ingredients abounded, as did the ice-cream bootlegger selling inferior products in a known maker's cabinet. The customer, assuming that the known maker's ices had deteriorated, would switch to another brand. This practice was almost uncontrolled and was only stopped when economic conditions improved.

By the late 1930s the ice-cream industry was again buoyant. From 1937 sales started to achieve new records every year, only to level off once America joined the Second World War. During the war American servicemen used a number of interesting and ingenious ways to make ice cream. Aircrews placed an ice-cream mix in the large cans that were stored in the rear gunner's compartment in the B 29s and when the aeroplanes returned from their sorties, ice cream had been made by a combination of the vibration and the freezing temperatures of high-altitude flying.

In 1943, the U.S. Armed Forces were the world's largest ice-cream manufacturers and in 1945 the U.S. Navy produced a floating barge that was an ice-cream parlour with a manufacturing capacity of 10 gallons per second. Ice cream was not made in Britain during the war as Lord Woolton, the Food Minister, had banned the manufacture to save transport and manpower. Instead an ice cream substitute was sometimes sold under the old name of Hokey Pokey (see page 29).

In Britain the market was dominated by Walls, Lyons and Eldorado after the wartime ban on making ice cream ended. Ice-cream sales continued to grow in the 1950s and 1960s but it was not until the 1970s and 1980s that new formulations began to appear at the opposite ends of the calorie scale, with yoghurt at the low end and super premium at the top end. Since then ice-cream sales have continued to grow with more and more extravagant formulations and greater demands from the various pressure groups for low cholesterol, and from the public for quality ice cream.

Serving ice cream and the birth of the ice-cream cone

Ice creams and ices were regarded as little short of magic by diners in the seventeenth and eighteenth centuries. Ices were rare, expensive to make and had a short life; early ices were made and eaten as quickly as possible, as they could be neither properly hardened nor stored for more than a few hours. Such a unique delicacy had at first no suitable dish in which to be presented that would give it the prominence required. By 1754 a special cup for serving ice cream was available. In that year, on 23 June, Madame de Pompadour ordered "un petit plateau blanc et or, et quatre tasses pour mettre des glaces" at a cost of 60 livres from Vincennes (*Livre Journal de Lazare Duvaux*). In the following year King Louis XV ordered a dinner service which included "plateau" with five or seven "tasses à glace". These small cups, no more than 6.5 cm (2¼ inches) high, were beautifully painted and jewel-like. In *L'Art de Bien Faire* by Emy, published in 1768 (see below), he describes and illustrates "Goblets à glace", together with their "plateau", which he lists in the index as being made of glass, crystal and porcelain. These cups and goblets were in a variety of styles with no handles, one handle or two handles. In Italy they were referred to as "giarre".

The Sèvres dinner service for Catherine the Great, delivered in 1779, was for 60 settings and included 20

"Gobelets à glace", made from crystal, glass or porcelain. The forerunner of the penny lick.

A curious object which, we believe, is an English sorbet glass, *c.* 1780. It is pontilled inside and out and the sealed airspace ensures that the sorbet does not melt from the heat of the user's hand.

plateaux for 116 ice-cream cups and 10 ice-cream coolers. Their style of decoration matches the rest of the service but with the additional decoration of gilded icicles around the edge. The Louis XVI Sèvres dinner service commissioned in 1783 for use at Versailles had single-handled ice-cream cups on round platters. This set, probably the most extravagant ever produced in the Sèvres factory, was planned to take twenty-three years to finish, but was never completed. The half that was made was later acquired by the Prince of Wales (later King George IV) in 1794 and is now in the collection of Her Majesty the Queen (see pages 22 and 23).

Ices were served with a flourish of icy peaks as described by the seventeenth-century Tuscan poet, Francesco Redi, in his poem *Arianna Infirma*: "Finest frozen snow rising from the rims of the goblets in hillocks".

In the 1825 Boilly print from Paris (right) two people are shown eating their ice cream with a spoon; the third is eating straight from a glass goblet. These goblets are cone-shaped and have no handles. It was from the crystal and glass "goblets à glace" that the "penny lick" was to evolve. In 1745 the Glass Excise Tax in Britain was levied on the raw materials used in the making of glass, thus increasing the cost of the finished product. Further glass taxes were imposed throughout the century until in 1845 the Glass Excise Tax was abolished and cheaper glass products could be made.

By the second half of the nineteenth century ice-cream production had developed to such an extent that it was available on a commercial scale. At the same time improvements in manufacturing inexpensive glass containers led to the rapid success of the penny lick. In time they proved so popular and so widely available that a smaller halfpenny lick and a larger two-penny lick were created together with other styles such as the reversible halfpenny and penny licks (see page 20). The alternative method of serving ice cream was to wrap ices, cut from a brick, in paper and sell them to be taken away and eaten from the wrapper (see page 20).

Aware of the possibilities of greater profits, ice-cream sellers promoted licks in which the bowl became increasingly filled with glass to the point, in some cases, where it was almost solid. This created an optical illusion, with the glass reflecting the ice and giving the appearance of a goblet full of ice cream. A further impression of larger servings was achieved by shaping the ice cream into the traditional peak with a wooden paddle. The cost of the various licks bore no guarantee as to the quantity provided – the size of the serving depended on the generosity or otherwise of the ice-cream vendor.

"Les mangeurs de glaces" by L. Boilly, Paris 1825.

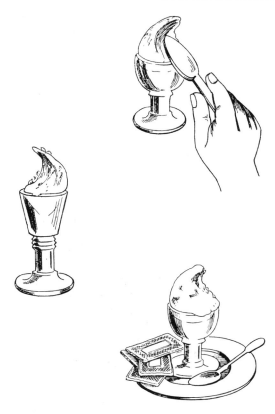

How to serve penny licks.

The ice-cream seller, often to be found at the seaside, favoured the glass licks which could be repeatedly used, frequently without being washed. They would last for years and created no litter, unlike the paper used for wrapping Hokey Pokey (see page 28). A further advantage of serving ice cream in the lick was that customers, instead of continuing their promenade along the beach, would be obliged to stand around the ice-cream seller creating a crowd, until they had finished their ice cream and returned the lick.

Licks remained popular even after the invention of the ice-cream cone. This was probably due to the cost of the cones, the inconvenience of storage and the ease with which they broke. Licks remained in widespread use until 1926 when they were finally outlawed in London for spreading diseases, particularly tuberculosis. Over the next few years bans followed in various towns throughout the country.

The origins of the ice-cream cone are full of controversy and the stories which abound have become part of ice-cream folklore. The most plausible origin for the cone was entirely evolutionary. Ice-cream manu-facturers, faced with the challenge of creating a

England could legitimately claim a first for ice cream cones as Mrs Marshall features "cornets" in her book *Fancy Ices*, 1894. Christina Cornets (above) were filled with ¾ pint of vanilla ice cream mixed with two ounces of finely diced dried fruits, cinnamon, ginger and Maraschino; the cornets were piped with royal icing and then dipped in chopped, blanched pistachio nuts and frozen. Margaret Cornets were filled with ginger water ice and apple ice cream to "serve for a dinner sweet or dessert". The implication is that they were eaten with a spoon and fork so that although they pre-date the claimed American invention, the claim may be disallowed on the grounds that they were not picked up and eaten.

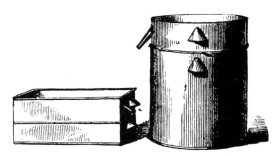

Ice Caves. All sorts of shapes were available for a variety of moulds. *Above*: early ice caves from Francatelli's Royal Confectioner, 1874.

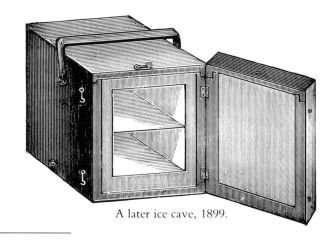

A later ice cave, 1899.

Agnes B. Marshall, a handsome woman and in our opinion a better cook than Mrs Beeton.

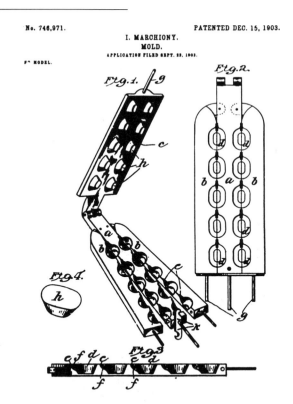

Copy of Marchioni patent, applied for on 22 September 1903.

container, at a very low cost, turned to their skills as confectioners and pâtissiers and produced biscuit, wafer and waffle cones. Italian ice-cream sellers in England and the United States may well have been inspired by the old Sicilian and Neapolitan tradition of cutting open a briosca (a type of brioche) and filling it with ice cream or granita and eating it on the way to work in the morning. (In Naples, the Gelateria della Scimmia still serves for breakfast a briosca filled with an ice that relies on cream alone for its flavour.)

The most popular story concerning the origins of the ice-cream cone follows a certain Ernest A. Hamwi, a Syrian from Damascus who came to St Louis in 1903 and obtained a concession at the 1904 World's Fair to sell zalabia, a Persian pastry baked on a waffle iron. His stall was next to an ice-cream maker who was selling his ice creams in small dishes. During the fair the ice-cream seller ran out of dishes and the enterprising Hamwi rolled his wafers into cornucopias and put a scoop of ice cream inside. The "World's Fair Cornucopia" was apparently an instant success. Another claimant is Abe Doumar who also was one of the fifty ice-cream concessionaires at the 1904 World's Fair.

On 28 April 1954, the International Association of Ice Cream Manufacturers held a special convention at the Chase Hotel, St Louis, to celebrate fifty years of the ice cream cone and its inventor, Ernest A. Hamwi. However, on 29 October 1954, the *New York Times* carried an obituary reporting the death of one Italo Marchiony, an Italian immigrant who not only claimed to have been *selling* cones in 1896, a claim that there is no evidence so far to support, but certainly had *applied* for a patent on 22 September 1903 (see patent above), well before the 1904 World's Fair. Examination of this patent shows that it was for a multiple cone-maker, making 10 cones at a time, which certainly suggests an earlier date for the invention by Marchiony. His grandson, William Marchiony, writing in 1984 in the N.I.C.R.A. *Bulletin* (National Ice Cream Retailers Association) says that Italo, who had a restaurant on Wall Street, was none too successful a restaurateur and decided to sell lemon ice, during the hot New York summers, from a cart in the street. These he served in "thick bottomed oversize whiskey shot glasses". Washing up was a problem (U.S. hygiene laws were ahead of those in Britain) and the glasses were being stolen, so he changed to paper cones which were an instant success. Next he added ice cream to the lemon (water) ice and in 1903 had the inspiration to make an edible cone. This was not a cone as we know it today but "was pre-baked dough that remained soft enough to be rolled into a cone at the time of sale". This was also a success and Italo went on further to develop the machine that would bake the cone. This was a considerable time-saver and produced a neater "package". Orders poured in for the cones, and he moved to New Jersey, disbanded his fleet of push carts and concentrated on manufacturing cones. He purposely designed a machine to manufacture cones with an overlapping seam that would look hand-rolled. Marchiony also claims his grandfather was the first person to make an ice-cream sandwich (wafer) by putting a slice of ice cream between waffle squares cut from a sheet.

The development of the cone and wafers took many directions. One of the most creative was in Scotland where they still have today a wide range of unusual ice-cream wafer shapes.

★ *Ice Cream Scoops All*, National Dairy Council leaflet, 1944
★ Elizabeth David, *Italian Food*

(right) Ice-cream container from a set made for Catherine the Great, 1779. From the Wallace Collection, London (height 20.5 cm, 8 inches).

(above) Single-handled ice-cream cup from a set made for King Louis XVI of France for Versailles in 1784 and subsequently purchased by the Prince of Wales, later King George IV (height 6.4 cm, 2½ inches).

CHAPTER 2

Ices

In the whole array of terms used in the culinary art, there are few of larger application or
more uncertain meaning than the word sherbet.

COMPTON DENE (FRED T. VINE),
Ices Plain and Fancy, London, 1890

A statement not only applicable to sherbet but to just about every other ice you care to name. Ices have evolved over a period of some seven centuries and across countries in Asia, the Middle East, Europe and America. So the field is vast, the boundaries blurred and the permutations infinite, and all for a very particular food that after all comprises so few basic ingredients.

At the same time as wanting to know the differences between various ices, people seem eager to know how they might all be connected or interrelated. Casting around for a simple way to convey this mixed bag of information, at first the notion of a family tree seemed the natural format. But the sprawling variety of ices resists all normal, neat categories and it took some time to evolve the simple diagram shown here. Even so it needs some explanation.

To show the relationship between the various ices it was first necessary to decide on the definitive recipe for each named ice. These were arrived at after substantial research and the recipes, tempered to today's ingredients and equipment, form the basis of the recipes in this book. The definitions of the individual ices are to be found in the glossary.

Americans may be surprised, even offended, to find a title well known to them given to quite another type of ice, e.g. parfait and sherbet. America took these two names and applied them to other types of ice; a good example of how different cultures can adopt and completely change an ice yet keep the name.

Ices, milk/cream and water-based, are made up of two or more of the following ingredients: sugar, milk, cream, water and sometimes whole, or separated eggs.

All ices contain water and sugar, even those such as rich super-premium ices; water in these is present as a natural constituent in the milk or the cream. For simplicity, we have combined sugar and water under the heading of sugar syrup in the diagram.

All ices, plain or composite, can now be fitted into this scheme since they are all based on some combination of both the ingredients and the types of ices named in the diagram.

The absence of eggs in the diagram might seem curious. Although they are essential in many ices, surprisingly they are not necessary to show the interrelationship of the various types of ices.

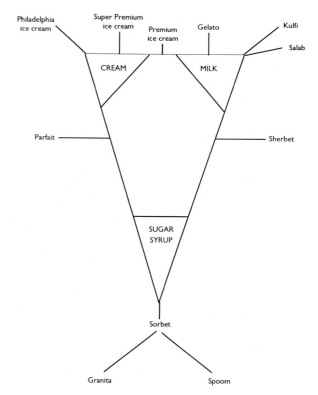

Ice-cream seller on Hampstead Heath, London, in May 1872. From the *Illustrated London News*.

CHAPTER 3

Glossary

Note: There are considerable difficulties in defining some terms due to widely differing local and national variations of meaning. For example, à la mode in France means something stylish and fashionable; in America, to serve with ice cream; and in England is a method of cooking beef.

À la mode   French expression that has been adopted and altered in America where it is used to indicate that a dessert is served with ice cream.

Age/ageing   An expression used in the ice-cream industry referring to the length of time the pasteurised liquid mix is held before churning. The smoothness of body (q. v.) and texture, resistance to melting and ease of whipping are improved by ageing. This process takes not more than 4 hours. Note: It is the *pasteurisation* of the made mix that effectively destroys all pathogens and bacteria and enables the safe storage of the mix (ageing) before churning. Home-made ice cream cannot be pasteurised therefore it is inadvisable to store the complete mix, with the cream added, even under refrigerated conditions. To keep bacterial action to a minimum you are strongly advised to quickly cool, then cover and refrigerate the custard mix, and not to add the chilled cream until just prior to freezing/churning.

Aqutaq   Eskimo ice cream originally made from animal fats such as seal oil, reindeer and caribou fat, sweetened and flavoured with berries and fruits. Modern versions use beef tallow, vegetable fats and butter.

Aufait   A term common at the turn of the century for a brick or moulded ice to which one or more thin layers of fruit (preserved or candied) have been added.

Banana Split   See page 185.

Batch freezers   Small ice-cream machines with an integral freezing unit capable of making a single batch of ice cream up to about 20 litres. For a greater output most small manufacturers switch to continuous freezers, but a discerning few stick to running a greater number of batch freezers which, although more labour-intensive and expensive, produce a better quality of ice cream with more character.

Biscuits glacés   *Considerable confusion exists with this and the two following entries. It is impossible to find any two books agreeing on the origins or nature of these ices. In particular, there seems to be no explanation of how the word bisque, a word usually used to describe a fish soup, ever had anything to do with ice cream.*

Term used in nineteenth-century and early twentieth-century books to describe ices frozen and served in paper containers in individual portions. Frequently made in layers of different flavours.

Biscuit Tortoni   Ice cream originating from the Café Tortoni in Paris, founded in 1804, and run by the Neapolitan ice-cream maker Tortoni. Consisted of ice cream, macaroons and rum.

Bisque   Ice-cream name popular in the nineteenth century and early twentieth century that is no longer in use. Baked goods, such as broken pieces of biscuits, macaroons, cake or meringues were added to an ice cream. The ice cream then became known as a bisque.

Bleeding   Term applied to the settling or separation of the sugar syrup at the bottom of a frozen container of sorbet, parfait or sherbet. The problem is caused by any combination of the following:- excessive overrun (q.v.) (due to overchurning and too much air), too much sugar or insufficient stabiliser.

Body   The body of an ice is the result of the combination of differing proportions of ingredients in relation to one another and the manner in which they are combined and the way they are churned and frozen. People's perception of the ideal body in an ice cream varies considerably. A manufacturer would look for both an acceptable firmness (density) when eaten, and, on leaving at room temperature, an acceptable rate of melt that leaves a smooth liquid similar in appearance and consistency to a sweet cream of about 40 per cent fat content.

Cassata gelata alla Siciliana   Cassata Siciliana is a traditional Sicilian dessert served at Easter and for weddings. Made in a hemispherical mould (Arabic, *quasat*) lined with pan de Spagna (a rich Madeira cake) and green-coloured marzipan, the centre containing a mixture of sweetened ricotta flavoured with crystallised fruits and chocolate. In short, a form of festive cheesecake. *Cassata gelata alla Siciliana* is a frozen edition of *Cassata Siciliana*. The classic recipe was agreed at the National Congress in Venice in 1963. Made in a stampo da spumone, a special domed mould with a lid, it is lined first with vanilla ice cream, then pistachio ice cream, then a layer of pan de Spagna soaked in rum. This is filled with a whipped egg white and cream mixture to which have been added candied fruits, orange and citrus peel and bitter chocolate. This is finished with a layer of vanilla and pistachio ice cream. It is then frozen and served decorated with candied fruit, whipped cream and orange peel. ★

College ice   A cheap type of sundae in that it comprises little or no ice cream but is made up of shaved or crushed ice flavoured with fruit syrup or crushed fruit.

Continuous freezers   A method by which commercial ice cream is made on a continuous basis. The liquid mix and air are passed continuously through a freezing chamber and emerge as ice cream. This process is non-stop for as long as the manufacturer cares to run the machine. Patented in 1913, it came into common usage in about 1922.

Coupe   Cup-shaped container, often on some sort of raised pedestal base, usually made of glass or silver-plated metal. Used to serve a composite dessert with ice cream as its main ingredient, e.g. Coupe Jacques.

Cream soda   Carbonated water to which flavoured syrup and milk or cream have been added. No ice cream is used.

★ Anna del Conte, *Gastronomy of Italy*, Bantam Press, 1989

Crème fraîche   A matured thick cream treated with a culture that gives it a light acidity without sourness. Minimum fat content is 35 per cent. This is standard cream in France.

Dasher   The part of the freezing machine that mixes and beats the mixture as it scrapes the ice cream from the walls of the freezing container. Hand or electrically driven. Usually referred to in Britain as the paddle.

Dip/dipper/disher   Ice-cream server (see scoops page 44).

Dixie cup   Paper drinking cups had been around since 1908 and were known as "Health Cups", as they were considered clean and hygienic to dispense and were, in addition, disposable. They became popular in ice-cream parlours and soda fountains as a way of serving ice cream in take-away portions.

In 1923, the manufacturer, the Individual Drinking Cup Company, started to market and sell individual portions of ice cream in a lidded, more tub-like version of the cup that had been waxed to prevent it softening and disintegrating. The company's president, Henry Moore, found that the cups weren't selling. A friend of his, Alfred Schindler, a manufacturer of dolls with the trade name Dixie, suggested it might boost trade if Henry called them Dixie cups. Thus was born one of America's most famous brand names.

There are many avid collectors of old Dixie cups in the U.S.A.

Eskimo ice cream   See Aqutaq.

Eskimo pie   Chocolate covered ice-cream bar invented and patented in 1921 by Christian Nelson in Onawa, Iowa. In partnership with Russell Stover who coined the name, Eskimo Pie, they formed a company that sold a million pies per day by 1922. Because the patent was declared invalid in 1928 many versions are still available in the U.S.A. today.

Float   Interpretations differ but a float is either based on a milkshake (i.e. flavoured syrup, milk and ice cream) or an ice-cream soda (i.e. flavoured syrup, soda water and ice cream). These are blended at high speed and poured into a tall glass. Dips/scoops of a complementary ice cream, sherbet or sorbet are floated on the top. Fruit or mint is sometimes added for decoration.

Frappé   Sweetened fruit juice or purée, frozen with water and liquidised to a soft mush and served immediately as a drink, or marginally harder, as a dessert with a spoon.

French ice cream A rich ice cream based on an egg custard, usually with a high ratio of cream to milk and eggs.

Fromage Early moulded ice creams were often referred to as fromages. Frequently divided into sections by strips of metal internally, or made in cheese-shaped slices as if cut from a round cheese. This allowed different coloured and flavoured ices to be made and joined together to make a complete round. The strips were later removed, the sections were gently pushed together and then lightly frozen as a whole.

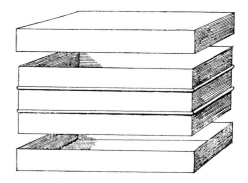

Gelateria Italian ice-cream parlour. Always look for the sign "Produzione Propria" which means made by the owner, and hope that it is true.

Gelato Gelato is an Italian term that is now used for both ice creams and sorbets, but strictly speaking it is an ice cream. See Italian Ice Cream.

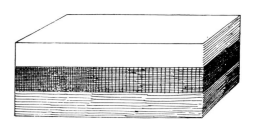

Good Humor bar Harry Burt Sr was a confectioner and candy seller in Youngstown, Ohio. There, in 1910, he invented the "Good Humor", a candy sucker/lollipop on a stick. He called it "Good Humor" as he considered that the humour of the mind was regulated by the palate.

Inspired by the success of the Eskimo Pie (q.v.), Harry Burt Sr went on to develop a chocolate-covered ice-cream bar. His daughter is reputed to have told him that his new chocolate-covered bar was too messy to eat so he tried putting a stick in it as he had done with the candy suckers, which is how his chocolate bars are sold to this day. So successful was this product that street ice-cream sellers became known as Good Humor Men.

Granita Italian coarse-textured, still-frozen water ice, 9–10° Baumé (see Saccharometer page 42). Do not be persuaded to make a granita with a higher sugar density than this as the classic granular ice texture will be lost. Instead the texture will be sticky and compact, rather in the manner of badly cooked rice.

Normally served in a tall glass with a spoon.

Hardening Refers to the additional freezing of a partially frozen ice.

When made commercially, ice cream leaves the machines and is packaged in its semi-fluid state and transferred to a hardening room where the temperature is swiftly lowered to harden (freeze) the ice. The swift freezing stops the formation of large ice crystals. The hardening of home-made ices is best carried out using a freezer with a fast-freeze switch. This effectively overrides the thermostat and reduces the temperature to around −30°C. Some domestic ice-cream machines will

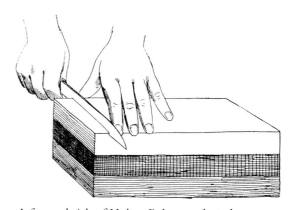

A frozen brick of Hokey Pokey ready to be cut up.

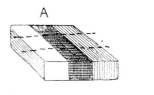
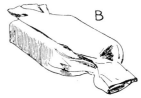

Instructions for making a Neapolitan brick and to shopkeepers on cutting and wrapping Hokey Pokey in wax paper.

freeze ices more effectively than others, i.e. will achieve a lower temperature. So, depending on the recipe used, some will produce ice cream that can be served directly from the machine while others will need a period of hardening in the freezer.

Hokey Pokey   The origins of the name are apocryphal; however, they are worth repeating. The Italian ice-cream sellers were reputed to use a number of cries; among them, "Gelati! Ecco un Poco" and "Gelati! Che un poco". It doesn't take much imagination to see that this could easily be corrupted by the English into Hokey Pokey. We would speculate that rhyming slang played a part in the derivation of the name, hokey pokey. This name spread to the United States, where there are clear references to hokey pokey in such books as *The Dispenser's Formulary*; however, later it was simply used as a slang name for ice cream (see page 30).

Hokey Pokey was a cheap Neapolitan-striped ice cream, usually in two or three colours, cut into small slices about 5×5×1.25 cm (2×2×½ inch) and wrapped in small squares of white, frequently waxed paper.

Ice cave   Early name for a freezer (see page 20).

Ice-cream soda   Made by putting fruit in syrup, or a flavoured syrup, with a soda spoon of ice cream, or whipped cream in a glass; pressurised soda water is added until the glass is three-quarters full, then two scoops of ice cream. The glass is then topped up with additional soda water and decorated with whipped cream. It is served with a long handled spoon and a straw.

Really skilful soda jerks balance one of the scoops of ice cream on the edge of the glass with the ice cream just touching the soda water.

According to the 1914 edition of the *Soda Fountain* magazine, the ice-cream soda was invented by Philip Mohr in his shop in Elizabeth, New Jersey, prior to 1872. The first record of an ice-cream soda being sold in London is surprisingly to be found in the *Newville, Pennsylvania Times*, 26 December 1894, and it apparently became a craze overnight.

Italian ice cream   Italian ice cream is a custard-based ice typically made with more eggs and milk and less cream than French ice cream. Because of the lower cream content less air is incorporated during churning or still freezing. So although the ice cream is not as rich, it is more dense and has a more intense flavour than its French counterpart.

Fred Saunders of Detroit, Michigan, claims the world record for selling 14,770 nickel (5 cent) sodas in one day in 1906 from his ice-cream parlour.

Jerk/soda jerk   Expression used to describe employees in soda fountains and ice-cream parlours due to their jerky actions when drawing soda water from the soda-water pumps.

Knickerbocker Glory   An English sundae, imported from the United States, that has become known as the ultimate example of the sundae-makers' art. New York used to be referred to as the Knickerbocker State, and the dessert seems to have grown from the Knickerbocker sundae. See page 185.

Kulfi   Indian ice cream (see page 104).

Lecithin   Phospholipid that occurs naturally in milk and egg yolks; additional small quantities are frequently added to commercial ice cream as a stabiliser.

Locust bean gum   Commercially produced natural stabiliser used in ice cream to prevent formation of large ice crystals.

Lolly   See Popsicle.

Mature   Confusing word, much misused. Correctly used to describe hardening (q.v.) it is not to be confused with ageing (q.v.).

Mellorine   U.S. term to describe any ice cream made without butterfat. In mellorine the butterfat is replaced with vegetable oil (coconut, cottonseed, soybean, corn or other plant fat) or non-dairy animal fat. Illegal in over 75 per cent of the U.S.A. and in the majority of the E.E.C. it unfortunately is allowed in Britain where it comprises over 75 per cent of the ice-cream market.

Mellow   Expression sometimes used to describe softening of ice cream from freezer temperature to an edible temperature. We prefer to describe this as softening (q.v.) as it leaves no room for doubt or confusion with maturing or ageing.

Milkshake   It is almost impossible to define a milkshake. However, there are some basic rules. Firstly the milk must be full cream milk, thoroughly chilled, in order that the ice cream will thicken the drink and not melt and thin it. Secondly, don't overmix; overmixing will also thin the shake.

A simple rule of thumb is 1 cup of milk (250 ml/8 fl oz) to 2 medium scoops of ice cream, whizzed briefly in a blender and served immediately (see page 185).

This is the most basic shake; the permutations of flavourings, syrups and fruits are almost limitless.

Hokey Pokey a penny a lump,
That's the stuff to make you jump.
Children's 19th century rhyme

Hokey Pokey is of a firmer material than the penny ice of the Italians; it is built up of variously flavoured layers. Sold in halfpenny and penny paper covered squares, kept until wanted in circular metal refrigerator pots surrounded by ice, Hokey Pokey has the advantage over its rival eaten in glasses, inasmuch as it can be carried away by the purchaser and consumed at leisure. . . Besides being variously flavoured, Hokey Pokey is dreadfully sweet, dreadfully cold, and hard as a brick. It is whispered that the not unwholesome Swede turnip, crushed into pulp, has been known to form its base, in lieu of the more expensive supplies from the cow, whose complex elaboration of cream from turnips is thus unceremoniously abridged.

Old London Street Cries, 1895

Moscovite (Crème à la) Victorian ice made with either isinglass or leaf gelatine added, moulded, and served partially frozen rather than hard frozen after about 2 hours in an ice cave. A rather rich cold dessert that tended more towards a jelly than an ice cream. No longer in use.

"The peculiarity of the Moscovite – or, to give it its proper name, the crème à la Moscovite – consists in the fact that, though iced from long burying in ice, it is not actually frozen, and owes some of its solidity to a certain proportion of either isinglass or leaf gelatine. It is, in consequence, decidedly to be recommended to such housekeepers as may not have freezing conveniences and wish to obey the fashion at the moment, which demands the presence of an iced sweet on every carefully arranged menu."

Horace Cox, *Queen Book of Ices*, London, 1899

M.S.N.F. Short for "Milk solids, non-fat". These solids, found in milk, cream and butter, consist of proteins (casein, albumin, globulin) 38 per cent, lactose 54 per cent, mineral salts and vitamins 8 per cent. Their presence in ice cream, in the right proportions, contributes smoothness, body and texture.

Neapolitan Style of ice cream brought from Naples in the 1850s by immigrants who set up small businesses making ice cream. The ice cream, in two or more lurid colours, was arranged in layers in a rectangular brick-shaped mould. It was then served sliced and wrapped in paper with the ends twisted, enclosing the ice cream rather like a boiled sweet. Originally made sweet, some Victorian cooks developed savoury Neapolitan ices (e.g. Mrs Marshall gives a recipe using artichoke, pea or cucumber and tomato to create the different layers).

See Hokey Pokey page 29.

Nesselrode Named after Count Nesselrode, the nineteenth-century Russian aristocrat, whose chef, Mouy, invented this pudding. It consisted of a cream-enriched custard mixed with chestnut purée, candied fruits, currants, raisins and Maraschino liqueur.

Overrun Manufacturers' term to describe the volume of churned ice cream obtained in excess of the volume of the unfrozen mix. Overrun is the result of the size of the barrel (diameter) and the speed of the dasher. The increase in volume is composed of air and is usually expressed as a percentage:

e.g. If 1 litre of unfrozen mix makes 1.25 litres of ice cream, the overrun is 25 per cent.

The equation to calculate overrun is as follows:-

$$\text{overrun percentage} = \frac{\text{volume of ice cream} - \text{volume of mix}}{\text{volume of mix}} \times 100$$

Overrun in domestically made ice creams varies from 5 to 25 per cent, and depends on whether an ice has been still frozen or churned.

The overrun range in commercial ice creams is 0–20 per cent in super premium ice creams, but can be up to 100 per cent or more for cheap bulk ice creams.

In U.S.A. the weight per gallon is legally enforced to prohibit excessive overrun. The weight per gallon of ice cream must not be less than 4.5 lb per gallon U.S. or more than 100 per cent overrun. Regrettably, this is not so in Britain.

Pareve Ice cream made without either dairy or animal ingredients but with vegetable oils.

There are also Kosher ice creams available. This means that the manufacturer is supervised or licensed by the Beth Din or Kedassi.

Parfait We have been unable to discover any documentation as to the origin and first use of this word to describe an ice cream. Popular in the nineteenth century, when a customer is reputed to have breathed the word "parfait" to describe this type of light ice cream made with sugar syrup, eggs and cream. Parfaits have fallen out of fashion as they are not easy to make. The word has also fallen into misuse in the U.S.A., where it is used to describe a range of fruit and ice-cream concoctions served in the traditional tall parfait glass (see page 185).

Pasteurise Pasteurisation is the process of heating a mix to a specific temperature for a specific time, then cooling it rapidly in order to kill off the pathogenic (harmful) micro-organisms present in milk, cream and eggs.

Any ice cream made for re-sale must be pasteurised. The temperatures and times required for pasteurisation are as follows:-

	Heat to:		Hold for:
	C	F	TIME
	60	140	30 minutes
or	71.1	160	10 minutes
or	79.5	175	15 seconds

The mix must then be cooled to less than 7.2°C/45°F within 1½ hours and must be stored at this temperature or lower until frozen.

Please note that the rapid cooling and subsequent storage is as important as the heating. So too is scrupulous cleanliness in all subsequent handling and packaging.

Since all our custard-based recipes require heating to 85°C/185°F and rapid cooling, you will be well within the limits of safety.

Pectin Natural, water-soluble stabiliser used extensively in commercially made sorbets. Our experiments with shop-bought powdered and liquid pectin, as a substitute for egg white, sadly have proved unsatisfactory. The flavour of the pectin is too obtrusive in all but the strongest-flavoured sorbets.

Philadelphia ice cream Philadelphia was surrounded on all sides by prime dairy counties and some of the abundant supply of cream was channelled into ice cream along with sugar and vanilla. Philadelphia ice cream has three main characteristics:

1. It has no custard base and is "uncooked".
2. It contains no eggs or milk (although eggs and milk started to appear in Philadelphia ice-cream recipes at the beginning of the twentieth century).
3. It has always contained specks of vanilla seed to show that true vanilla has been used rather than an inferior flavouring.

In the 1850s vanilla was a highly prized, expensive perfume and spice to which Philadelphia had access through its direct trading links with the Caribbean and South America as well as France. The fashionable ladies of Philadelphia in the late eighteenth and early nineteenth centuries followed the French mode and considered it a sign of extreme cultivation to be able to serve an ice cream flavoured with vanilla that had been grated against a cone of sugar. We are told that today Philadelphians will refuse their ice cream if it does not contain black specks.

True Philadelphia ice cream is slightly grainy due to the lack of the emulsifying effect of eggs.

Plombières There is no consistency in recipes for plombières. The name was presumably coined from the French "plomb" meaning lead, from which early pewter moulds were made. Wyvern (Colonel Kenney-Herbert) in *Sweet Dishes*, 1884, suggests it is a three-tier pyramid mould of different flavoured and coloured ice creams. Balzac refers to it in *Splendeurs et Misères des Courtisanes*: "At the end of the meal, ice cream called plombières was served. Everyone knows this ice cream contains small bits of delicate candied fruit sprinkled over the ice cream, and comes served in small cups which keep intact the pyramid shape of the ice cream. The ice cream had been ordered from Madame du Val-Noble in Tortoni whose famous shop was at the corner of Rue Taitbout on the main street."

Popsicle The Popsicle, or as it was originally called, the Epsicle, was first patented in 1923 by Frank Epperson, a lemonade seller in California. He maintained that in 1905 as a child, in New Jersey, he left some flavoured powder mixed in water with the mixing stick still in it, in a glass on the back porch. In the morning the liquid was frozen solid and Frank had a stick of frozen flavoured water to show to his friends at school. When he patented the idea in 1923 it precipitated a clash with Harry Burt Sr, the inventor of the Good Humor Bar (q.v.). A compromise eventually allowed Epperson to make sherbet or water ice on a stick and Burt to make ice cream on a stick.

It is a mark of the difference between our cultures that the origin of the iced lolly in Britain passed unnoticed and unrecorded.

Puckler German ice-cream combination named after the German megalomaniac traveller Prince Puckler-Muskau. A neapolitan-type layered ice cream with strawberry, vanilla, flavoured with maraschino or kirsch, and chocolate ice creams, and layers of crushed macaroons soaked in the same alcohol.

Punch Term derived from the Arabic, "panj", a word meaning five. It refers to the drink popular in the Persian Gulf made of five ingredients: grape juice, rosewater, sugar, lemon and ice. Under Western influence it developed both as a hot and a cold drink, both versions served with the addition of alcohol. The cold punch was used as a palate refresher during large multi-course dinners, frequently being served after the soup, before the roast meat. When served, cold punch was in a tall glass in a semi-frozen state. It developed, as methods of refrigeration improved, to become more frozen and solidified to the point that it had to be eaten from the glass with a spoon. At this stage it really was a water ice somewhere between a sorbet and a granita. Francatelli said punch "may be served hot or liquid, frozen similarly to a granita". Later recipes recommend making punch using sorbet with alcohol poured over and mixed in as well as the addition of Italian meringue.

Punch went out of fashion in mid-Victorian times as dining habits changed and attention switched to sorbets served as a dessert (see Sorbet).

Ripening This is the time needed to allow the flavour to mature and develop in ice cream. Vanilla, for example, requires up to two days to permeate properly through the product and develop a full flavour.

Sa'alab/salab/salap Persian ices (see page 142).

Scoop See Equipment page 44.

Semi-freddo Italian term used to describe light parfait-type ices made in a mould without an ice-cream making machine. Literal translation is semi-frozen. It is also referred to in Italy as *perfetti*. Due to composition of ingredients it does not freeze hard.

Sherbet A word that almost defies definition, so mangled has it become by the influences of nations, legislation, and ignorant usage. The word probably derives from the Arabic sharab meaning a cold, sweetened, non-alcoholic drink.

Briefly, nowadays, a sherbet is usually a water ice containing some milk or cream, whereas a sorbet is a non-dairy product and contains neither milk nor cream. This is the definition we have stuck to throughout this book, but in the United States the Food and Drug Administration, in their wisdom, have no classification for a sorbet. What Europe calls a sorbet the F.D.A. call a water ice and they have additional classifications for sherbet (where the milk-derived solids must be not less than 2 per cent and not more than 5 per cent) and ice milk (where the total milk-derived solids are not less than 11 per cent).

Sorbet Water-based ice made without dairy products or egg yolks but nowadays frequently containing egg whites. Made to a density of 14–17° Baumé if they contain alcohol and 17–20° Baumé without alcohol. Served as an appetite stimulant/palate refresher between courses or as a dessert.

Escoffier advised that they should be served between courses to prepare the stomach for the roast, and suggested that they were eaten at an almost drinkable consistency (see Punch).

Sorbetto Italian sorbet.

Spongada Italian ice based on whipped cream and flavouring, partially frozen and usually not moulded. Sometimes referred to as a spumante in the nineteenth century.

Spoom Sorbet base with half its volume of French meringue added. It is then frozen without further agitation.

Spumoni Italian ice moulded in two layers in a hemisphere, claimed to originate from both Acireal in Sicily and Naples. The outside layer is usually a custard-based ice cream flavoured vanilla, chocolate or strawberry. Inside there is a semi-freddo or parfait of alcohol, coffee, nut or fruit.

Still frozen Method of freezing ices without an ice-cream machine, where the milk is not agitated or stirred continuously during freezing. It is, however, beaten by hand with a fork or electric hand whisk or in a food processor a number of times at various stages during the freezing (see page 48).

Stir frozen A process whereby ices are frozen in a machine and are agitated/stirred continuously as the temperature of the mix is lowered. These machines range from the simplest hand-cranked machine to the batch machines and the continuous process factory machines.

Sundae Ice-cream dessert with syrup or sauce, fruit or nuts made according to a number of classic formulae, or according to the taste or the mood of the server, or under the direction of the customer. Whatever the combina-

ICE CREAM GLASSES

Sundae Cup

Peach Cup

Sundae Cup

Parfait

Knickerbocker
Glory

Coupe Jacques

Banana Split

Ice cream glasses *c.* 1925, still in use today.

2. The second theory is a little more convoluted. In the 1890s a George Hallauer walked into his local soda fountain in Two Rivers, Wisconsin, and asked the owner, Ed Berner, to pour the chocolate syrup normally reserved for making chocolate ice-cream sodas on to a nickel (5c) portion of ice cream. Its fame and price spread to the adjoining town where the soda fountain owner, George Giffey, was so concerned that there was no profit to be made from it at 5 cents that he restricted its sale to Sundays only. The "ae" was added later to differentiate it from the day.

Super premium ice cream Late twentieth-century term used to describe highest quality, most expensive ice creams. These are usually high fat, low overrun ice creams containing only natural ingredients.

There are no regulations in Europe or America yet to control the use of this term.

Syrup Simple or stock syrup used in making all sorbets, parfaits and granitas (see Chemistry of Ices page 177). There is no single accepted classic formula for simple syrup; the ratio of sugar to water varies, which is not very helpful when recipes for successful ices very much depend on the correct amounts of sugar and water. We have opted for a formula which is the easiest to remember and use: 1 litre water to 1 kilo of sugar.

Tempering Expression sometimes used to describe softening of ice cream from freezer temperature to an edible temperature. We prefer to describe this as softening as it leaves no room for doubt.

Total solids There are *two types* of solids in milk or cream – butterfat, and those solids which comprise M.S.N.F. (milk solids non-fat) (q.v.).

The total solids refers to the addition of these two and it is necessary to know these numbers separately and then in total in order to achieve the correct balance in planning recipes for ice creams.

Tutti frutti Finely chopped fruit marinated in maraschino and worked into a vanilla-based ice cream after churning and before hardening. It is Italian in origin.

Water ice Flavoured ice, made with fruit, herbs, spice, alcohol, etc., without any dairy products or egg yolks. It may have lightly beaten egg whites added as a stabiliser. Term used in U.S.A. where the F.D.A. have no classification for sorbets.

tion, it is served on a dish and eaten with a spoon (see page 185).

The origin of the word sundae is hotly contested by public relations departments of many cities and towns in the U.S.A., eager to claim the original sundae as their own. However, from the small amount of reliable information available, it would seem that one or other of the following theories is likely:

1. Since early soda fountains and churches were the only places open for the young to meet on Sundays, the soda fountains were inevitably seen by the churches as competition.

In 1890, Evanston, Illinois, was the first community to legislate against the "Sunday soda menace". The local soda-fountain owners got round it by selling a sodaless sundae/Sunday using ice cream and syrup – but no soda.

CHAPTER 4

Ingredients

A gourmet who thinks of calories is like a tart who looks at her watch.

JAMES BEARD 1903–85

Naturally, while making ices, the few common ingredients have come in for close scrutiny. As a result of much testing and tasting, we have refined our ideas down to some specifics. These, and any additional hints and information that might be of help, are given below.

Almond extract

When buying, look for the word natural, and the list of ingredients should say almond oil and alcohol. Avoid everything else. Be extremely cautious using natural bitter almond essence, the minutest amount is sufficient. Dip a fine skewer into the liquid and add single drops from the point.

Chocolate

In order to fully understand the qualities of chocolate, it is necessary to know something of the manufacturing process. Briefly, cocoa kernels are pulverised to produce cocoa mass. This is then refined to produce cocoa butter and cocoa powder, which are together frequently described on chocolate wrappers as cocoa solids.

The cocoa butter retains about 2 per cent of cocoa powder and in this state is off-white and almost flavourless. The cocoa powder retains some 20–22 per cent cocoa butter.

Individual manufacturers re-combine cocoa butter with cocoa powder and some of the original cocoa mass to produce their own distinctive types of chocolate. Since cocoa butter is a useful commodity, especially to the cosmetic industry, some manufacturers sell this off and substitute cheaper vegetable fats and oils, such as soya, palm and coconut.

It is the percentage of cocoa solids in chocolate, therefore, that gives it its chocolate taste.

It has proved surprisingly difficult to produce a good chocolate-flavoured ice cream that is strong and round enough in flavour, without any rawness, and with good consistency that is not too dense or chewy. All tests using milk chocolate, which contains less cocoa solids than plain chocolate, were unsatisfactory, so milk chocolate has not been used in this book.

In order to get a good, positive, chocolate flavour it is necessary to use a good-quality plain chocolate with a high cocoa solids content. (In the U.S.A. plain chocolate is frequently referred to as semi-sweet or bitter-sweet chocolate.) However, buying a good quality chocolate is not as straightforward as it may seem; whereas good quality is reflected in the price, price alone does not guarantee the quality. Before buying a dark plain chocolate look on the back of the packet at the ingredients and their percentages. If this information is absent, do not buy the chocolate – manufacturers should feel sufficiently confident of their product to print the contents for all to see. Do not buy chocolate if it lists the cocoa solids at under 45 per cent.

We normally use Menier, which is readily available. Some supermarkets have excellent "own brands" which contain 50 per cent and higher. Other quality chocolates we would recommend are Lindt bitter-sweet, Fauchon and Callebaut; the last two, once difficult to find, are becoming increasingly available.

WHITE CHOCOLATE

Chocolatiers do not consider white chocolate to be real chocolate, since the only part of the cocoa bean the product contains is cocoa butter. The rest of the chocolate is made up of milk solids, sugar and flavouring. Some brands do not even contain cocoa butter: again this is replaced with vegetable fat and oils such as soya, palm and coconut oil. To avoid low-quality chocolate look on the packet to check that the contents contain at least 25 per cent cocoa *butter*. Less than this, the chocolate may not melt at all, or insufficiently to be incorporated into the ice-cream mix.

In the U.S.A. white chocolate cannot be legally sold as chocolate. If it contains no cocoa butter, it is sold as confectioner's or summer coating. *So, never buy white chocolate unless it gives the percentage of cocoa butter on the package.*

Cocoa

When the cocoa butter has been removed from the pulverised cocoa bean kernel (cocoa mass) the result is cocoa. Although a dry powder, the best cocoa still retains some 20–22 per cent cocoa butter. In this raw state it is a greyish-red colour, acidic, and without the addition of sugar is practically inedible.

Most cocoa for the domestic market is then "alkalised" or "Dutch processed". This treatment, which removes the acidity, was invented by Coenraad Johannes Van Houten in 1828. To this day, Van Houten remains arguably the best quality cocoa and most widely available in Britain, Europe and the U.S.A.

Having said all this, if you look on a container to see if it is alkalised or non-alkalised, in most cases this information is not given. Rest assured, in Britain all cocoa is alkalised. **U.S. readers should be alert to the fact that some main brands available in the United States are non-alkalised.**

We have achieved undeniably better results from alkalised cocoa powder and now use it exclusively in ices.

Cream

To keep the recipes simple and successful for the widest possible public, with few exceptions the cream used throughout the book is of the type called **whipping** cream in Britain (legal minimum fat content 35 per cent).

This cream is known as **heavy** cream in the U.S.A. (legal minimum fat content 36 per cent). This choice of cream was made at the outset of writing the book because it gave sufficient fat content for most types of ice cream whether still frozen or churned; it was readily available, or if not, other creams could easily be adapted down to this fat content by the addition of milk; furthermore, sticking to just one type of cream keeps shopping simple and the fridge uncluttered.

Lovers of super-rich ice cream should not be tempted to use double cream willy-nilly in the assumption that it will make the ice cream "better". It does not. A cream of higher fat content, in some recipes, is likely to run to butter in an ice-cream maker, or at best, produce an ice cream with a very crumbly texture. Using a cream of lower fat content will of course give a less rich ice cream, but before all the dieters opt for this they should know that it will also give a rather hard, icy-textured ice cream.

In other words, for the best results use whipping cream (or heavy cream in U.S.A.) or be prepared to adjust the volumes of ingredients using the formulae in Chapter 9: The Chemistry of Ices (see pages 172–179).

Having said all that, it does not make life any easier to discover that whipping cream is not so widely available as double cream (legal minimum fat content 48 per cent). However, by diluting double cream with whole milk (legal minimum fat content 4 per cent) it can be reduced to the fat content of whipping cream. The formula is:

3 parts double cream to 1 part whole milk
= 37 per cent fat content

PLEASE NOTE: In practice, creams are almost always a few percentage points above the minimum legal fat contents given above.

Those interested in the physics and chemistry of ice cream will see that this important fact is taken into account in our calculations.

Caution: Do not use U.H.T. or ultra-heat-treated creams or milks in making ice cream. The heat processing that these products receive alters their proteins and adversely affects the churning, freezing and taste of an ice cream.

Neither do we recommend using the type of cream which is labelled "extra thick".

Eggs

For easy availability in both Europe and the U.S.A. we have used Size 2 (average weight 67 g) eggs. These correspond with Extra Large eggs in the U.S.A., which on the basis of 27 oz per dozen, works out at 2.25 oz each or 63.8 g.

If you are left with a number of egg whites in a bowl it is useful to know that one egg white = approximately 35 ml. This can be more accurately measured using a small medicine measure available from chemists, usually free, and used for sorbets, spumantes or spooms, or for tuiles to accompany ice creams.

Gelatine

From the turn of the century up to the First World War gelatine was extensively used as a stabiliser in commercial ice cream. Then technology provided cheaper and more efficient substitutes. In this book we have largely avoided using gelatine because we find it gives a curious boiled-milk flavour to ice creams, acceptable up to a point in vanilla ice creams but cloying and deadening in, for example, a fruit-flavoured ice cream.

The quality of gelatine varies. The transparent sheets (leaf gelatine) are generally of a higher quality but not readily available. The granular form is available in most supermarkets and is therefore the type we have used.

(If sorbets are correctly made gelatine is not necessary.)

Milk

Unless otherwise specified in the recipe always use full cream milk (U.S.A. whole milk) with a minimum legal fat content (Britain 4 per cent, U.S.A. 3.9 per cent). Do not use skimmed or Long Life or Ultra Pasteurised milk as these upset the flavour and the texture of the ices. (For further information see Chapter 9: The Chemistry of Ices pages 172–179.)

Sugar

Most of the recipes use sugar in the form of sucrose which is obtained from either sugar cane or sugar beet. All white sugar is refined to 99.9 per cent sucrose and in this form there is absolutely no difference between beet and cane. Since granulated sugar with its medium-sized crystals is the most common and inexpensive sugar, we have used it in the majority of recipes, where heating ensures the dissolving of the crystals anyway. Where the ingredients are not heated, but simply stirred together and frozen, caster/ultra-fine sugar has been used – the smaller crystals of sugar dissolving more readily without the application of heat.

NOTE: All 99 per cent refined sucrose, weight for weight, has the same sweetening power whatever the degree of granulation. Because of this you can substitute granulated for caster sugar in Britain. However, *do not* substitute icing/confectioner's sugar as there is a small proportion of anti-caking agent added.

Vanilla sugar

This is normally made by burying three or four vanilla bean pods in a container of sugar. Within a week the sugar has taken up the flavour and aroma of the beans and is ready to use. This provides a very subtle background flavour in ice creams.

Ours is a more skinflint approach; given the high price of vanilla beans and not wishing to use them more than once for infusing custard, we rinse and dry these used beans and put them into the sugar and go on doing this until there are almost more beans than sugar. We then throw them out and start the process all over again.

Rose-petal sugar

Rose-petal sugar is a delightful thing to have around. Use petals from highly scented roses (see list on page 140). Spread out the petals and allow them half a day to dry, then fill a container with alternate layers of sugar and petals, cover with a tight-fitting lid and leave aside for two weeks or so. The sugar will need sieving before use. The ratio of petals to sugar is not critical; as a rough guide use **1 oz petals to 225 g (1½ cups) sugar**.

Sugar syrup

See page 47.

Vanilla

As the tomato is to Italian cookery so vanilla is to ices. A superb flavour in its own right, it is unique in its capacity to act as a passive background for other flavours, sometimes accentuating even rather reticent ones.

The best vanilla flavour to be had is indisputably from the bean. The pods are green/yellow when picked from the climbing orchid *Vanilla planifolia*. They are some

"...and eight tubs of vanilla. Vanilla
still seems to be the favorite."

HENRY MARTIN

Water

This may seem an extraordinary entry in a list of ingredients, but without water you could not have ices and unhappily it is a sign of the times that we have to consider the taste and quality of water. If you don't drink the water from your tap, don't make ices with it. Or, if you live in an area where you know that the water is highly chlorinated, or suspect it is high in phosphates, we suggest that you use bottled water.

Yoghurt

People who are calorie-conscious and who hope to cut down on calories may be rather disappointed to find that all the yoghurt ices contain a full fat creamy Greek-style yoghurt, about 10 per cent fat content. This enables the ice cream to be frozen or stored before eating. You can use low-fat as long as you eat it as soon as it has reached a suitable ice-cream consistency, be it churned or still frozen. Otherwise due to the low milk-solid and fat content, and therefore high water content, it will freeze hard and have a rough icy consistency and lack roundness of flavour. Commercial yoghurt ices are bristling with stabilisers and emulsifiers to overcome this problem.

In the U.S.A. Greek-style yoghurts are frequently referred to as Russian-style yoghurts.

Ice cream fork, a sorbet spoon, an ice cream spoon and a
sherbet spoon, Tiffany, New York, c. 1880.

12.5–25 cm/5–10 inches long, about 2.5 cm/1 inch in circumference and have no vanilla flavour or fragrance. It is only the laborious and time-consuming process of continually sweating and drying that develops the vanillin, which in combination with other substances (gums, resins and oils) gives vanilla its typical wonderfully seductive, sweet and spicy smell. Beans carrying a dusting of white vanillin crystals are considered to be of high quality, but despite some fifty years of combined cooking experience we have only once come across them. We are happy when we find highly aromatic, dark, fat, moist, luscious beans and cheerfully pay the high price.

As to what are the best beans, experts say Mexican ones are excellent. High quality Madagascar beans are widely available, but sadly only Americans seem to have access to the highly perfumed, aromatic Tahitian beans.

In the absence of the bean, vanilla extract is the next best thing, but a poor second in our opinion. The best quality is made by soaking beans in an alcohol-water solution to extract the flavour. In the United States avoid "imitation vanilla" and buy only the product that is labelled "vanilla extract" which ensures it is derived from vanilla beans. In Britain the standard of vanilla extract is not required to be so high as that sold in the U.S.A. and wording on the labels can be confusing. You are best advised to look for the word "natural" in the wording on the label. However, high quality bourbon beans and natural vanilla extract from U.S.A. are available in Britain by mail order (see Useful Addresses page 184).

CHAPTER 5

Equipment

The equipment with which people choose to cook is as personal to them as the clothes they wear, their jewellery, or the paintings they hang on their walls. You buy what suits you best and what is best for one person can be wholly unsuccessful for another.

Here is our equipment selection for making ices.

Blender   See Food processor/liquidiser/blender

Bombe/ice-cream moulds   All moulds made specially for ice cream have a lid and are usually metal; the lid helps prevent the formation of ice crystals on the surface of the ice cream; metal is the most efficient conductor of heat, i.e. when the ice is put into the freezer or when it is unmoulded.

Simple bombe moulds are readily available in good kitchenware stores. The cheapest are aluminium. Much

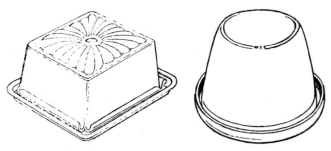

more expensive ones are made of copper lined with tin. They have screw-in plugs that act as bases on which the moulds can stand. When they are filled, to turn out the frozen ice the plug is unscrewed, which releases the vacuum, enabling the ice to slide out. Middle of the range in price and decoration are the square-shaped moulds with a fluted pattern on the base. These are now sometimes made in stainless steel. Very ornate ice-cream moulds are only available from specialist shops in France (see Useful Addresses page 184).

For advice on the most successful shapes to use see Chapter 8: Bombes and Moulded Ices page 167.

NOTE: **Do not use antique or reproduction moulds unless you are absolutely sure that they are not made with lead-based pewter. Most are. Do not use copper ones unless the tinning is in good condition.** Do not use glass or ceramic moulds as they may split with the expansion during freezing or during unmoulding.

Do not mistake chocolate moulds for ice-cream moulds. For more information see pages 167–168.

Bottle brush   Necessary for the scrupulous cleaning of funnels and the central columns of dashers in many electric ice-cream machines.

Bowls   We recommend heatproof glass bowls and a minimum of:

1. Two 30 cm/12 inch heat-proof glass bowls, for making parfaits.

2. One medium-sized heat-proof bowl, for making a basic custard.

3. One small bowl, for separated eggs.

Cone form (wood)   This enables a number of cones to be made more easily and lessens the chance of your fingers getting burned. Electric cone/pizelle makers often supply a wooden cone form with the machine. These are rather too slim to ensure a closure at the tip of the cone, and the cones rather too small to give a satisfactory portion.

Our slightly larger cone form, developed specially by Randal Marr, more readily forms a leak-proof cone and takes a sensible portion of home-made ice cream (see Useful Addresses page 184).

Cone maker   See pizelle.

Coolbags and freezer boxes   Once you discover the flavours of home-made ice creams the natural reaction is to want to share them and that involves transporting ice cream. This has to be done in a coolbag or box.

The most effective bag we have come across is made from Flectalon® and is insulated with the same material. Flectalon is an ultra-lightweight metallised coating on a fabric that reflects the heat and maintains the cold.

Use in conjunction with freezer packs (see below).

Freezer boxes. Although hardly a thing of beauty they are effective, more so than a coolbag. Especially if you pack the base and top with freezer packs and put a folded newspaper directly on top before the lid is put on.

The cheapest boxes have an air space between the inner and outer skins. These are not nearly as effective as the ones where the cavity is filled with either foam or expanded polystyrene or fibreglass.

Cup measures   Please note that these are **American cup measures** based on the comparatively new "full" cup measure that is equal to 250 ml or 8 fl oz. (Measuring cups vary in capacity depending on whether the manufacturer has rounded the conversion of 8 fl oz up or down.)

A set of measuring cups can consist of up to 6 different-sized cups. In addition to the 1 cup size we have used ½ cup/125 ml, ⅓ cup/80 ml, ¼ cup/60 ml. We prefer stainless steel ones, but check that the handles are firmly attached.

To measure liquids stand the cup on a level surface to fill. With solids (e.g. sugar), dip the cup measure in, and sweep off the excess with the back of a knife.

Dippers   See Scoops.

Dishers   See Scoops.

Double saucepans   A double saucepan is something of a luxury, but if you are an inexperienced cook and intend making ices in some quantity, we recommend you buy a good quality double saucepan, but not aluminium, as this discolours egg-based sauces.

NOTE: The top pan should never come into contact with the water in the base.

In the absence of a double saucepan, select a saucepan that will comfortably contain two-thirds of a heatproof bowl; the base of the bowl should not come into contact with the water. See also Saucepans.

Eprouvette   See Saccharometer.

Food processor/liquidiser/blender   You probably already have a food processor. But, if you haven't, in most cases a sieve and spoon will do.

Freezer box   See Coolbag.

Freezer packs   We recommend 4 of the larger type to make freezer boxes more effective.

Fridges and freezers   See page 47.

Funnel   If you have one of the canister-insert ice cream machines that has a comparatively small aperture in the cover, a large funnel is very useful to quickly and cleanly fill the machine.

Heat-diffuser mat   When making custards it is safest of all to use a double saucepan. The next best way is to use an ordinary saucepan over a heat-diffuser mat. Look for the perforated metal sandwich with a handle, rather than the metal gauze type.

Ice-cream makers   The hardest part of making ice cream at home is to get enough air into the ice cream. Machines help considerably to achieve this. They will also produce an ice cream with less fuss (with the exception of the type that uses ice and salt) and of a higher standard. But having said that, **there are NO ices in this book that MUST be made in a machine**. They can all be still frozen (i.e. stirred occasionally by hand or machine-beaten with an electric hand whisk or using a food processor) once or twice during freezing (see Still Freezing page 48).

There are four basic types of ice-cream maker. We have worked with all the types of machines. Here we describe their main characteristics and our personal view of the performance of each type.

1. *The old-fashioned bucket type* that uses ice and salt. The wooden buckets have now largely disappeared from the market, except for those lined with fibreglass. The buckets are instead made of plastic or fibreglass. A

stainless steel or galvanised freezing canister with a removable lid sits centrally in the bucket and a stationary plastic paddle or dasher fits inside the canister and gently scrapes the inside wall as the canister rotates. The liquid ice mix is poured into the canister, the dasher inserted, the lid fitted, then the canister is put into the bucket. The cranking mechanism is locked in place on top, and ice and salt are packed round it.

In almost all machines, the canister is then rotated by either a hand-crank or an electric motor. Hand-cranked models are considerably cheaper than the electric ones.

The hand-cranked version is the machine for the purist who may feel that the ice cream is imbued with a superior

quality by virtue of the hard work. It may also be the choice for those who nostalgically yearn for ice cream like they think they remember as a child. Mom made it in a hand-cranked machine so it is the only way to make *real* ice cream. This type of machine is comparatively cheap and has the virtue of producing quite a large quantity (3½ –4½ litres/4–5 American quarts) of ice cream at fairly low cost. It can be used anywhere, as long as ice and salt travels with it.

The serious disadvantages of this type of machine, whether hand or electrically operated, are the amount of ice and salt needed and the time to set up and clean up. Be careful that no brine gets into the canister when dismantling and removing the dasher from the container of freshly churned ice cream. If it is to be used within an hour, scrape the ice cream from the dasher and pack it down into the canister. The ice cream can then be hardened by repacking the canister in the bucket with additional ice and salt; then wrap the bucket with a blanket, or transfer the canister to a freezer if your freezer is large enough.

Crushed ice and salt ratios for making and hardening ices are given on page 182.

2. *Fridge/freezer or freezer type often called sorbetières.* This unit fits into the freezing compartment of a refrigerator or in a deep freeze. The flattened power cord comes out through the closed door and operates an electric motor that churns the mix as well as driving a small fan to circulate the cold air around a canister which remains stationary.

These machines are comparatively cheap and are a fairly small unit to store. But our experience of using them is that when operating they generate a considerable amount of condensation in the freezer and take some 30 minutes to produce rather small quantities.

A satisfactory machine for those people who occasionally want to make ice cream in small quantities.

3. *Prefrozen canister.* The new concept in ice cream machines. The canister has a surrounding hollow jacket in which is sealed a coolant, liquid at room temperature and solid when frozen; the principle is the same as that of freezer packs. The container needs freezing overnight to chill sufficiently. It is then put into, or locked on to, the machine and the dasher inserted before the chilled ice mix is poured in. An electric motor then rotates either the

dasher or the complete canister, depending on the design of the machine.

Hand-cranked versions are also available. These are of a limited capacity, right down to individual portions for children.

For the serious home ice-cream maker this type of machine is probably the best buy. They are moderately priced and make a smooth ice in about the shortest time.

We have tried out a number of these and find them excellent. However, you need to think ahead as the canister requires up to eight hours in the freezer before you make an ice.

The alternative is to keep the canister permanently in the freezer to allow for impromptu ice-cream making, but this does occupy valuable freezer space.

Also bear in mind that the canister is only good for making one batch, which can be a problem if the recipe makes too much for the capacity of the machine. For this reason, we strongly recommend buying two canisters, and storing them permanently in the freezer – if you have the freezer capacity.

The only other disadvantage we have found is that the coolant is so efficient that once the ice has churned to a satisfactory consistency the machine should be stopped and the ice scraped out as quickly as possible or it will freeze hard on to the sides of the canister, making its removal difficult and the overall texture of the finished ice uneven.

Enormous fun can be had with the small ice-makers that use this pre-chilled canister principle. Some are designed specifically to be used by children and process little more than a single portion of ice cream. We have even heard that some enterprising restaurants use these tiny machines to make up single portions to order.

4. *Self-contained ice-cream machine with integral refrigeration unit.* These have refined ice cream and sorbet making down to the turn of a switch. All these machines normally require is 5–10 minutes to allow the compressor to chill the machine to the operating temperature, the

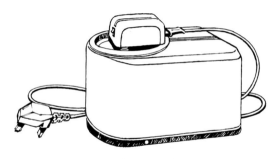

dasher is then inserted and set in motion, then the liquid ice mix poured in.

This is the Rolls-Royce end of the ice-cream machine market, and this fact is reflected in the price. They are all in excess of £200.00 ($300.00).

This type is for the very serious ice-cream maker or the small restaurant, as you can go on making ices all day long. If you are buying one for the home, make sure you are going to get your money's worth out of it; these machines are too big and too expensive to consign to the cupboard under the sink after the first flush of enthusiasm. In fact, because they contain their own refrigeration unit, these machines are large and the greatest disadvantage is the amount of space they take up on a counter in the kitchen, or when stored. This also makes them heavy; and, for the compressor's sake, they should be kept upright all the time, and adjusted so that they are level when in use.

Some have an optional removable bowl; you would be well advised to consider this. On the one hand it somewhat reduces the efficiency of the machine (i.e. making a batch of ice cream takes longer) and this requires the addition of a salt or alcohol solution to create a seal between the bowls. On the other hand, having a removable bowl makes both the serving and transfer of the ices easier and the cleaning of the machine much simpler. Careful cleaning is very important as this type of machine can easily start smelling sour.

Use a washing-up brush and a standard solution of the type used for sterilising babies' bottles. NOTE: Take extra care of the lids as they are fragile, and can be troublesome and expensive to replace.

Jugs Measuring jugs are a necessity and something you almost cannot have too many of but they can take up a lot of storage space. You need an assortment that includes:

1. Two × 2½ litre/80 fl oz jugs, one lidded.

2. Two × 1¼ litre/40 fl oz.

3. One × 250 ml/8 fl oz.

We prefer unbreakable plastic jugs, the polypropylene type. These are opaque, so it is slightly harder to see the level of the liquid inside the jug, but durability wins over visibility. Check that the graduations are clearly marked in the sort of measurements you both understand and will use.

Don't then put the jugs in the dishwasher as the graduations will become illegible. Tall narrow jugs are best for fridge storage, bowl-shaped ones are good for mixing.

Kulfi moulds If you go to the trouble of making kulfi it is nicer to use the correct moulds (see Useful Addresses page 184).

They are inexpensive and available in either plastic or aluminium. We prefer the plastic ones because the screw tops seem more efficient. A lolly mould of approximately the same shape that comes in a tray of six could be substituted. It is available in some supermarkets and kitchen stores.

Labels Use freezer-proof labels with extra strong adhesive backing; ordinary labels simply peel off in the cold of the freezer. Always label everything you put in the fridge or freezer, with both description and date, using a freezer pen (see pens).

Liquidiser/blender See Food processor/liquidiser/blender.

Lolly moulds Various sorts are available but the type shown on the right is really worth searching out. They

are available in a tray of six in some supermarkets and are easy to stand in the freezer. The lids act as both cover and lolly stick (see Useful Addresses page 184).

Measuring spoons All spoon measurements are based on:
1 tablespoon = 15 ml
1 teaspoon = 5 ml
½ teaspoon = 2.5 ml
¼ teaspoon = 1.25 ml

The sort we prefer to use come in a five-piece set and includes an eighth of a teaspoon. We particularly like the type with a flat base that will sit on the work surface.
All spoon measurements are level.
(See also cup measures.)

Mixer For the non-professional cook who probably lacks the muscles, an electric hand mixer is essential for making parfaits. But a balloon or rotary whisk will substitute for whipping cream or egg whites.

Moulds See bombe and kulfi.

Paper Greaseproof or silicone paper is needed to cover ices during chilling, to reduce evaporation, stop skin formation on custards and exclude air from ices being stored in the freezer. If making any quantity of ice cream have a supply of paper pieces ready cut to size to fit the plastic boxes you plan to use.

Pens Get a special freezer pen to write on labels and on freezer boxes. With these your writing will neither dissolve nor run.

Pizelle A very thin, Italian waffle biscuit that can be rolled to make an ice-cream cone.

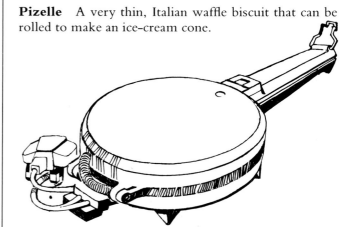

Pizelle maker We bought our machine in Williams-Sonoma in Washington D.C. We have not found these anywhere in Britain. They are a luxury, but they certainly speed up the making of professional-looking cones and also enable you to make your own wafers, pizelle and cones to accompany ices. Try our recipe for cones on page 158 for excellent results.

Saccharometer/hydrometer If you want to stray outside the recipes in this book, or are interested in the technical side of making ices, we strongly advise you to purchase a saccharometer.

The reason for this is that successful water ices depend on the correct ratio of sugar to liquid. The amount of sugar present in a liquid increases the density.

If it were only a matter of having to know the quantity of sugar in any amount of water, weighing the sugar and measuring the water would suffice. However, water ices are more complicated liquids, made up, for example, of various puréed fruits, fruit juices and alcohol as well as the basic sugar and water.

Each additional ingredient brings its own sugar and water and it is the **resulting density of these ingredients combined that you need to know**; only a saccharometer will tell you this.

A saccharometer is a glass instrument about 15 cm/ 6 inches long that looks like a thick clinical thermometer with a large bulb at the base, which is weighted. This means that when put into a liquid the calibrated stem floats above the surface of the liquid to a greater or lesser degree, depending on the density.

The reading is taken at the point where the instrument leaves the liquid.

Saccharometers are obtainable in wine-making accessory shops and good kitchen equipment shops.

They are calibrated either in specific gravity or according to the Baumé scale. The latter is an old system of measuring the strength of syrups, in whole numbers referred to as e.g. 18° Baumé. The scale is named after the French chemist, Antoine Baumé (1728–1804), who invented it. Although it is getting quite difficult to find Baumé saccharometers it is worth searching hard for one as it is so much easier to use the clearly marked whole numbers than the sometimes minute and complicated markings of decimals denoting specific gravity or density.

It is probably the simplicity of this system that maintains its popularity over specific gravity, density and other measuring systems such as Brix in the U.S.A.

There seems to be a lot of confusion vis-à-vis hydrometers and saccharometers.

A saccharometer is a refined type of hydrometer, that is calibrated on a scale especially suitable for measuring sugar syrups.

If you buy a hydrometer it will cover a much wider range of densities for all liquids but it may not clearly cover the small part of the scale you require for sugar syrups and may not be that easy to read.

With the saccharometer you would do well to buy a density-measuring cylinder. Known as an éprouvette in France, a much prettier word, this is a tall cylinder about 19 cm/7½ inches high and 4 cm/1½ inches in diameter with a wide-footed base for stability and a loop handle.

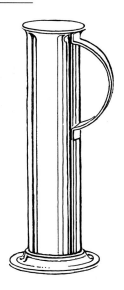

They are made of metal, usually tinned or in stainless steel. This gives sufficient depth to float the saccharometer in a small amount of mix. These are more readily found in France (see Useful Addresses, page 184). However, we have recently come across a slightly larger clear plastic/styrene measuring cylinder some 25 cm/10 inches high and 4 cm/1½ inches in diameter with no handle. This does exactly the same job for a fraction of the price. These are to be found in shops specialising in home-made wines and beers.

Saucepans Since in the majority of recipes the cooking is confined to custards, we suggest you buy a good quality non-stick or enamel medium-sized 20 cm/8 inch pan. (See also Double saucepans.)

PLEASE NOTE: Aluminium pans discolour egg-based sauces. White Opal glass saucepans, particularly the French Arcopal ones, are ideal as the handles can be removed for refrigerator and microwave use.

Scales Not essential but always useful. In the U.S.A. a pair of scales is a rarity in the kitchen. We have therefore avoided the use of weights for the U.S. measurements except where they are likely to be encountered in the supermarket.

The most important requirement of a pair of scales is that it is accurate (to within 5 g) *and remains so*. We prefer a commercial size of the old-fashioned balance scale and have both metric and imperial weights.

Scoops/dippers/dishers There are two types; mechanical and non-mechanical. The mechanical type relies on pressing the ice into a hemispherical spoon. Squeezing and releasing the double handle then sweeps a bar across the bowl of the spoon and releases the ice.

These come in all sorts of shapes and sizes and the better quality ones are numbered according to the

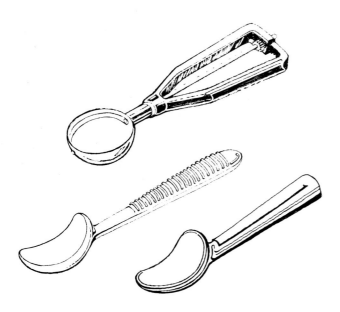

number of scoops to be had from a pint or quart or litre, depending on the origin and date of manufacture.

NOTE: Since metrication, scoops made in Britain will be numbered according to how many scoops can be had from a litre. American scoop numbers are based on the American quart (i.e. 32 fl oz).

Cheap scoops are a false economy; they either do not operate smoothly or lock in one position. The best quality ones will be expensive but they will work smoothly and last almost for ever.

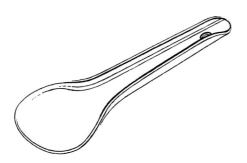

Non-mechanical scoops are cheaper, the best contain a liquid to stop the ice sticking. These scoops are drawn across the surface of the ice cream, forming the scooped-up layer into a ball, in the manner of a butter curler.

A flat stainless-steel paddle type of server can sometimes be found. Surprisingly, we bought one locally which was imported from Sicily, and in a local café the Italian proprietor still uses exactly the same paddle to fill the ice-cream cones. They are also useful for packing ice cream into containers.

Sieves You need:

1. A set of three nylon sieves. (These are used to avoid taint or discoloration to acid mixes or red berry fruits.)

2. A set of three fine metal sieves (for straining fibres and fragments of pips from purées.)

3. A plastic "tea strainer" sized sieve for straining lemon juice.

4. A fine mesh chinoise, or pointed sieve, which strains custards neatly from the tip.

5. A large colander, liberally perforated, which allows soft fruits to be rinsed with the minimum damage.

Spatulas Some ice-cream machine makers supply a spatula that fits the curve of the machine canister exactly; use it, as it is quicker and more efficient than anything else.

A selection of hard and soft, plastic and rubber spatulas is essential. The slightly bowl-shaped flexible rubber spatulas are worth searching out (see Useful Addresses page 184.)

Spoons (cooking) To avoid the wrong flavours creeping into ices, reserve a range of different size wooden spoons and put a blob of coloured paint on the tip of the handles to ensure that they are used exclusively for sweet mixes. Or you can use heatproof melamine spoons that carry no flavours if you don't mind their rather unsympathetic hardness.

Storage boxes Find a local supplier for these if you can, or buy them by mail order. When purchased in packs of ten they are quite cheap, which is good because you can use a lot of them. 1 litre/32 fl oz and 500 ml/16 fl oz boxes are best. Smaller ones are not much use (see Useful Addresses page 184).

Thermometer As with an oven, it is important to know if your fridge and freezer are at the correct temperatures. If you do not have thermometers in them we would advise that you get them; the results might surprise you. Small self-adhesive thermometers are obtainable in most supermarkets and freezer stores.

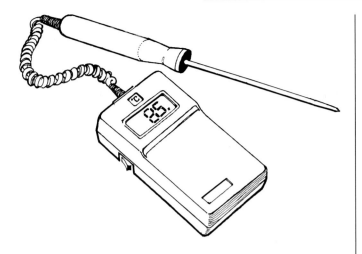

You also need a cooking thermometer that reads from 20–190°C/50–375°F. This will cover all your needs outside the freezer. Don't ever plunge a glass spirit thermometer straight into hot or cold liquid or it will fracture. Warm it in hot water before measuring the temperature of a hot liquid. Cool on a dry surface before washing.

A real luxury we have discovered is a digital-probe thermometer. These vary in temperature range but one that reads from −49°C to 199.9°C covers everything you could want in a kitchen and is ideal for checking custards, freezers and internal temperatures of ices (see Useful Addresses page 184).

Whisks Plastic or wood, small, light balloon-type whisks are good to stir custards in a non-stick pan. Also, in the absence of an electric hand mixer, a good-sized stainless steel balloon whisk can be used.

Zester A really good stainless steel zester is very useful but surprisingly hard to find; Victorinox make a particularly good one (see Useful Addresses page 184.) If unobtainable, use a sharp potato peeler; then cut the strips very, very finely. However, if you remove some of the bitter white pith with the zest (the coloured part only), shave this off, using a sharp knife angled almost flat against the peel.

Small spades used for serving ice cream, WMF Germany, *c.* 1900.

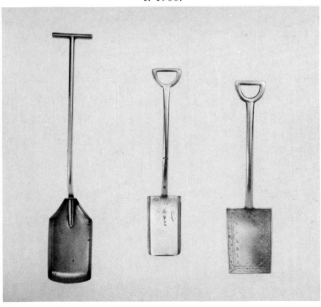

CHAPTER 6

Recipes

Introduction

There are a number of basic recipes and techniques in making ices and to avoid needless repetition these are given in detail below. However, before starting to make any ices, please read our advice on hygiene and the proper handling and storage of ices, as well as the instructions concerning fridges and freezers; these basics are important.

A typical caricature of an Italian vendor, at odds with the language, selling both penny licks and Hokey Pokey (note the discarded wrappers on the ground). Postmarked 1906.

Hygiene

Firstly, all equipment used in the making of ices should be kept scrupulously clean. Ideally, those items that can, should be put through a dishwashing machine. Otherwise, they should be washed in hot soapy water, rinsed in very hot water and left to dry in the air, rather than dried with a cloth.

We carry out this washing process before and after each session. So, in effect, all items are doubly clean.

Always refer to the manufacturer's instructions concerning the cleaning of machine parts. After each ice-making session we recommend the machines themselves

are wiped over with a clean cloth wrung out in sterilising solution; the sort and strength that is used for sterilising babies' bottles.

Ices, if badly handled, can provide an ideal breeding ground for all sorts of undesirable organisms, so it is important to bear in mind a few fundamental principles. These are, that food-borne bacteria can be destroyed by heat and are rendered inactive and unable to multiply by cold. **They multiply most rapidly at temperatures around human blood heat.** At temperatures slightly above or below they can still multiply, but at a slower rate. At temperatures below 10°C/50°F they are not killed but the rate of multiplication slows considerably as the temperature drops from this point; above 63°C/145°F they start to die.

For the maker of ices the main aim and object is to move the mixture through this critical temperature range, around blood heat, as quickly as possible, thereby minimising the potential for bacterial growth. Therefore we recommend that as soon as a custard has reached 85°C/185°F and is thickened, it should be cooled to below 10°C/50°F as quickly as possible. To do this, plunge the pan containing the custard into a bowl of cold water. Leave, stirring occasionally, until the custard is cool enough to put into the fridge.

NOTE: It may be necessary to change the water in the bowl if it becomes tepid.

The custard can now be transferred to a jug, covered and refrigerated. In this state it is perfectly safe to store overnight in the fridge as long as it is kept well away from any strongly smelling or uncooked or raw foods.

In uncooked ices such ingredients as cream and milk should be pre-chilled before mixing together, then frozen as soon as possible. We recommend that the ice cream be eaten within 1–2 days.

The only other area that should give rise to concern is when a made ice is taken from the freezer and thawed sufficiently to eat, and the remainder then re-frozen. From the health aspect, it is unwise to carry out this process more than twice. It will also interfere with the consistency of the ice. Do not attempt to re-freeze any ice that has fully thawed to a liquid state.

FRIDGES AND FREEZERS

Most people do not know the running temperature of either their fridge or freezer; we advise the purchase of thermometers (see Equipment page 44) so that you can get to know the variations of temperature, according to use and season. This can be quite an eye-opener.

The recipes in this book are based on the running temperature of a fridge at 4°C/39°F and freezer at −18°C/0°F.

Remember: an overloaded or iced-up fridge or freezer will not function properly. They also need to be level to operate efficiently.

Always check before you start that there is sufficient space in the freezer to accommodate the newly made ice. If you are using a canister-type machine, allow enough time for the insert to be completely frozen.

If you have a fast-freeze button or switch on your freezer, use it; switching it on ahead of time, if necessary. The use of this facility is particularly beneficial when still freezing to ensure the fast growth of small ice crystals to give a smooth-textured ice.

Basic recipes

WATER ICES

All the recipes for water ices (i.e. sorbets and granitas), as well as the hybrid sherbets and the parfaits, are based on a sugar syrup.

SUGAR SYRUP

Sugar syrup is a combination of sugar and water, also referred to by cooks and chefs as simple or stock syrup. This is made in varying strengths so even if a recipe calls for stock/simple syrup for a sorbet or parfait it is impossible to know what the writer intended – which is absurd when the success of an ice depends on it.

We have used a standard sugar syrup instead of different quantities of sugar and water in each recipe because it is quicker and easier to use a syrup rather than measuring and mixing small quantities of sugar and water each time. More importantly, a standard syrup establishes a basis from which any fruit, vegetable or herb can be formulated into a successful recipe for sorbets, granitas and spooms; follow the guidelines on page 178.

Our sugar syrup is:

1 kilo of sugar to 1 litre of water *or*
5 cups sugar to 4 cups water *or*
2 lb 3 oz sugar to 32 fl oz water

This makes

1600 ml/6⅔ cups/54 fl oz of syrup

The chart on page 177 gives the measurements for making smaller quantities of this syrup, if necessary.

There are elaborate instructions in some books on making syrups, boiling and skimming them for anything up to 10 minutes. This is simply not necessary. Sugar syrup in small quantities can be made with cold water taken straight from the tap, if you can be bothered to stand there and stir it until the sugar has dissolved. This has the advantage that, once the sugar has dissolved, the syrup is immediately ready for use. However, for quantities like the basic recipe we prefer to put a vanilla bean in a measuring jug, pour in a litre of boiling water, then add the sugar. Stir until the sugar has dissolved, which takes less than half a minute. Cool, cover, then refrigerate. That is all you need to do.

Boiling simply evaporates some of the water and increases the density of the syrup to a greater or lesser degree, depending on the diameter of the saucepan. Only those people living at 6,000 feet or over will have any trouble with our technique. At this altitude it is necessary to heat the sugar and water in order to get the sugar to dissolve.

Once made and cooled, the syrup should be kept in a lidded or covered jug in the refrigerator, with the vanilla bean in it.

The syrup will keep for 2–3 days at kitchen temperature or at least 2 weeks in a refrigerator. It will probably keep much longer as the only cause of deterioration is the growth of yeast spores picked up from the air. Yeast growths will make the syrup cloudy, so do not use the syrup if it is anything other than clear.

The concentration of this sugar syrup is measured by the density. It will be 28° on the Baumé scale or 1.241 on a decimal scale (see page 177).

SORBETS

Sorbets are made using a proportion of the above basic sugar syrup plus flavouring. The ratio of sugar syrup varies according to the amount of liquid that is contained in the flavouring.

EGG WHITES

For advice on the health aspect of raw egg whites in sorbets please see Warning page 4. However, not all sorbets need the addition of raw egg whites. Surprisingly, egg white really only needs to be added to stabilise and/or lighten those sorbets which are prone to quick melting or have a dense texture because of a low proportion of pectin or fibre in the flavouring fruit.

Egg white should be lightly beaten with a fork to merely loosen it before adding. It is not necessary to beat it any further than this, *certainly not* to the point of a foam.

DE'

SORBETTI

S A G G I O

DEL DOTTOR

FILIPPO BALDINI

Profeſſor di Medicina , e Membro di varie Regali Accademie Italiane, e Oltramontane.

SECONDA EDIZIONE

Corredata di nuove Aggiunte , e di alcune Oſſervazioni intorno all' Ananas.

****
******
*****
***
*

IN NAPOLI MDCCLXXXIV.
CON LICENZA DE' SUPERIORI

De' Sorbetti was the first book devoted to sorbets. Written in Naples, 1794.

STILL FREEZING

Still freezing is the method of freezing ice without an ice-cream machine.

For successful still freezing we strongly recommend that you check the temperature of your freezer (see fridges and freezers page 47).

Pour the chilled mixture into a strong polypropylene container, a sandwich or cake-box shape, 23×16×8 cm/ 9×6×3 inches, to give a depth of mix of approximately 4 cm/1½ inches. Cover with a lid and put in the coldest part of the freezer. Check after 1–1½ hours; the mixture should have frozen to a firm ring of ice around the sides and base of the box, with a soft slush in the centre. Then either:

1. Beat for a few seconds with a sturdy electric hand beater until the mixture forms a uniform slush.

or

2. Quickly process in a food processor to a uniform slush.

Quickly return the ice to the box, cover and put back in the freezer.

Repeat the beating or processing at least twice at intervals of 1–1½ hours. After the third beating, the ice will need freezing for a further 30–60 minutes to be sufficiently firm to serve. If freezer space is limited it may be more convenient to transfer it to a deeper, smaller box after the third beating.

Once frozen solid, transfer the sorbet to the main body of the fridge for about 20 minutes before serving.

NOTE: Alcohol-flavoured ices will take longer to freeze and you are best advised to make them the day before. However they will require less time to soften in the fridge and can sometimes be served almost directly from the freezer.

STIR FREEZING (OR CHURNING)

If you are using an electric machine, switch on and allow a pre-chilling time, if necessary. Pour in the chilled, flavoured syrup and churn for 10–15 minutes until frozen to a soft slush. At this stage the lightly beaten egg white can be added while the machine is in motion. Continue churning until the mixture has achieved a soft ice that will hold its own shape in the manner of softly whipped cream.

If you wish to serve immediately, continue churning for up to 5 minutes longer to enable the ice to become firm enough to serve, in the manner of stiffly beaten cream.

If the sorbet is not to be served immediately, stop at the softly whipped cream stage and quickly transfer it to a plastic storage box. Cover with waxed or greaseproof paper or freezer dividing tissues placed directly on the exposed surface of the ice to exclude any air. Cover with a lid, label, then freeze until firm enough to serve, approximately 1–2 hours. If frozen solid, transfer the sorbet to the fridge for approximately 15–30 minutes to soften sufficiently to serve.

Using a machine, there is an enormous temptation to overchurn a sorbet as you see the volume increase. Try and resist this as it introduces too much air into the frozen mixture and will result in a fluffy consistency, more like compressed snow than a frozen water ice.

GRANITAS

Make the granita according to the recipe and thoroughly chill the liquid mixture in the fridge. When ready, pour into one or more strong polypropylene containers, a sandwich or shallow cake-box shape is ideal, approximately 25×25×8 cm/10×10×3 inches, to give a depth of mix of approximately 2 cm/¾ inch, then cover with a lid, and freeze. The aim is to achieve uniformly small separate ice crystals throughout, so the liquid will now need beating with a table fork at regular intervals during freezing. Use as shallow a box as you can find.

First freeze for 1 hour or until the liquid has formed an iced rim around the edge and is starting to freeze on the base. Scrape this away with a fork and combine evenly with the remaining liquid. Repeat this scraping and mixing process every 30 minutes for the remaining 2½ hours or until the mixture forms a smooth consistency of identifiable ice crystals. Ideally, it should be eaten at once, but it can be held at a good consistency for up to 4 hours if stirred once or twice to break up any clumps of ice crystals that form, especially around the edges.

If kept overnight, allow to defrost slightly in a fridge for 30 minutes; beat again with a fork to get an even consistency then re-freeze for about 30 minutes. You may need to fork and re-freeze once more to regain a good granita texture.

This may seem like a lot of work, especially if you have read recipes telling you to break the mixture up in a food processor once it has gone solid. Of course you can do this, but the consistency will become too fine, like a very icy sorbet, rather than the rougher texture of a true granita.

To achieve the perfect granita, there is no substitute for the fork technique.

PARFAITS

There are many techniques for making parfaits, all of which we have tried. In our opinion, the recipe below gives the best result for an alcohol-flavoured parfait. It may seem rather painstaking and detailed, but if you follow it to the letter the result will be excellent.

We have tried and recommend the following flavours: Cointreau, dry sherry, Strega, Amaretto, Pernod, Mandarine Napoléon and whisky. The amount of alcohol needed for this recipe will vary between 15–60 ml/1–4 tablespoons, according to taste. However, do not try to add more than the upper limit as it will prevent the parfait freezing.

The classic flavour for a parfait is coffee. This requires a slightly different technique than an alcohol-based parfait (see Coffee Parfait page 85), as does Chocolate Parfait (page 73).

PARFAITS

Parfait

This recipe can be adapted to use any fortified wine or liqueur of your choice, see above.
The recipe is precise in order to get a perfect result.

INGREDIENTS

	Metric	U.S.	Imperial
Egg yolks	4	4	4
Sugar syrup (see page 47)	185 ml	¾ cup	6 fl oz
Whipping/heavy cream (36 per cent fat)	250 ml	1 cup	8 fl oz
Alcohol	1–4 Tbsp	1–4 Tbsp	1–4 Tbsp
Makes about	1.25 litres	5 cups	40 fl oz

For this recipe you will need a thermometer, a three-speed electric hand mixer and, preferably, a double saucepan. Failing this, select a large heatproof bowl which will sit snugly into a saucepan. Into the bowl put the yolks and use the electric mixer to whisk them until light and pale.

Warm the syrup to 30–40°C/86–104°F (around blood heat), then whisk this, a few tablespoons at a time, into the egg yolks. Try not to take this stage too fast or the eggs will scramble. Now, either position the bowl over, not in, a saucepan of barely simmering water, or pour the mixture into the top of a double saucepan positioned over, but not in, scarcely simmering water. Cook, stirring occasionally to make sure the mixture is not over-cooking on the base or in the angles of the pan. Heat either until the temperature reaches 85°C/185°F or until the mixture has thickened sufficiently to coat the back of a spoon. It will take up to 20–25 minutes.

Now remove the mixture from over the water and pour into a large, deep mixing bowl. Using an electric beater, beat on high speed for about 1 minute. Then adjust to medium speed and continue for a further 3–4 minutes. Finally, turn down to low speed for 5 minutes. By this stage the volume will have increased by about 50 per cent. The mix will be almost cold and thick enough to hold a ribbon of mixture trailed over the surface. Put the bowl containing the mix, and a second empty bowl, plus the whipping cream, into the fridge and leave to chill for at least 1 hour.

When ready remove the empty bowl, pour in the chilled cream and beat until it forms soft peaks. Now remove the yolk/syrup mixture from the fridge and gently fold in the whipped cream in about four stages. After the second lot of cream has been added, sprinkle in the alcohol and continue to fold in the remaining cream until all has been added and is evenly mixed. Pour into a plastic freezer box and cover with waxed or greaseproof paper and a lid. Finally label, then freeze for at least 2 hours. A parfait, if frozen solid, will need about 15–20 minutes in the fridge to soften sufficiently to serve.

If the parfait is being used in a bombe, pour into a prepared bombe mould (see page 38) and proceed as for bombe making.

The only drawing of the original Pêche Melba, 1899.

ICE CREAMS

French Vanilla Ice Cream

These are our favourite custard-based ice creams.

INGREDIENTS

	Metric	U.S.	Imperial
Milk	300 ml	1¼ cups	10 fl oz
Vanilla bean	1	1	1
Granulated sugar	100 g	½ cup	3½ oz
Egg yolks	3	3	3
Whipping/heavy cream			
(36 per cent fat)	250 ml	1 cup	8 fl oz
Makes about	800 ml	3¼ cups	26 fl oz

Rich French Vanilla Ice Cream

INGREDIENTS

	Metric	U.S.	Imperial
Milk	375 ml	1½ cups	12 fl oz
Vanilla bean	1	1	1
Granulated sugar	90 g	½ cup minus 1 Tbsp	3¼ oz
Egg yolks	5	5	5
Whipping/heavy cream			
(36 per cent fat)	185 ml	¾ cup	6 fl oz
Makes about	800 ml	3¼ cups	26 fl oz

Combine the milk, vanilla bean (split in half lengthwise) and half the sugar in a medium-sized saucepan and bring to just below boiling point. Remove the pan from the heat, cover and leave aside for a minimum of 15 minutes to allow the vanilla flavour to develop.

Meanwhile, in a medium-sized heatproof bowl, combine the egg yolks with the remaining sugar and beat, preferably with an electric hand mixer, until the mixture is pale and thick enough to hold the shape when a ribbon of mix is trailed across the surface. Bring the milk back to boiling point, then pour it in a thin stream on to the egg yolks and sugar, whisking steadily as the milk is added.

The bowl can now be placed over a pan of simmering water, or the custard can be returned to the saucepan, which is then put on top of a heat-diffuser mat so that it is not in direct contact with the heat. Only if you have an accurate thermometer and/or are confident that you will not overheat the sauce, should you put the saucepan over a gentle direct heat. Use a small wooden spoon or spatula to stir the custard. As it heats over water, the custard will not suffer as long as it is stirred frequently and it will take from 5–30 minutes (depending on the thickness of the bowl or the pan) to thicken sufficiently, or reach 85°C/185°F.

Over direct heat the custard needs constant attention and will take about 8–10 minutes. Without a thermometer: to judge if the custard has thickened sufficiently, remove the spoon and tilt the back of it towards you. Look first at the way the sauce coats the spoon. If it forms only a thin film, try drawing a horizontal line across the back of the spoon. This should hold a clear shape. If not, continue cooking the custard until it coats the back of the spoon more thickly and holds a clear line.

As soon as the custard has reached the right tempera-

The Original Pêche Melba

Inspired by a performance of *Lohengrin*, in which Madame Melba took the role of Elsa, Escoffier created a new sweet as a surprise for the brilliant singer, who was dining at the Savoy the following day.

Peaches and vanilla ice cream were served on a silver dish set between the wings of a swan, recalling the famous scene from the opera; this swan was carved from a block of ice and covered with "sucre filé" (spun sugar). The sweet was named "Les Pêches au Cygne".

The necessity of carving the swan out of ice, using hot irons, chisels and knives, prevented the sweet from becoming generally popular. It was not until some eight years later on, 1 July 1899, to celebrate the opening of the Carlton Hotel in London's Haymarket, that Escoffier added the raspberry purée to this recipe and told a waiter to set it before Melba. She enjoyed it so much she asked its name and Escoffier sent back a request. "Would she allow him to call it Pêches Melba?" Thus was created the true Pêche Melba.

ture and thickened sufficiently remove the pan from the heat and plunge the base in a few inches of cold water. On no account should the custard be allowed to overheat or boil as the mixture will curdle. (For how to deal with an overheated custard see below.) Leave to cool, stirring occasionally until the mixture feels as though it has never been heated.

HOW TO DEAL WITH AN OVERHEATED CUSTARD

If the custard overheats, at a temperature of about 88°C/190°F, the protein in the egg will coagulate and harden, and the custard will take on a velvety look. If this begins to happen, or the mixture boils, immediately remove from the heat and plunge the pan or basin into cold water. Whisk vigorously for 1 minute or so until the temperature drops below the danger point. Continue carefully as per the recipe.

In our opinion, it is better to avoid using cornflour. The temperature required to cook out cornflour is much higher than eggs can stand. And to add enough cornflour to hold the eggs at a sufficiently high temperature for a long enough time to thicken the cornflour completely changes the nature of the custard. Life is much easier if you use a thermometer.

Remove the pan from the cold water bath and transfer the custard to a bowl or jug, leaving the vanilla bean in the custard. Cover and chill in the fridge. The mixture can be left overnight at this stage. When ready, start the ice-cream machine. Use a teaspoon or the back of a knife to separate the tiny black vanilla seeds from the bean. Stir into the custard with the chilled cream and pour into the ice-cream machine. Either still freeze (see page 48) or churn until the ice cream is the consistency of softly whipped cream.

STILL FREEZING

Still freezing is the method of freezing ices without an ice-cream machine.

For still freezing the ice creams, see the instructions for sorbet still freezing page 48.

STIR FREEZING (OR CHURNING)

If you are using an electric machine, switch on and allow a pre-chilling time, if necessary. Set the machine in motion before pouring in the mixture. (NOTE: Some machines have an awkward aperture and it is difficult to pour in the mix fast without spilling it. Use a large plastic funnel to solve this problem.) Pour in the liquid ice-cream mix, to fill the canister not more than ¾ full, to allow for overrun. Churn for 15–20 minutes or until frozen to a consistency that is stiff enough to hold a shape. There is an enormous temptation to overchurn the ice cream. The

longer it is churned beyond this time the greater the chance of the ice cream being spoiled by butter flecks as the cream begins to turn to butter.

If the ice is not to be served immediately, quickly transfer it to a plastic freezer box, and cover with waxed or greaseproof paper or freezer dividing tissues placed directly on the exposed surface of the ice to exclude any air. Cover with a lid. Finally label, then freeze until firm enough to serve, approximately 30–60 minutes.

When ready to serve transfer the ice cream to the fridge for approximately 20–30 minutes to soften sufficiently to serve.

STORAGE

Boxes
While the large, shallow, flatter boxes are better for making granitas and still freezing other ices, they take up a lot of space in an average-sized freezer.

Since it is preferable to fill boxes to capacity with an ice and thereby exclude as much moisture-laden air as possible, we recommend storing ices in polypropylene boxes of 1 litre/32 fl oz and ½ litre/16 fl oz capacity (see Equipment page 38).

These should be filled to within 6 mm/¼ inch of the top to allow for expansion during freezing, and the surface of the ice covered with waxed or greaseproof paper, or freezer dividing tissue, which will minimise the formation of ice crystals.

It is extraordinary how quickly you forget what is in the freezer and how long it has been there. For this reason, be meticulous about labelling all ices that go into the freezer.

Shelf life
Although ices will keep for years in a well maintained freezer and remain safe to eat, the eating qualities of such ices would leave a lot to be desired. We feel that as a general rule home-made ices are best eaten within 1–2 days of making. Uncooked ices should definitely be eaten within this period and cooked ones we tend not to keep for more than 1 month. Beyond this period flavours develop unpredictably.

Serving
Advertising has done a great disservice to ice cream in portraying hoardings and photographs of rock-hard balls of ice cream. In order to get the full flavour from ices, they need to be served one degree removed from melting.

Almond Granita

It is very difficult getting the almond flavour in a water ice and we have tried many methods, but this one really does achieve it. It produces a wonderfully refreshing granita, which relies on orgeat, a syrup made from almonds, sugar and flower water that is used extensively in cocktail-making. We expressly recommend French orgeat and no other. Using almonds simply produces a gritty, rough ice with a rather unpleasant aftertaste.

INGREDIENTS

	Metric	U.S.	Imperial
Sugar syrup (see page 47)	250 ml	1 cup	8 fl oz
Orgeat	8 Tbsp	8 Tbsp	8 Tbsp
Water, chilled	700 ml	2¾ cups	22 fl oz
Lemon juice	3 Tbsp	3 Tbsp	3 Tbsp
Slivered almonds for decoration			
Makes about	1 litre	4 cups	32 fl oz

Combine the chilled syrup, orgeat and chilled water in a jug and stir thoroughly. Add 2 Tbsp of the lemon juice, taste and add the third, if necessary. Do not worry if it tastes rather flat, freezing and the texture improve the taste out of all recognition.

For detailed instructions on how to prepare the perfect granita see page 49.

Serving
Decorate with the slivered almonds.

Sister Theresa went to the freezer
To get herself a granita.
When she got there,
The freezer was bare,
'cos Sister Anita had beat 'er.

Anon

Amaretto Parfait

See page 49.

Angelica Sorbet

Associating angelica with the crystallised green bits on the top of trifle and butter-creamed cakes, we were unsure whether fresh angelica would make a good sorbet. Though the result is not to everyone's taste we were agreeably surprised. We found the flavour very complementary to other fruits, such as rhubarb and apple, and exquisite with soft red berries and peaches.
We originally tried angelica leaves, but young or old they are inclined to be bitter when used in the quantity needed to flavour a sorbet. Using the fresh stalks alone gave us exactly the flavour we were looking for.

INGREDIENTS

	Metric	U.S.	Imperial
Fresh angelica stem 1.25 cm or ½ inch thick	22 cm	9 inch	9 inch
Sugar syrup (see page 47)	250 ml	1 cup	8 fl oz
Water	125 ml	½ cup	4 fl oz
Lemon juice	2 Tbsp	2 Tbsp	2 Tbsp
Dry white wine	65 ml	¼ cup	2 fl oz
Makes about	500 ml	2 cups	16 fl oz

Wash carefully, dry and cut the angelica stem in 2.5 cm/ 1 inch pieces. Put them in a non-reactive saucepan with the sugar syrup and the water. Bring to the boil and boil gently for 2 minutes. Remove from the heat, add the wine and lemon juice and cool overnight in the fridge. When ready, strain the mixture and still freeze (see page 48) or start the ice-cream machine. Pour in the mixture and churn for about 20 minutes until the ice is firm enough to serve. If it is to be stored, quickly scrape the ice into plastic freezer boxes, and cover with a piece of waxed paper and a lid. Finally, label, then freeze. Once the ice becomes solid it will need about 20 minutes in the fridge before it is soft enough to serve.

NOTE: Angelica plants (*Angelica archangelica*) can be bought at nurseries specialising in herbs, but beware – they grow very large.

A diamond is the only type of ice that keeps a girl warm.

Elizabeth Taylor

Bramley Apple Ice Cream

As firm champions of British apples, and cooking apples in particular, we were trying to get a no-nonsense Bramley flavour to come through in this ice cream. We achieved it by marbling the apple purée through the vanilla ice cream.

INGREDIENTS

	Metric	U.S.	Imperial
Milk	500 ml	2 cups	16 fl oz
Vanilla bean	1	1	1
Granulated sugar	200 g	1 cup	7 oz
Egg yolks	6	6	6
Bramley apples	500 g	1¼ lb	1¼ lb
Grated lemon zest	1 tsp	1 tsp	1 tsp
Lemon juice	1 tsp	1 tsp	1 tsp
Water	2 Tbsp	2 Tbsp	2 Tbsp
Granulated sugar	2 Tbsp	2 Tbsp	2 Tbsp
Makes about	1 litre	4 cups	32 fl oz

Using the above quantities of milk, vanilla, sugar and egg yolks, prepare and cook custard according to the method for making French Vanilla Ice Cream (see page 51). Once the custard has thickened strain it, cover and chill in the fridge.

To prepare the apple pulp, peel, quarter and core the apples and slice immediately into a pan containing the grated zest, lemon juice and water. Toss the apple slices in this as you work to prevent them browning.

Transfer the pan to the heat and cook, covered, over a very low heat, until they have softened to a pulp; about 15 minutes. Remove the pan from the heat, stir in the 2 Tbsp of sugar then re-cover, cool and chill in the fridge. When ready to make the ice cream, either still freeze (see page 48) or start the ice-cream machine. Pour in the chilled custard and allow it to churn and freeze to the consistency of softly whipped cream. Quickly scrape into a rectangular plastic freezer box at least 1 litre/4 cup/32 fl oz capacity and fold in the chilled apple pulp. Do not worry if this is not done evenly, marbling adds

character to the ice cream. Level the surface, cover with a piece of waxed paper and a lid, then freeze. Serve within 1 hour or if frozen solid, allow 30 minutes in the fridge to soften sufficiently for serving.

Serving
Good served with Cider Sorbet (see page 80), and/or Light Lemon and Sultana Sauce (see page 165) or hot and fragrant stewed blackberries. A little esoteric but well worth trying: serve with hot elderflower fritters and lemon sauce minus the sultanas.

Apple and Verbena Sorbet

Verbena is a herb that is not used very often, perhaps because it needs such careful use; too much in the wrong place calls to mind the smell of soaps and cosmetics, and the association can ruin the enjoyment of the food. It is an unusual lemon flavour, slightly old-fashioned, but one that works very well with apples, making a sorbet that marries well with a vanilla ice cream.

NOTE: *The apple contributes a fair amount of pectin and fibre to this sorbet, making it more dense when frozen, so it will need some 30 minutes in the fridge before it is sufficiently soft to serve.*

INGREDIENTS

	Metric	U.S.	Imperial
Sprigs of verbena	2×13 cm	2×5 inch	2×5 inch
Sugar syrup (see page 47)	250 ml	1 cup	8 fl oz
Granny Smith apples	675 g	1½ lb	1½ lb
Juice of lemons	2	2	2
Water	125 ml	½ cup	4 fl oz
Makes about	750 ml	3 cups	24 fl oz

Rinse the sprigs of verbena and pat dry. Put one sprig into a medium-sized saucepan with the syrup and bring slowly to simmering point. Meanwhile peel, quarter and core the apples. Then immediately slice them thinly directly into the hot syrup to limit the browning of the apples. Bring back to simmering point, then cover and cook gently until the apple slices are tender. Remove the pan from the heat and leave to cool for 15 minutes.

Remove the sprig of verbena from the poached apples and transfer the contents of the saucepan to a food processor or blender. Add a further dozen leaves from the remaining sprig of verbena, the strained lemon juice and the water. Blend until the apples are reduced to a smooth purée and the verbena is finely chopped. Taste to assess the verbena flavour, and add up to a further dozen leaves, if liked. Blend again to chop down the fresh leaves. Transfer the purée to a jug, cover and chill in the fridge. When ready still freeze (see page 48) or start the ice-cream machine. Freeze until the mixture is firm enough to serve. To store, quickly scrape into plastic freezer boxes and cover with waxed or greaseproof paper and a lid. Finally label, then freeze. Once the sorbet becomes solid, it will need about 30 minutes in the fridge to soften sufficiently to serve.

Pippin and Rose Petal Ice Cream

This is an ice cream for an Indian summer, when roses start to look blowzy and the first of the Cox's Orange Pippins arrive in the shops. We used the petals of a small, pale pink, scented rose, a hybrid musk called Felicia, both to infuse the cream and torn up in the made ice cream, and found it combined with the flavour of the apples to produce an exquisite ice. However, do not worry if you cannot get this particular variety, simply use any highly scented rose variety available. (For suggested varieties see page 141.) Decorate the ice with a few crystallised rose petals scattered over each serving. Admittedly a very feminine ice cream.
NOTE: *Please be sure that you use untreated roses i.e. unsprayed roses only, and that they are freshly plucked.*

Valentine's Day cards frequently featured ice creams.

INGREDIENTS

	Metric	U.S.	Imperial
Rose heads	4	4	4
Whipping/heavy cream (36 per cent fat)	500 ml	2 cups	16 fl oz
Cox's Orange Pippins/ Pippins	450 g	1 lb	1 lb
Lemon	½	½	½
Caster/Ultra fine sugar	150 g	¾ cup	5¼ oz
Makes about	1 litre	4 cups	32 fl oz

Take 3 heads of roses and pull away the petals on to a plate. Sort through them carefully (they can carry a

surprising amount of wildlife) and discard any damaged outer petals. Put them into a saucepan with the cream and bring to the boil, then remove from the heat, cover and leave to infuse. Taste after 30 minutes to see if the flavour is strong enough to flavour both the cream and the apple. How long this will take varies considerably, according to the type of rose.

Peel, core and slice the apples thinly. If possible, cook them in a microwave as this method needs no additional water. Simply put the apple slices into a large shallow casserole so that they are distributed in a thin layer. Squeeze the lemon juice over the apples, cover and microwave on full heat for about 4 minutes or until the apple forms a soft pulp. Otherwise, cook gently with an additional 30 ml/2 Tbsp of water in a covered saucepan until the apples are soft.

Transfer the pulp to a food processor or blender, add the sugar and blend to a smooth purée. Pour into a bowl, cover and chill in the fridge until ready to use. When ready, still freeze (see page 48) or start the ice-cream machine. Strain the cream, pressing the rose petals firmly to extract all the cream and flavour. Combine with the apple purée and pour into the machine. While the ice cream is left to churn prepare the remaining rose head in

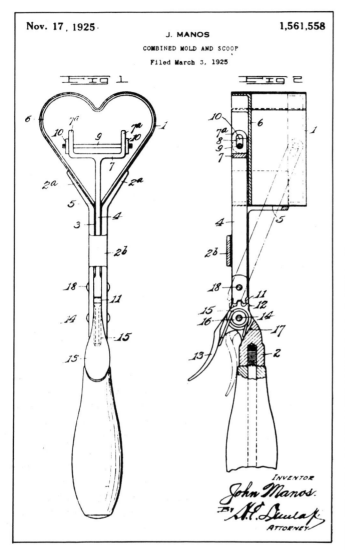

Nov. 17, 1925.   1,561,558

J. MANOS

COMBINED MOLD AND SCOOP

Filed March 3, 1925

A working model of this scoop was sold in 1990 for $6,000.

the same way, then tear the petals into small pieces. As soon as the ice has churned to the consistency of whipped cream, quickly scrape into plastic freezer boxes, sprinkling with the rose petals as you go.

Stir once or twice to mix evenly, then smooth the surface. Cover with waxed or greaseproof paper and a lid. Finally label, then freeze for a minimum of 1 hour. Allow approximately 20 minutes in the fridge before serving, if frozen hard. Serve this ice cream as fresh as possible.

Apricot and Cardamom Sherbet

A light, clean combination of milk, fresh apricots and a subtle spicing of cardamom.

INGREDIENTS

	Metric	U.S.	Imperial
Fresh apricots	450 g	1 lb	1 lb
Sugar syrup (see page 47)	250 ml	1 cup	8 fl oz
Cardamom pods	2	2	2
Milk, chilled	250 ml	1 cup	8 fl oz
Lemon juice	generous squeeze		
Egg white	1	1	1
Makes about	750 ml	3 cups	24 fl oz

Rinse, drain, halve and stone the apricots. Put the fruit in a pan with the sugar syrup and lightly crushed cardamom pods. Bring to the boil. Then cover and simmer gently for 5–10 minutes or until the fruit is just tender. Remove from the heat and leave to cool. Discard the cardamom pods before transferring the contents of the pan to the food processor or blender. This is because if the cardamom pods are puréed with the fruit the flavour could be a little too strong. Blend the fruit to a smooth purée, then check the consistency; some varieties of apricot can be fibrous in a way that neither food processors nor blenders can break down, so it may be necessary to sieve the purée at this stage. Transfer to a bowl then cover and chill in the fridge.

When ready, still freeze (see page 48) or start the ice-cream machine. Combine the apricot purée, chilled milk and sugar syrup, then taste and flavour with a squeeze of lemon juice. Pour into the machine and churn until the mixture is just starting to become icy. Using a fork, beat the egg white until loosened and add to the sherbet with the machine still running. Continue churning until the sherbet is firm enough to serve. Or to store, quickly scrape into plastic freezer boxes, and cover with waxed or greaseproof paper and a lid. Finally label, then freeze. Once the sherbet becomes solid it will need about 20 minutes in the fridge to soften sufficiently to serve.

Apricot, Honey and Yoghurt Ice

An excellent store-cupboard ice cream that is easily made.

INGREDIENTS

	Metric	U.S.	Imperial
Canned apricots in			
syrup	425 ml	15 fl oz	15 fl oz
Honey, clear	3 Tbsp	3 Tbsp	3 Tbsp
Granulated sugar	75 g	⅓ cup	2½ oz
Cornflour	2 tsp	–	2 tsp
or			
cornstarch	–	2 tsp	–
Apricot brandy	1 Tbsp	1 Tbsp	1 Tbsp
Greek/Russian style			
yoghurt	360 g	1½ cups	12¾ oz
Makes about	1.25 litres	5 cups	40 fl oz

Pour the contents of the can of apricots into a food processor or blender. Add the honey, then the sugar mixed with the cornflour and blend until smooth. Pour into a pan and bring to the boil, stirring. Boil gently for 2–3 minutes then remove from the heat and cool. Stir in the apricot brandy and the yoghurt and chill in the fridge. When ready still freeze (see page 48) or start the ice-cream machine. Pour in the mixture and churn until the ice is firm enough to serve. If it is to be stored, quickly scrape the ice into plastic freezer containers and cover with a piece of waxed or greaseproof paper and a lid. Finally label, then freeze. Once the ice cream becomes solid, it will then need about 20 minutes in the fridge before it is soft enough to serve.

RIDDLE

**As I was going o'er London Bridge,
I heard something crack;
Not a man in all England
can mend that!**

Answer is ice.

Apricot Sorbet

Apricots are one of the most disappointing of the soft fruits. They promise much but so seldom deliver – the flavour being woolly and elusive. By contrast dried apricots are much more reliable and suffer no seasonality.

INGREDIENTS

	Metric	U.S.	Imperial
Dried apricots	250 g	8 oz	8 oz
Boiling water	750 ml	3 cups	24 fl oz
Sugar syrup (see page			
47)	375 ml	1½ cups	12 fl oz
Juice of lemons,			
strained	3	3	3
Bitter almond extract	2 drops	2 drops	2 drops
Egg white	1	1	1
Makes about	1 litre	4 cups	32 fl oz

Rinse the apricots and put them in a medium-sized saucepan. Pour in the boiling water, cover and leave aside for 1 hour. Place the pan over the heat and bring to the boil. Now adjust heat to a gentle simmer and cook covered for about 15 minutes, or until the apricots are tender. Put straight into a food processor or blender; blend to a smooth purée, then sieve and add the sugar syrup and the strained lemon juice. Add 2 drops only of bitter almond essence, as this flavouring should be very subtle with only you knowing that it is there and no one else able to detect it. Taste and add more lemon juice, if preferred.

When ready, still freeze (see page 48) or start the ice-cream machine. Pour in the mixture and churn for about 10 minutes until just beginning to freeze very softly. Beat the egg white in a small bowl with a fork until loosened. Pour into the sorbet as it churns and leave the machine in motion until the ice is firm enough to serve. If it is to be stored, quickly scrape the ice into plastic freezer boxes and cover with a piece of waxed or greaseproof paper and a lid. Finally label, then freeze. Once the ice becomes solid it will need about 20 minutes in the fridge before it is soft enough to serve.

Avocado Ice Cream

That an avocado is not a starter, forever wedded to vinaigrette, prawns or crab, is still inclined to shock. If you might be facing this sort of resistance, slip this ice cream into a selection of Honey and Toasted Walnut (see page 101), Espresso coffee (see page 84), and Buttermilk (see page 66).

INGREDIENTS

	Metric	U.S.	Imperial
One recipe French Vanilla Ice Cream (see page 51), omitting the vanilla bean and substituting			
Vanilla extract	¼ tsp	¼ tsp	¼ tsp
Avocados/Haas, fully ripe	3	3	3
Lemon juice	1 tsp	1 tsp	1 tsp
Makes about	1 litre	4 cups	32 fl oz

Make the custard following the instructions for French Vanilla Ice Cream (see page 51), substituting the vanilla extract for the vanilla bean. Stir in the vanilla extract when the thickened custard is removed from the heat.

Leave the pan containing the custard sitting in cold water whilst you halve and scoop the avocado flesh from the shells into a food processor or blender. Pour in the warm custard and blend until smooth. At this stage, it is best to strain the mixture through a sieve into a bowl to remove small lumps of avocado and any flakes of brown skin from the stone which are inclined to get in. It will need stirring to persuade the mixture through the sieve as it is quite a thick consistency. Taste the custard and add sufficient lemon juice to bring forward the taste of the avocado. Then insert a piece of buttered greaseproof paper to lie directly on the surface of the custard and seal it to the edge and up the side of the bowl; this excludes the air and stops the avocado discolouring in the fridge.

NOTE: Because the avocados are prone to discolour it is best to make the ice cream as soon as the mixture has chilled. The colour will deaden and brown, the longer the mixture is left.

When ready, still freeze (see page 48) or start the ice-cream machine. Pour the custard into the machine and churn for about 10 minutes until the mixture is the consistency of thick cream. Quickly scrape into plastic freezer boxes, level the surface and cover with a piece of waxed or greaseproof paper and a lid. Finally label, then freeze. Serve within 1 hour or, if frozen solid, allow 30 minutes in the fridge to soften sufficiently for serving.

Avocado and Coffee Ice Cream
Es Krim Adpokat

This startling combination for a dessert ice cream comes from Thailand. Don't attempt it unless the avocado pears are bordering on the overripe; soft to the touch but undamaged.

INGREDIENTS

	Metric	U.S.	Imperial
Milk	625 ml	2½ cups	20 fl oz
Granulated sugar	225 g	1 cup plus 1 Tbsp	8 oz
Instant coffee granules	1 tsp	1 tsp	1 tsp
Vanilla extract	½ tsp	½ tsp	½ tsp
Avocados/Haas, really ripe (4)	800 g	1¾ lb	1¾ lb
Makes about	900 ml	3¾ cups	30 fl oz

Combine the milk, sugar and coffee together in a saucepan and bring to just below boiling point. Remove the pan from the heat and stir in the vanilla extract. Leave on one side whilst you halve the avocados and remove their stones. Then use a spoon to scoop out the flesh into a food processor or blender. Blend until smooth then, with the machine still running, pour in the milk mixture via the funnel. If the food processor is not large enough to take all the liquid, simply add as much as it will accommodate. When the mixture seems smooth, strain it to remove any pieces of avocado or flakes of brown skin from around the stone. Whisk in any remaining milk mixture. This mixture will lose its luminous green and discolour the longer it is left, so cover closely with buttered greaseproof paper, pushing it down directly on to the surface of the liquid and on to the sides of the jug to exclude as much air as possible. Then refrigerate. Once the mixture has cooled sufficiently, still freeze (see page 48) or churn in the ice-cream machine as soon as possible. When it has the consistency of thickly whipped cream stop the machine and quickly scrape the mixture into plastic freezer boxes. Level the surface and cover with waxed or greaseproof paper and a lid. Finally, label, then freeze. Serve within 1 hour. If frozen, allow about 30 minutes in a fridge to soften sufficiently to serve.

Serving
Serve with Chocolate Fudge Sauce (see page 165) for a real surprise.

Bailey's® Original Ice Cream

A very simple, very successful recipe. Thanks to the Bailey's, the ice cream has quite a high alcohol content, which has the effect of lowering the point at which the mixture will freeze. This means the ice cream never reaches a firm enough stage to serve from the churn. It will definitely need overnight in the freezer to get cold enough and harden sufficiently. Do not be tempted to add more Bailey's to the ice-cream mixture as, if you do, it will probably never freeze in a normal domestic fridge. Better to pour some Bailey's over the ice cream when it is served.

INGREDIENTS

	Metric	U.S.	Imperial
Whipping/heavy cream			
(36 per cent fat)	500 ml	2 cups	16 fl oz
Milk	500 ml	2 cups	16 fl oz
Caster/Ultra fine sugar	200 g	1 cup	7 oz
Bailey's® Original Irish			
Cream	125 ml	½ cup	4 fl oz
Makes about	1.25 litres	5 cups	40 fl oz

Combine the ingredients and stir occasionally until the sugar dissolves. Cover and chill in the fridge. When ready, still freeze (see page 48) or start the ice-cream machine. Pour in the mixture and churn for not more than 20 minutes. Quickly transfer the ice cream to plastic freezer containers and cover with waxed or greaseproof paper and a lid. Finally label, then leave to freeze and harden overnight. To serve, allow 5–10 minutes in the fridge if it needs time to soften. This will depend on the temperature of your freezer. In many cases it can be served directly from the freezer.

Serving
Bailey's lovers will like an additional helping spooned over each scoop.

Banana Ice Cream

Dead simple, no problems and excellent result. The only thing is to keep your nerve with the bananas. Let them ripen to the stage where they are about two-thirds black and the flavour of the ice cream will be excellent.

INGREDIENTS

	Metric	U.S.	Imperial
Bananas, very ripe	4	4	4
Lemon juice	1 Tbsp	1 Tbsp	1 Tbsp
Vanilla sugar (see page			
36)	200 g	1 cup	7 oz
Milk	250 ml	1 cup	8 fl oz
Whipping/heavy cream			
(36 per cent fat),			
chilled	250 ml	1 cup	8 fl oz
Makes about	1 litre	4 cups	32 fl oz

Peel the bananas and cut into chunks. Put them into a food processor or blender with the lemon juice and sugar and blend until smooth. Add the milk and process again, briefly. Pour into a jug and insert a piece of clingfilm directly on top of the liquid, sealing the clingfilm right up to the edge then up the side of the bowl. Excluding the air in this way will minimise the discoloration of the banana. Chill in the fridge. When cold enough, combine with the chilled cream. Then either still freeze (see page 48) or start the ice-cream machine and pour in the liquid. Churn until the mixture is the consistency of thick cream. Quickly scrape it into plastic freezer boxes, level the surface and cover with a piece of waxed or greaseproof paper and a lid. Finally label, then freeze. Serve within 1 hour. Or, if frozen solid, allow 20 minutes in the fridge to soften sufficiently for serving.

Variation

BANANA AND GIN

NOTE: The banana flavour not only marries well with rum but also with gin. Add the alcohol gradually after the chilled cream, a tablespoon at a time, tasting as you go. Even if you like it strong, it will probably not need more than 4 tablespoons.

Banana, Brown Sugar and Peanut Brittle Ice Cream

INGREDIENTS

	Metric	U.S.	Imperial
One recipe Banana Ice Cream (see page 59), omitting the vanilla sugar and substituting soft brown sugar			
One recipe Peanut Brittle (see page 163)			
Makes about	1 litre	4 cups	32 fl oz

Make the banana mixture following the instructions for Banana Ice Cream (see page 59), substituting the soft brown sugar for the vanilla sugar. Seal closely with clingfilm and leave to chill in the fridge.

Meanwhile, prepare the Peanut Brittle following the instructions on page 163, and leave to cool and harden. Break the solidified brittle into small nugget-sized pieces by pounding, not too forcefully, in a mortar and pestle. It is best not to reduce it to a powder as this dissolves in the ice cream; much better to come across crisp bits of nutty caramel. When ready, still freeze (see page 48) or start the ice-cream machine and pour in the liquid. Churn until the mixture is the consistency of thick cream. Quickly scrape it into plastic freezer boxes, sprinkling in the peanut brittle as you go. Then stir two or three times before levelling the surface, cover with a piece of waxed or greaseproof paper and a lid. Finally label, then freeze. Serve within 1 hour. Or, if frozen solid, allow 20 minutes in the fridge to soften sufficiently for serving.

Banana and Fudge Ripple Ice Cream

See page 165.

Banana Yoghurt Ice

INGREDIENTS

	Metric	U.S.	Imperial
Bananas, peeled (4 or 5)	350 g	12 oz	12 oz
Honey, clear	2 Tbsp	2 Tbsp	2 Tbsp
Greek/Russian style yoghurt	240 g	1 cup	8½ oz
Juice of lemons, strained	1½	1½	1½
Makes about	750 ml	3 cups	24 fl oz

Cut the bananas into chunks, put them in a food processor and blend with the honey. Liquidise until smooth then add the yoghurt and blend again, until smooth. Stop the machine and add strained lemon juice to taste. Chill in the fridge.

When ready, still freeze (see page 48) or start the ice-cream machine. Pour in the mixture and churn until the ice is firm enough to serve. Or, to store, quickly scrape into plastic freezer containers and cover with waxed or greaseproof paper and a lid. Finally label, then freeze. Once frozen, allow 30 minutes in the fridge to soften.

Basil Granita/Sorbet

See Herb Granitas/Sorbets pages 99 and 100.

Fresh Bay Leaf Ice Cream

We have come to think of bay leaves as a flavouring for savoury dishes alone, but in Victorian times they were commonly used to flavour "cold forms", such as cornflour moulds. As it is preferable to use most herbs fresh, we have used fresh bay leaves here, but dried ones can be substituted. The flavour of bay is unlike any other herb. Many herb books refer to the fresh leaf as being strongly scented, spicy and bitter, and to counteract particularly the bitterness suggest leaving the leaves to dry out for a few days before using. This has posed no problem in flavouring ice cream; perhaps the fat content sufficiently subdues any bitterness and freezing takes care of flavour excesses. The resulting ice cream is unusual, and unusually good, especially when served with warm poached fruits such as pears, or rhubarb, or dried fruit compotes. Accompany with crisp, thin shortbread biscuits.

INGREDIENTS

	Metric	U.S.	Imperial
One recipe French Vanilla Ice Cream (see page 51), omitting the vanilla bean and substituting			
Bay leaves, fresh	3	3	3
Makes about	750 ml	3 cups	24 fl oz

Make the custard following the instructions for making French Vanilla Ice Cream (see page 51), substituting the bay leaves for the vanilla bean.

Leave the bay leaves to infuse in the custard throughout the cooking, cooling and chilling, removing them just prior to churning and freezing the ice cream. Freeze the ice cream as directed then store in a plastic freezer box covered with waxed or greaseproof paper and a lid.

Bay Leaf, Lemon and White Wine Granita

The flavour of bay is usually associated with savoury recipes, but its strange flavour, best described by Tom Stobart as "balsamic", works very well in sweet dishes. If you use dried bay leaves start with six and taste carefully. Dried bay leaves are not very consistent in flavour. See Fresh Bay Leaf Ice Cream above.

INGREDIENTS

	Metric	U.S.	Imperial
Bay leaves, dried	6	6	6
Water	250 ml	1 cup	8 fl oz
Granulated sugar	100 g	½ cup	3½ oz
Asti Spumante	500 ml	2 cups	16 fl oz
Fresh lemon juice	250 ml	1 cup	8 fl oz
Fresh lime juice	4 Tbsp	4 Tbsp	4 Tbsp
Makes about	1 litre	4 cups	32 fl oz

Put the bay leaves and water into a small saucepan. Bring to the boil and boil gently for 3 minutes. Remove the pan from the heat. Add the sugar. Stir, cover and leave aside until cold. Stir in the remaining ingredients, cover and chill in the fridge.

For detailed instructions on how to prepare the perfect granita see page 49.

Japanese Red Bean Ice Cream

In Japanese cooking adzuki (or azuki) beans, boiled, mashed and sweetened, are a base for many sweets and cakes from the traditional yokam, a jellied sweetmeat served with tea, to a much more Western-based newcomer, red bean ice cream. Served as a dessert, it is generally available in Japanese hotels and ice-cream parlours, a recent import to Japan. The sweetened red bean paste can be made at home, but to try this ice cream for the first time it is simpler to buy a can of the ready cooked, sweetened red beans from a Japanese food shop. The brand we use is called Santa and the can reads, "Prepared red beans, 'Yude Azuki'." Mirin, a very sweet rice wine, can also be bought from Japanese food shops; buy the type labelled hon-marin, meaning naturally brewed. Don't be put off if the result looks like frozen Mexican re-fried beans, the flavour is delicious.

INGREDIENTS

	Metric	U.S.	Imperial
One can prepared red beans (sweetened)	235 g	8¼ oz	8¼ oz
Mirin	3 Tbsp	3 Tbsp	3 Tbsp
Sugar syrup (see page 47)	125 ml	½ cup	4 fl oz
Whipping/heavy cream (36 per cent fat)	185 ml	¾ cup	6 fl oz
Salt	pinch	pinch	pinch
Lemon juice	1–2 tsp	1–2 tsp	1–2 tsp
Makes about	625 ml	2½ cups	20 fl oz

Empty the contents of the can into a measuring jug and use a good old-fashioned potato masher to half-crush the beans. Stir in the remaining ingredients, then cover and leave to chill in the fridge. When ready, still freeze (see page 48) or start the ice-cream machine and pour in the red bean mixture. Leave to churn until the mix has frozen to the consistency of whipped cream.

Quickly scrape it into a plastic freezer box. Give the mixture a good stir to distribute evenly the pieces of bean before covering with waxed or greaseproof paper and a lid. Finally label, then freeze for about 2 hours before serving. Remove the ice cream from the freezer and leave in the main body of the fridge for 15 minutes so that the ice cream and particularly the beans are sufficiently soft to serve.

Bellini Sorbet

See page 127.

Blackberry Granita

Make according to the recipe for Blackberry Sorbet (see page 63), adding an additional 375 ml/1½ cups/12 fl oz of water with the Crème de Mûre and lemon juice. Mix well.

For detailed instructions on how to prepare the perfect granita see page 49.

Blackberry Ice Cream

Blackberry is a flavour that is all too easy to lose. But in this light and simple, no-cook ice cream it comes over loud and clear. Helped, it has to be said, by the addition of Crème de Mûre, which costs about the same as a cheap bottle of wine from one of the large supermarket chains. But failing this, you will still have a well-flavoured ice cream of an almost fuchsia colour.

INGREDIENTS

	Metric	U.S.	Imperial
Blackberries	450 g	1 lb (about 3 cups)	1 lb
Caster/Ultra fine sugar	150 g	¾ cup	5¼ oz
Juice of lemon, strained	½	½	½
Crème de Mûre	2 Tbsp	2 Tbsp	2 Tbsp
Whipping/heavy cream (36 per cent fat)	500 ml	2 cups	16 fl oz
Makes about	1 litre	4 cups	32 fl oz

Pick over the blackberries carefully, then transfer them to a colander and sluice them thoroughly with cold water. Drain, and turn out on to a double thickness of kitchen paper; spread out the berries and leave to dry. Now put them in a food processor or blender with the sugar and blend for about 1 minute. Position a nylon sieve over a bowl and strain the blackberry pulp, rubbing the last stage through the sieve until all that is left is the seeds. Flavour the purée with the strained lemon juice and Crème de Mûre. Taste, and add a little more lemon juice, if liked. Chill in the fridge.

When ready, still freeze (see page 48) or start the ice-cream machine. Beat the cream into the flavoured blackberry purée, pour it into the machine and allow it to churn and freeze to the consistency of softly whipped cream. Quickly scrape into plastic freezer boxes, level the surface and cover with a piece of waxed or greaseproof paper and a lid. Finally label, then freeze. Serve within 1 hour, or, if frozen solid, allow 20 minutes in the fridge to soften sufficiently for serving.

Goutez mes glaces, c'est la banquise

Blackberry Sorbet

The deep colour of blackberry sorbet always looks wonderful. As blackberries are only available for a short time each year it is well worth freezing them either as whole blackberries or cooked in the proportion of fruit to sugar syrup given in the recipe below. Then you can quickly make a blackberry sorbet, or with the addition of some water, a granita any time during the winter.

INGREDIENTS

	Metric	U.S.	Imperial
Blackberries	450 g	1 lb	1 lb
Sugar syrup (see page 47)	250 ml	1 cup	8 fl oz
Crème de Mûre	2 Tbsp	2 Tbsp	2 Tbsp
Juice of lemons	2½	2½	2½
Makes about	1 litre	4 cups	32 fl oz

Rinse the blackberries in cold water, drain, then spread out the berries on a double layer of kitchen paper and leave until dry. Put into a non-reactive saucepan with the sugar syrup, heat to boiling point and simmer for 2–3 minutes. Allow to cool for a few minutes then pour into a food processor or blender and liquidise, then strain to remove the pips. Allow to cool, then add Crème de Mûre, and lemon juice to taste. Cover and chill in the fridge. When ready, still freeze (see page 48) or start the ice-cream machine. Pour in the mixture and churn for about 15 minutes until the sorbet is firm enough to serve. If it is to be stored, quickly scrape the sorbet into plastic freezer boxes, cover with waxed or greaseproof paper and a lid. Finally label, then freeze. Once the ice becomes solid it will need about 20 minutes in the fridge before it is soft enough to serve.

Variation
This can be used to make Blackberry Spoom and Sorbet Bombe (see page 170).

Blackcurrant Ice Cream

Although a summer fruit, blackcurrants seem curiously suited to winter eating. Maybe this is a childhood association with blackcurrant syrup and its vitamin C, which was used to ward off winter colds.
Blackcurrants are far better employed in ice creams and sorbets. Freezing some for the winter makes sense, especially as you cannot guarantee they will be in every supermarket freezer. Incidentally, freeze the whole berries by all means, but try freezing a small batch or two puréed. Put the berries through a fine sieve or mouli, rather than liquidising them, as crushed seeds will give a bitter flavour. The purée can be diluted and sweetened and served as a purée, or used to make ices or sauce for ice cream. But be careful, the flavour is powerful and it may need some judicious reining in.

INGREDIENTS

	Metric	U.S.	Imperial
Blackcurrants	450 g	1 lb	1 lb
Granulated sugar	315 g	1¼ cups	11 oz
Water	125 ml	½ cup	4 fl oz
One recipe French Vanilla Ice Cream (see page 51)			
Granulated sugar, additional	5 Tbsp	5 Tbsp	5 Tbsp
Makes about	1 litre	4 cups	32 fl oz

If fresh, use a fork to strip the berries from their stalks into a colander or sieve. Sluice with cold water, drain and dry on kitchen paper. Put the prepared blackcurrants, sugar and water in a non-reactive saucepan. Simmer gently, covered, for about 5 minutes, then put through a nylon sieve to remove the pips.

Take the sieved blackcurrant pulp and mix with the French Vanilla Ice Cream (see page 51). Check the sweetness and add up to 5 Tbsp of sugar, depending on the tartness of the blackcurrants. Then chill in the fridge. When ready, still freeze (see page 48) or start the ice-cream machine. Pour in the mixture and allow it to churn and freeze to the consistency of softly whipped cream. Quickly scrape into plastic freezer boxes, level the surface, cover with a piece of waxed or greaseproof paper and a lid. Finally label, then freeze. Serve within 1 hour or, if frozen solid, allow 20 minutes in the fridge to soften sufficiently for serving.

Blackcurrant Sorbet with Mint

INGREDIENTS

	Metric	U.S.	Imperial
Blackcurrants	450 g	1 lb	1 lb
Sugar syrup (see page 47)	315 ml	1¼ cup	10½ fl oz
Water	125 ml	½ cup	4 fl oz
Sprigs of mint	4×10 cm	4×4 inch	4×4 inch
Egg white	1	1	1
Makes about	1 litre	4 cups	32 fl oz

Prepare the blackcurrants as described in the recipe for Blackcurrant Ice Cream (see page 63). Put in a non-reactive saucepan with the syrup and water and simmer gently, covered, for about 5 minutes. Cool a little before rubbing through a nylon sieve to remove the pips. Add the rinsed and dried mint to the warm blackcurrant purée, cover and leave to cool.

Taste and, if necessary, allow the mint to steep longer while chilling in the fridge. Remove the mint sprigs when the mint flavour is strong enough; it should not overwhelm the blackcurrant flavour.

When ready, still freeze (see page 48) or start the ice-cream machine. Pour in the mixture and churn for about 10 minutes, until the sorbet begins to become icy. Then add the lightly beaten egg white and continue churning until the sorbet is firm enough to serve. If it is to be stored, quickly scrape the sorbet into plastic freezer boxes and cover with waxed or greaseproof paper and a lid. Finally label, then freeze. Once the ice becomes solid it will need about 20 minutes in the fridge before it is soft enough to serve.

Blueberry and Buttermilk Sherbet

Too easily, the fresh flavour of blueberries can be lost, or comes through tasting like one of the poorer quality, mass-marketed fruit yoghurts, and these delicious berries deserve a better fate.

INGREDIENTS

	Metric	U.S.	Imperial
Blueberries	350 g	2⅓ cups	12 oz
Sugar syrup (see page 47)	250 ml	1 cup	8 fl oz
Buttermilk, chilled	250 ml	1 cup	8 fl oz
Lemon juice	1 tsp	1 tsp	1 tsp
Egg white	1	1	1
Makes about	1.1 litres	4½ cups	36 fl oz

Sort through the blueberries, discarding any damaged fruit or stalks. Transfer the remaining fruit to a colander, sluice with water, drain thoroughly and transfer to a medium-sized saucepan. Add the sugar syrup and bring to the boil. Cover, remove from the heat and leave to cool before transferring to the fridge to chill. When ready, mash the fruit (quite literally; use a potato masher) to reduce it to a very rough pulp, then stir in the buttermilk and lemon juice. Still freeze (see page 48) or start the ice-cream machine. Pour in the fruit and churn until the sherbet is just starting to get icy. Using a fork, beat the egg white until loosened and add to the sherbet with the machine still running. Continue churning until the sherbet is the consistency of thick whipped cream. If it is to be stored, quickly scrape the ice into plastic freezer boxes and cover with a piece of waxed or greaseproof paper and a lid. Finally label, then freeze. Once the ice becomes solid it will need about 30 minutes in the fridge before it is soft enough to serve.

Brown Bread Ice Cream

Perhaps this ice cream was born as a result of Victorian good housekeeping when a woman, driven by the need to use up stale bread, came up with the idea of making it into an ice cream. If this was the case, it is certainly noteworthy as it displays a certain sort of culinary lateral thinking of which great dishes are made. But what is far more extraordinary is the rapturous reception this ice cream gets; especially from men. We must confess to being somewhat underwhelmed by this ice cream, but due to the pressure of public opinion, kept on testing and eventually came up with a very respectable recipe, but using two techniques.

Method 1 is straightforward, quicker and easier to make than Method 2 which needs more time and careful attention.

Method 1 produces an ice with a nutty bread flavour; Method 2 has much more of a caramel flavour with the partially melted sugar combining with the breadcrumbs and remaining in praline-like pieces in the ice cream.

Should you feel the urge to experiment you would do well to avoid using any other brown breads: cracked grains, rye, sourdough or pumpernickel; better to stick to wholemeal.

INGREDIENTS

	Metric	U.S.	Imperial
Wholemeal breadcrumbs	45 g	¾ cup	1½ oz
Whipping/heavy cream (36 per cent fat)	500 ml	2 cups	16 fl oz
Demerara sugar	180 g	1 cup	6½ oz
Dark rum	3 Tbsp	3 Tbsp	3 Tbsp
Vanilla extract	¼ tsp	¼ tsp	¼ tsp
Makes about	750 ml	3 cups	24 fl oz

Method 1. Spread the crumbs out evenly on a large baking tray and toast under the grill, turning them at short intervals so that they brown evenly. Measure the cream into a jug and stir in the cooled, browned crumbs and the remaining ingredients; cover and chill for 1 hour to give the crumbs a chance to soften.

Method 2. Combine the crumbs with an equal quantity (135 g/¾ cup/4¾ oz) of Demerara sugar. Spread out evenly on a large baking tray. Preheat the grill on medium to high, then position the baking tray 7.5–10 cm/ 3–4 inches from the heat source.

From now on do not leave the grill but continue toasting and regularly and evenly re-spreading the crumbs until the mixture is an overall colour – just one stop lighter than muscovado sugar. As it browns the mixture will get stickier as the sugar melts, but try to spread it as evenly as possible. When sufficiently browned, remove and leave to cool. When cool, pound the lumps of crumb/sugar mix until reduced to the size of Demerara sugar crystals. Measure the cream into a jug and stir in the crushed crumb/sugar mix and the remaining ingredients, including the remaining Demerara sugar. Cover and transfer to the fridge to chill for 2 hours. This gives the crumb mix a chance to soften, but leaves a minimal crunch in the finished texture of the ice cream. When ready, either still freeze (see page 48) or start the ice-cream machine, giving the mix a good stir before pouring it into the machine. Churn until the mixture has the consistency of softly whipped cream. Now quickly scrape into plastic freezer boxes and cover with a piece of waxed or greaseproof paper and a lid. Finally label, then freeze. Serve within 1 hour. If the ice becomes solid it will need about 30 minutes in the fridge before it is soft enough to serve.

The shades of night were falling fast,
The child had gone to sleep at last,
We knew that now no more he'd weep,
But still he murmured in his sleep:
"Oh you Ice Cream."

A pint that night alone he ate;
We feared next day he'd "pay the freight"
He woke next morn, sat up in bed,
And yelling lustily he said:
"Oh you Ice Cream."

The moral now is simply told –
Ice cream is good for young and old.
To make Ice Cream is quite a fuss,
But that's our business. Call on us.
"Oh you Ice Cream!"

Poem on menu of New England Ice Cream Manufacturer's Association Annual Dinner, 19 January 1916

Soft Brown Sugar Ice Cream with Peanut Brittle

This ice cream is delicious on its own – but even better with the brittle.

INGREDIENTS

	Metric	U.S.	Imperial
Milk	300 ml	1¼ cups	10½ fl oz
Dark soft brown sugar	100 g	½ cup well packed	3½ oz
Egg yolks	3	3	3
Whipping/heavy cream (36 per cent fat)	250 ml	1 cup	8 fl oz
Vanilla extract	¼ tsp	¼ tsp	¼ tsp
One recipe Peanut Brittle (see page 163)			
Makes about	750 ml	3 cups	24 fl oz

Using the above quantities of milk, brown sugar, egg yolks and cream, prepare and cook a custard according to the method for making French Vanilla Ice Cream (see page 51).

Continue up to the stage where the chilled custard is combined with the cream and add the vanilla extract. When ready, either still freeze (see page 48), or start the ice-cream machine and pour in the custard mix. Leave to churn for about 20 minutes or until the consistency of thick cream.

While the ice cream is freezing crush the peanut brittle in a pestle and mortar until the pieces are approximately the size of coffee sugar crystals. Then either sprinkle the brittle into the ice cream as it churns, allowing just 2 or 3 more revolutions before switching off the machine, or fold into the still frozen ice cream. Immediately scrape into plastic freezer boxes, smooth the surface flat, then cover with waxed or greaseproof paper and a lid. Finally label, then freeze for a minimum of 2 hours until firm enough to serve. Once it has frozen solid allow about 20 minutes in the fridge to soften sufficiently before serving.

> The manufacture of ''ice Cream'' by the use of homogenised milk and butter has been stopped in California by the new State Law which went into effect January 1. Under the provisions of this act only pure cream flavoured, sweetened and frozen will be allowed the name of ice cream.
>
> California State Law, 1914

Buttermilk Ice Cream

A delightful, clean-tasting, fresh-flavoured ice cream with one disconcerting trait; it separates if the finished custard is left to stand before churning. Ignore this, it will not affect the ice cream in any way.

INGREDIENTS

	Metric	U.S.	Imperial
Eggs	3	3	3
Granulated sugar	250 g	1¼ cups	8¾ oz
Vanilla bean	1	1	1
Whipping/heavy cream (36 per cent fat)	250 ml	1 cup	8 fl oz
Buttermilk	750 ml	3 cups	24 fl oz
Lemon juice	1 Tbsp	1 Tbsp	1 Tbsp
Makes about	1.25 litres	5 cups	40 fl oz

In a large heatproof mixing bowl whisk together the eggs and sugar. Split the vanilla bean in half lengthwise and put it in a saucepan with the cream. The vanilla bean remains in the custard until it is ready to churn. Bring to the boil then pour slowly into the bowl containing the beaten eggs and sugar in a thin stream, beating constantly. Transfer to a double saucepan or position the bowl over a pan of barely simmering water and continue to heat, stirring frequently, until the custard reaches 85°C/185°F. Remove from the heat and lower the temperature of the custard quickly by sitting the top of the double saucepan or the heatproof mixing bowl in cold water. On no account should the custard be allowed to overheat or boil as the mixture will curdle. (For how to deal with an overheated custard see page 52.) Stir from time to time, testing the temperature. When it feels positively cold, remove the bowl, cover and chill in the fridge, preferably overnight to allow the flavours to develop.

When ready, remove the vanilla bean and use a teaspoon to scrape the vanilla seeds from inside the pod; stir into the custard followed by the buttermilk and the lemon juice. Still freeze (see page 48) or start the ice-cream machine and pour in the custard mix.

Leave to churn and freeze for about 20 minutes or until the consistency of thick cream; if the ice cream is left to churn until thicker it will start to become buttery. Quickly scrape into plastic freezer boxes, smooth the surface flat and cover with waxed or greaseproof paper and a lid. Finally label, then freeze overnight. Once it has frozen solid allow about 30 minutes in the fridge to soften sufficiently to serve.

Buttermilk, Rum and Sultana Ice Cream

INGREDIENTS

	Metric	U.S.	Imperial
Dark rum	125 ml	½ cup	4 fl oz
Sultanas/Golden raisins	120 g	¾ cup	4¼ oz
1 recipe Buttermilk Ice Cream (see page 66)			
Makes about	1.75 litres	6¼ cups	50 fl oz

Combine the rum and sultanas in a small saucepan and bring to the boil. Cover the pan with a lid, remove from the heat and leave, preferably overnight, to allow the sultanas time to absorb the rum.

When ready, still freeze (see page 48) or churn the Buttermilk Ice Cream as described in the recipe for Buttermilk Ice Cream (see page 66). Have ready a rectangular plastic freezer box about 18×23×7.5 cm/7×9×3 inches. Quickly scrape the ice cream into the box, stirring in the rum-soaked sultanas at the same time. Smooth the surface, seal and freeze as described in the recipe for Buttermilk Ice Cream.

Caramel Ice Cream

With the exception of deep-fat frying, caramel is the hottest and most potentially volatile thing to deal with in the kitchen, so please take care. Never leave caramel to cook, always watch it like a hawk from start to finish. The dangerous stage in this recipe is when water is added to the medium brown liquid caramel (about 180°C/356°F). Remove the pan from the heat the instant the sugar reaches this stage. Have the water ready standing by, and the hand and arm grasping the pan wrapped in a protective cloth. Then slowly add the water, standing well back. There will be a considerable noise and ferment in the pan, but once this subsides the rest is easy and the result is a superbly flavoured ice cream.

NOTE: *For this recipe it is necessary to use really fresh cream. If less than fresh, the cream is likely to curdle when mixed with the rather acidic caramel.*

INGREDIENTS

	Metric	U.S.	Imperial
Granulated sugar	200 g	1 cup	7 oz
Water	2 Tbsp	2 Tbsp	2 Tbsp
Whipping/heavy cream (36 per cent fat)	185 ml	¾ cup	6 fl oz
Milk	375 ml	1½ cups	12 fl oz
Vanilla bean	½	½	½
Egg yolks	3	3	3
Makes about	750 ml	3 cups	24 fl oz

Pour into a small, heavy saucepan about 60 g/⅓ cup/2 oz of the measured sugar. Taking full account of how to deal with caramel (see above), place the saucepan over a moderate heat.

As the sugar begins to liquefy and brown around the edge, stir once or twice so that the sugar continues to caramelise evenly. As soon as it is a uniform medium brown (180°C/356°F), remove the pan from the heat and slowly add the water. When the bubbling subsides, pour in the cream, stir and leave aside to allow the caramel to complete dissolving in the cream, then chill.

Meanwhile put half of the remaining sugar in a separate pan with the milk and split vanilla bean. Bring to just below boiling point then cover and leave aside to infuse for 30 minutes. Now follow the method for making French Vanilla Ice Cream (see page 51) to freeze.

Caviar Savoury Ice
Black or Red Lumpfish Roe
Savoury Ice

We advise still freezing (see page 48) this ice as it keeps the roe intact. If you do use an ice-cream machine the churning action will break down the roe and you will get the colour more dispersed in the ice. This looks fine with the red but distinctly unappetising with the black!

INGREDIENTS

	Metric	U.S.	Imperial
Shallots	2	2	2
Sour cream	250 ml	1 cup	8 fl oz
Caviar or lumpfish roe	50 g	1¾ oz	1¾ oz
Lemon juice	1 Tbsp	1 Tbsp	1 Tbsp
Vodka	2 Tbsp	2 Tbsp	2 Tbsp
Makes about	375 ml	1½ cups	12 fl oz

Chop the shallots very finely indeed, and mix them with the sour cream in a glass bowl. Add the caviar or lumpfish roe, keeping back one teaspoonful for garnish, then the lemon juice and the vodka, and mix carefully. Taste, and add more lemon juice if necessary. Either still freeze (see page 48) or if red, churn in an ice-cream machine for about 5–8 minutes then store in the freezer. Place the red or black ice in a plastic freezer box and cover the surface with greaseproof or waxed paper. Finally label, then freeze. After 1 hour, stir with a fork to disperse the solidified ice around the edges and on the base of the box. Serve after about 1 more hour. If frozen overnight, allow 20–30 minutes in the fridge to soften before serving. Cut into slices and decorate with the teaspoonful of caviar or lumpfish roe. Serve with lemon wedges.

**Mary had a little lamb,
It was a greedy glutton,
She fed it on ice cream all day,
And now it's frozen mutton.**

parody on Old English Nursery Rhyme

Morello Cherry Ice Cream

If there is a market for both the sweet and sour varieties of gooseberry, why is there no market for the sour cherry? In Britain, in or out of season, sweet dessert cherries are everywhere but never an acid cooking cherry to be had. Which is a great shame, because the cooked flavour of these far outdoes that of sweet dessert cherries, fresh or cooked. So bottled sour cherries it has to be, and preferably pitted to save time, mess and sanity. Try to buy from an outlet that has a good turnover as sometimes jars are left a long time and the cherries turn mushy.

INGREDIENTS

	Metric	U.S.	Imperial
Whipping/heavy cream (36 per cent fat)	375 ml	1½ cups	12 fl oz
Egg yolks	3	3	3
Vanilla sugar (see page 36)	90 g	½ cup minus 1 Tbsp	3½ oz
Sour cream	185 ml	¾ cup	6 fl oz
Morello cherries (sour)	450 g	1 lb	1 lb
Makes about	1 litre	4 cups	32 fl oz

Pour the cream into a saucepan and heat to just below boiling point. Meanwhile, in a heatproof bowl, combine the egg yolks and the vanilla sugar and beat until they are paler in colour and a lighter consistency. Pour the hot cream in a thin stream on to the yolks and the sugar, whisking steadily all the while. The bowl can now be placed over a pan of simmering water, or the custard can be returned to the saucepan, which is then put on top of a heat-diffuser mat, so it is not in direct contact with the heat. Only if you have an accurate thermometer and/or are confident that you will not overheat the custard should you put the saucepan over a gentle, direct heat. Stir until the custard reaches 85°C/185°F or thickens sufficiently to coat the back of a spoon. As soon as the custard reaches this stage plunge the base of the pan into cold water. On no account should the custard be allowed to overheat or boil as the mixture will curdle. (For how to deal with an overheated custard see page 52.) Once cool, the custard can be covered with a circle of lightly buttered greaseproof paper and transferred to the fridge to chill.

Just before churning, lightly beat the sour cream into the custard. Put the drained and pitted cherries into a food processor or blender and blend briefly so that the cherries are reduced to a rough pulp, rather than a purée. Whisk this into the custard.

Now either still freeze (see page 48) or start the ice-cream machine. Pour in the cherry mixture and leave to churn for about 15–20 minutes or until the ice cream has the consistency of softly whipped cream. Quickly scrape into plastic freezer boxes, smooth the surface flat and cover with waxed or greaseproof paper and a lid. Finally label, then freeze for about 1 hour before serving. If frozen overnight, allow about 30 minutes in the fridge to soften sufficiently to serve.

And in an evening he (James Stevens Cox) loved to sit in an ice cream parlour or in a soda-fountain eating luscious concoctions of marshmallows and talking . . .

Hubert Nicholson,
Half My Days and Nights, London, 1941

I have heard from unimpeachable authorities that as a young man my father not infrequently consumed sixteen ice-cream sundaes at a sitting. His record is believed to be eighteen Neapolitan sundaes topped with fresh fruit. He then adjourned to an eating house and consumed a steak, onions and baked potatoes. On several occasions he has visited ice-cream factories in America; and in January 1965, I saw him eat a *gallon* of ice cream while waiting for a *bus in a snow storm* at Norwalk, Connecticut. This behaviour must not be attributed to exhibitionism – only one person, apart from myself, witnessed the last incident (a buxom negress who disappeared into the distance laughing) – but rather to a Rabelaisian proclivity for his favourite dish. In short, I think that the reader will appreciate that J.S.C. is well qualified to edit a monograph about ice creams. His love of the stuff remains and he can be seen consuming his favourite varieties every day, summer and winter, at Maison Carré in St Peter's Port. As soon as he approaches this ice cream pleasure-house, unbidden but knowing his desire, the dark-eyed beauties of the café make ready his daily manna.

George Stevens Cox,
Preface to *Ice Creams in Queen Victoria's Reign*

CHESTNUTS

Because the chestnut season is so short and peeling fresh chestnuts is such a thankless task, we have included recipes using both fresh chestnuts and canned crème de marrons (chestnut spread). Truth be told, there is very little difference between the two ice creams . . . !

Serve with Pear Ice Cream (see page 127) or Chinese Walnut Brittle Ice Cream (see page 155) or in the manner of a Montblanc, topped with whipped cream and Chocolate Fudge Sauce (see page 165).

Fresh Chestnut Ice Cream

INGREDIENTS

	Metric	U.S.	Imperial
Fresh chestnuts	225 g	½ lb	½ lb
Milk	300 ml	1¼ cups	10½ fl oz
Egg yolks	4	4	4
Vanilla sugar (see page 36)	200 g	1 cup	7 oz
Whipping/heavy cream (36 per cent fat)	250 ml	1 cup	8 fl oz
Makes about	800 ml	3¼ cups	26 fl oz

Rinse the chestnuts and cut a slit in each one. Put them into a saucepan and cover generously with cold water. Bring to the boil then cover and boil gently for 30 minutes. By this time the chestnuts will be tender. Drain and leave until cool enough to handle, then shell and peel.

Put the peeled nuts into a food processor or blender with 65 ml/¼ cup/2 fl oz of the milk and blend until reduced to an uneven paste. Then switch off, leaving the bowl or goblet in place. Bring the remaining milk to the boil. Meanwhile, in a medium-sized heatproof bowl, combine the egg yolks with the sugar and beat, preferably with an electric hand mixer, until the mixture is pale and thick. Pour the hot milk in a thin stream on to the egg yolks and sugar, whisking steadily all the while.

The bowl can now be placed over a pan of simmering water, or the custard can be returned to the saucepan which is then put on top of a heat-diffuser mat, so it is not in direct contact with the heat. Only if you have an accurate thermometer and/or are confident that you will not overheat the sauce, should you put the saucepan over a gentle direct heat. Stir the custard until it reaches 85°C/185°F or until it has thickened sufficiently to coat the back of a spoon. On no account should the custard be allowed to overheat or boil as the mixture will curdle. (For how to deal with an overheated custard see page 52.) As soon as the custard reaches this point, remove the pan from the heat, set the food processor or blender in motion and pour in the hot custard via the funnel on to the chestnut paste. When all the custard has been poured in, stop and scrape down the bowl before starting the machine again; leave it to run until the mixture is smooth. Then pour it into a jug, cover and chill in the fridge.

When ready, still freeze (see page 48) or start the ice-cream machine. Strain the chestnut mix through a fine sieve, combine with the cream, and pour into the machine. Churn until it has the consistency of softly whipped cream. Quickly scrape into plastic freezer boxes, smooth the surface flat and cover with waxed or greaseproof paper and a lid. Finally label, then freeze for about 1 hour before serving. If frozen overnight, allow about 25–30 minutes in the fridge to soften sufficiently to serve.

Crème de Marrons Ice Cream

We find that Clément Faugier® crème de marrons (chestnut spread) works perfectly for this ice cream.

INGREDIENTS

	Metric	U.S.	Imperial
Milk	250 ml	1 cup	8 fl oz
Whipping/heavy cream			
(36 per cent fat)	250 ml	1 cup	8 fl oz
Egg yolks	4	4	4
Caster/Ultra fine sugar	65 g	⅓ cup	2¼ oz
1 can Crème de			
Marrons	250 g	8¾ oz	8¾ oz
Makes about	750 ml	3 cups	24 fl oz

Combine the milk and cream in a medium-sized saucepan and bring to just below boiling point.

Meanwhile in a medium-sized, heatproof bowl combine the egg yolks with the sugar and beat, preferably with an electric hand mixer, until the mixture is pale and

thick. Pour the hot milk/cream in a thin stream on to the egg yolks, whisking steadily as it is added. The bowl can now be placed over a pan of simmering water, or the custard can be returned to the saucepan which is then put on top of a heat-diffuser mat, so it is not in direct contact with the heat. Only if you have an accurate thermometer and/or are confident that you will not overheat the sauce, should you put the saucepan over direct gentle heat. Stir the custard until it reaches 85°C/185°F or until it has thickened sufficiently, to coat the back of a spoon. As soon as the custard has reached the right temperature and thickened sufficiently, remove the pan from the heat. On no account should the custard be allowed to overheat or boil as the mixture will curdle. (For how to deal with an overheated custard see page 52.)

Have the crème de marrons ready in a separate medium-sized bowl. Gradually stir in the hot custard, a little at a time, until it is all smoothly incorporated. Leave to cool to room temperature, then cover and transfer to the fridge to chill.

When ready, still freeze (see page 48) or start the ice-cream machine. Pour in the chilled chestnut mix and churn until it is the consistency of softly whipped cream. Quickly scrape into plastic freezer boxes, smooth the surface flat, cover with waxed or greaseproof paper and a lid. Finally label, then freeze for about 1 hour before serving. If frozen overnight, allow about 25–30 minutes in the fridge to soften sufficiently to serve.

Chestnut Fudge Ripple

See page 165.

PROCOPE
Café Procope is the oldest café in the world, founded in 1686 in Paris by the Sicilian, Francesco Procopio dei Coltelli. It is still open on its original site although the name of the street is now Rue de l'Ancienne Comédie, renamed after the Comédie Francaise opened on the far side of the street. Cotelli sold chocolate, coffee and perfume and was among the first people to sell ices, which were then considered a strange novelty from Italy.

Everyday Chocolate Ice Cream

This Philadelphia, no-cook style ice cream is ideal for children, for everyday use, and for mixing with other ingredients for say Rocky Road (see page 77) or Chocolate and Fresh Mint Ice Cream (see page 74). It can also be used for Chocolate Ice Cream with Rosemary (see page 75), Chocolate and Spice Biscuit Ice Cream (see page 75), Chocolate and Hazelnut Ice Cream (see page 76), Chocolate Brownie Ice Cream (see page 76) and Chocolate Malted Ice Cream (see page 76). It is easy and fast to make.

INGREDIENTS

	Metric	U.S.	Imperial
Cocoa powder★ (unsweetened)	30 g	⅓ cup	1 oz or 5½ Tbsp
Granulated sugar	100 g	½ cup	3½ oz
Sweetened condensed milk	125 ml	½ cup	4 fl oz
Milk	375 ml	1½ cups	12 fl oz
Vanilla extract	1 tsp	1 tsp	1 tsp
Whipping/heavy cream (36 per cent fat)	250 ml	1 cup	8 fl oz
Makes about	1.1 litres	4½ cups	36 fl oz

★ See Ingredients page 35.

There are two ways of cooking the cocoa mixture. The first method takes a short while and needs constant attention. The other takes a lot longer and needs very little attention. In both techniques the essential thing is to cook the cocoa mix sufficiently to get rid of any trace of raw powderiness. So, either put the cocoa, sugar, condensed milk and ordinary milk in a saucepan, bring to the boil then simmer gently for 5 minutes, *stirring constantly*. Or, use a double saucepan, combine the same ingredients in the top half of the pan, bring to the boil over direct heat, stirring constantly, then transfer to cook over simmering water. Then leave it to cook for 30 minutes, stirring once or twice. When the cocoa mix has cooked transfer the pan to cold water in order to cool it quickly.

When ready, still freeze (see page 48) or start the ice-cream machine, add the vanilla extract and stir in the chilled cream. Strain the mixture into a jug and pour into the machine. Leave to churn until the ice cream is the consistency of whipped cream, about 20 minutes. Quickly scrape into plastic freezer boxes, level the surface and cover with waxed or greaseproof paper and a lid. Finally label, then freeze. Serve within 2 hours. If frozen solid, allow about 20–25 minutes in the fridge before serving.

Rich Chocolate Ice Cream

This is a good straightforward chocolate ice cream that can be used for all sorts of occasions. Not as rich as the Ultimate Chocolate Ice Cream (see page 72), but ideal for ordinary occasions and for making bombes.

INGREDIENTS

	Metric	U.S.	Imperial
Cocoa powder★ (unsweetened)	3 Tbsp	3 Tbsp	3 Tbsp
Granulated sugar	80 g	½ cup minus 1 Tbsp	2¾ oz
Milk	375 ml	1½ cups	12 fl oz
Plain/semisweet chocolate,★★ chopped fine	100 g	3½ oz	3½ oz
Egg yolks	3	3	3
Vanilla extract	1 tsp	1 tsp	1 tsp
Whipping/heavy cream (36 per cent fat)	250 ml	1 cup	8 fl oz
Makes about	750 ml	3 cups	24 fl oz

★ See Ingredients page 35.
★★ See Ingredients page 34.

In a small bowl combine the cocoa powder and half the sugar. Pour in sufficient of the measured milk to form a thin paste and bring the rest of the milk to the boil. Pour the hot milk on to the blend, whisking all the while, then immediately return the mixture to the pan. Now, with the pan positioned on a heat-diffuser mat, bring the cocoa mixture slowly to simmering point, stirring constantly. Once it reaches simmering point, continue to cook gently, stirring, for 6 minutes. This stage is very important, as the long slow cooking ensures all the powdery flavour of the cocoa is cooked out. (We have lost count of the "reputable" chocolate ice creams we have tasted where a raw, powdery taste is unpleasantly prominent.) So take it slowly, and keep stirring, because the cocoa blend will catch on the base of the pan the moment your attention wanders. Remove the pan from the heat and stir in the chopped chocolate.

In a separate bowl beat together the egg yolks and remaining sugar until pale. Pour in the chocolate mixture, beating vigorously, then immediately return the mixture to the pan. Again working with the saucepan on a heat-diffuser mat, heat slowly, stirring until the temperature reaches 85°C/185°F.

Remove the pan from the heat. Add the vanilla extract and sit the base of the pan in a few inches of cold water, until the mixture is cold. Strain (there will be bits in it), cover and chill in the fridge.

When ready, beat the cream into the chocolate mixture. Then still freeze (see page 48) or start the ice-cream machine and pour it in. Leave to churn until the ice cream is the consistency of whipped cream, about 20 minutes. Quickly scrape into plastic freezer boxes, level the surface and cover with waxed or greaseproof paper and a lid. Finally label, then freeze. Serve within 2 hours. If frozen solid, allow about 20–25 minutes in the fridge before serving.

The Ultimate Chocolate Ice Cream

Bertillon, on the Ile de la Cité in Paris, make the best commercially produced chocolate ice cream we have ever tasted. This started us out on the quest for the ultimate chocolate ice cream and this is it.

INGREDIENTS

	Metric	U.S.	Imperial
Cocoa powder* (unsweetened)	5 Tbsp	5 Tbsp	5 Tbsp
Granulated sugar	90 g	½ cup minus 1 Tbsp	3¼ oz
Milk	375 ml	1½ cups	12 fl oz
Plain/semisweet chocolate,** chopped fine	150 g	5¼ oz	5¼ oz
Egg yolks	3	3	3
Vanilla extract	1 tsp	1 tsp	1 tsp
Instant coffee granules	1 tsp	1 tsp	1 tsp
Sugar syrup (see page 47)	65 ml	¼ cup	2 fl oz
Whipping/heavy cream (36 per cent fat)	250 ml	1 cup	8 fl oz
Makes about	875 ml	3½ cups	28 fl oz

* See Ingredients page 35.
** See Ingredients page 34.

Follow the method for Rich Chocolate Ice Cream, (see page 71). but add not only the vanilla extract, but also the instant coffee granules and sugar syrup just before the mixture is cooled in a cold water bath. Continue with the method given for Everyday Chocolate Ice Cream to complete the making, chilling and freezing.

Variations
You may care to add a teaspoon of rum to it, if you like the suggestion of alcohol in your chocolate.

Serve this on its own. Forget the calories, just enjoy the experience.

Chocolate Parfait

Parfaits proper should be flavoured with coffee or alcohol. If you stray from these flavours, you are likely to end up with a less than perfect parfait. But we know that most people love chocolate, so here is our version. Although rich and slightly chewy, this has a light, quick and clean flavour with none of the heaviness you usually get with chocolate ice creams.

INGREDIENTS

	Metric	U.S.	Imperial
Sugar syrup (see page 47)	250 ml	1 cup	8 fl oz
Cocoa powder,★ sieved	3 Tbsp	3 Tbsp	3 Tbsp
Plain/semisweet chocolate,★★ chopped	50 g	1¾ oz	1¾ oz
Egg yolks	4	4	4
Whipping/heavy cream (36 per cent fat)	250 ml	1 cup	8 fl oz
Makes about	750 ml	3 cups	24 fl oz

★ See Ingredients page 35.
★★ See Ingredients page 34.

In a heavy-based thick saucepan combine the sugar syrup and sieved cocoa powder. Bring slowly to the boil, stirring frequently to make sure that it does not catch. Then, simmer gently for 5 minutes. Alternatively, using a double saucepan, combine the same ingredients in the top half of the pan, bring to the boil over direct heat, stirring constantly, then transfer to cook over simmering water in the base of the pan. Leave to cook for 30 minutes, stirring once or twice.

Remove from the heat and add the chopped chocolate, stirring well to ensure it is completely melted. Allow to cool to 35–40°C/95–104°F (around blood heat). Then proceed exactly according to the method for making parfaits (see pages 49 to 50).

My tongue is smiling.

Abigail Trillin aged four after eating chocolate ice cream
Calvin Trillin
Alice, Let's Eat

Chocolate Sherbet

This chocolate sherbet is very rich and has a strong chocolate flavour. Chocaholics love it as it contains no cream and so has less cholesterol and fewer calories than ice cream.

INGREDIENTS

	Metric	U.S.	Imperial
Cocoa powder★			
(unsweetened)	55 g	⅔ cup	2 oz
Granulated sugar	100 g	½ cup	3½ oz
Milk	500 ml	2 cups	16 fl oz
Vanilla extract	1 tsp	1 tsp	1 tsp
Salt	pinch	pinch	pinch
Makes about	500 ml	2 cups	16 fl oz

★ See Ingredients page 35.

In a bowl mix together the cocoa and sugar. Then gradually stir in sufficient of the measured milk to give a smooth, thin paste. Bring the rest of the milk to the boil and pour into the cocoa blend, whisking all the while. Immediately return the mixture to the pan and put the pan on a heat-diffuser mat. Bring to the boil over a gentle heat, then continue to simmer gently for about 6 minutes, stirring all the while. Remove the pan from the heat, stir in the vanilla extract and salt. Then cool the mixture quickly by sitting the base of the pan in a few inches of cold water. Cover and chill in the fridge.

When ready, still freeze (see page 48) or start the ice-cream machine and pour in the chilled mixture. Leave to churn until the sherbet holds its own shape, about 20 minutes. Quickly scrape into plastic freezer boxes, level the surface and cover with waxed or greaseproof paper and a lid. Finally label, then freeze. Serve within 1 hour. If frozen solid, allow about 15–20 minutes in the fridge before serving.

Serving
Serve on its own or with fresh raspberries, or with Raspberry Ice Cream (see page 135).

North Pole advertisement, *c.* 1936.

Chocolate and Fresh Mint Ice Cream

Why do so many recipes for chocolate and mint ice cream contain mint essence when fresh mint is widely available all year round and gives a much better, more subtle, rounded flavour? The intensity of the mint will vary though, according to variety and season. Just taste the mix carefully at intervals, leaving the mint to infuse the mix a little longer if you think it could be stronger – but don't overdo it.

INGREDIENTS

	Metric	U.S.	Imperial
One recipe Everyday Chocolate Ice Cream (see page 71)			
Fresh mint sprigs	4×10 cm	4×4 inch	4×4 inch
Makes about	1.1 litres	4½ cups	36 fl oz

Make up and simmer the chocolate mixture according to the recipe for Everyday Chocolate Ice Cream (see page 71). Whilst it simmers, quickly rinse and dry the mint. Bruise the sprigs with a rolling pin, then put them into a measuring jug.

As soon as the chocolate mixture has cooked, pour it on to the mint in the jug. Leave to cool, then cover and chill overnight in the fridge. Keep tasting, and as soon as the flavour reaches the right strength, remove the mint if you are not quite ready to make the ice cream. When ready, still freeze (see page 48) or start the ice-cream machine, and strain the mint and chocolate mix via a sieve straight into the machine.

NOTE: Firmly pressing the mint in the sieve can extract more last-minute flavour, if needed.

Churn and freeze according to the instructions for Everyday Chocolate Ice Cream.

Chocolate Ice Cream with Rosemary

The inspiration for this combination originated from a dessert recipe by David Wilson of the Peat Inn, Fife, in Scotland. If the idea of combining chocolate and rosemary was all his own, the man is little short of a genius; the combination is excellent.

INGREDIENTS

	Metric	U.S.	Imperial
One recipe Everyday Chocolate Ice Cream (see page 71), omitting the vanilla extract and substituting			
Sprig fresh rosemary	1×15 cm	1×6 inch	1×6 inch
Makes about	1.1 litres	4½ cups	36 fl oz

Make up and simmer the chocolate mixture according to the recipe for Everyday Chocolate Ice Cream (see page 71). Whilst it simmers, quickly rinse and dry the rosemary. Bruise lightly with a rolling pin and put in a measuring jug.

As soon as the chocolate mixture has cooked pour it on to the rosemary in the jug. Leave to cool, then cover and chill overnight in the fridge. Keep tasting, and as soon as the flavour reaches the right strength, remove the rosemary if you are not quite ready to make the ice cream. When ready, still freeze (see page 48) or start the ice-cream machine, and strain the rosemary and the chocolate mix via a sieve straight into the machine. Churn and freeze according to the instructions for Everyday Chocolate Ice Cream.

Chocolate and Spice Biscuit Ice Cream

It could be a deterrent to find that the biscuits need baking before you make the ice cream. However, since there is nothing on the market which is remotely like the flavour of these biscuits, and the combination of spices with the chocolate ice cream is so good, we just had to include it. We particularly liked the crisp consistency that the biscuits retain in the ice cream.

INGREDIENTS

	Metric	U.S.	Imperial
One recipe Everyday Chocolate Ice Cream (see page 71)			
Allspice Biscuits (see page 163), diced	160 g	2 cups	5¾ oz
Makes about	1.5 litres	6 cups	48 fl oz

Follow the recipe for Everyday Chocolate Ice Cream (see page 71) up to the stage where the ice cream has just completed churning. As it is transferred to the plastic freezer boxes, sprinkle in the diced biscuits. Stir briefly to distribute the pieces of biscuit evenly throughout the ice cream. Then cover and store as directed in the recipe for Everyday Chocolate Ice Cream.

Chocolate Brownie Ice Cream

Most people have their own favourite chocolate brownie recipe, but fudgy or cakey it does not matter, all varieties seem to work in this ice cream – even packet-mix brownies. Pecans, walnuts, hazelnuts and salted peanuts can be added to the brownie mix, but coconut gets a definite thumbs down.

INGREDIENTS

	Metric	U.S.	Imperial
One recipe Everyday Chocolate Ice Cream (see page 71)			
Chocolate brownies, diced, approximately	160 g	2 cups	5¾ oz
Makes about	1.5 litres	6 cups	48 fl oz

Follow the recipe for Everyday Chocolate Ice Cream (see page 71) up to the stage where the ice cream has just completed churning. As it is transferred to the plastic freezer boxes, sprinkle in the diced brownies. Stir briefly to distribute the pieces of brownie evenly throughout the ice cream then cover and store as directed in the recipe for Everyday Chocolate Ice Cream.

Chocolate and Hazelnut Ice Cream

We have tried other nuts in combination with chocolate ice cream but none are as successful as hazelnuts.

INGREDIENTS

	Metric	U.S.	Imperial
One recipe Everyday Chocolate Ice Cream (see page 71)			
Hazelnuts, chopped and toasted	140 g	1 cup	5 oz
Makes about	1.3 litres	5½ cups	44 fl oz

Follow the recipe for Everyday Chocolate Ice Cream (see page 71) up to the stage where the ice cream is just about ready to be served. At this point, add the hazelnuts. Leave the machine in motion or stir by hand just long enough to distribute the nuts evenly. Then quickly scrape the ice cream into plastic freezer boxes and store as directed in the recipe for Everyday Chocolate Ice Cream.

Chocolate Malted Ice Cream

For lovers of malted milk shakes, malted ice creams are a real surprise. Malted milk is sold under a number of brand names, but we have always used Horlicks®.

INGREDIENTS

	Metric	U.S.	Imperial
One recipe Everyday Chocolate Ice Cream (see page 71)			
Malted milk powder	8 Tbsp	8 Tbsp	8 Tbsp
Makes about	1.25 litres	5 cups	40 fl oz

Follow the recipe for Everyday Chocolate Ice Cream (see page 71). Just before churning put the mixture in a liquidiser and add the malted milk powder. Liquidise for about 30 seconds then freeze as usual. This produces a smoother, richer ice than Everyday Chocolate Ice-Cream.

Rocky Road

In 1929 the Dreyer's® Grand Ice Cream Company in Oakland, California, made history when its owner, William A. Dreyer, and partner Joseph Edy first added toasted almonds and marshmallows to a batch of chocolate ice cream. It appealed to the nation's taste to such an extent that today it is certainly one of America's best-selling flavours.

The partners certainly had the makings of a good team. Joseph Edy, who owned a candy store which also sold ice cream, had produced a very successful Rocky Road candy bar, a lumpy mixture of chocolate, almonds and marshmallows. William Dreyer, erstwhile Professor of Advanced Ice Cream Manufacturing at the University of California in Davis, noted the popularity of the bar and with simple genius substituted chocolate ice cream as a vehicle for the nuts and marshmallows. (Purists, please note: the original recipe did not contain chocolate chips!)

The tricky bit is the sticky bit: cutting up the marshmallows. This was a considerable labour for William Dreyer until a supplier took pity on him and developed miniature marshmallows. Unfortunately they are hard to find in Britain. In order to keep your sanity when cutting up the conventional size marshmallows, try regularly dipping the scissors into hot water and snipping them into eight.

INGREDIENTS

	Metric	U.S.	Imperial
One recipe Everyday Chocolate Ice Cream (see page 71)			
Whole skinned almonds	75 g	½ cup	2¾ g
Marshmallows, snipped	120 g	1 cup	4¼ oz
Makes about	1.5 litres	6 cups	48 fl oz

Make up the chocolate mix for Everyday Chocolate Ice Cream (see page 71) and leave to chill in the fridge. Meanwhile brown the almonds by roasting them on a baking tray in a preheated oven, 180°C/350°F/Gas Mark 4, for about 8 minutes. The instant you can smell them in the kitchen they are ready. Remove from the oven and leave to cool before chopping to the size of salt crystals. Snip each marshmallow into 8 as described in the introduction above. When the chocolate ice-cream mix is sufficiently chilled, still freeze (see page 48) or start the ice-cream machine. Pour in the mixture. As the ice cream reaches the final stage add the nuts, then the marshmallow bits, and stir carefully by hand or allow the ice cream 3 or 4 more revolutions before stopping the machine. Quickly scrape into plastic freezer boxes, level the surface and cover with waxed or greaseproof paper and a lid. Finally label, then freeze. Serve within 2 hours. If frozen solid, allow about 20–25 minutes in the fridge before serving.

Mars bar® Ice Cream

This is our answer to the phenomenon of the Mars® Ice Cream Bar. The success of this product rocked the British ice-cream industry by taking 10 per cent of the market in the first 22 months – an unprecedented achievement. Serve with Chocolate Fudge (see page 165) or Butterscotch Sauce (see page 164).

INGREDIENTS

	Metric	U.S.	Imperial
Mars bars® or in U.S. Snickers™ 65 g/ 2¼ oz	4	4	4
Milk	250 ml	1 cup	8 fl oz
Whipping/heavy cream (36 per cent fat), chilled	500 ml	2 cups	16 fl oz
Makes about	1 litre	4 cups	32 fl oz

Chop each Mars® bar in four and put in a saucepan with the milk. Heat gently, stirring frequently, until all but a few unmelted bits remain. Do not worry about these as they will disappear in the churning action of the ice-cream machine. Remove the pan from the heat and transfer to sit in a few inches of cold water to cool the mixture quickly.

When ready, still freeze (see page 48) or start the ice-cream machine. Stir the chilled cream into the Mars bar mixture and pour into the machine. Continue to churn for about 15 minutes, or until the ice cream has the consistency of thick cream. Then quickly scrape into plastic freezer boxes, cover with waxed or greaseproof paper and a lid. Finally, label then freeze for at least 1 hour. Allow about 30 minutes in the fridge to soften sufficiently to serve.

NOTE: MARS® is the registered trade mark of Mars Ltd., England.

White Chocolate Ice Cream

It proved quite difficult to produce an ice cream with an identifiable white chocolate flavour. Using as much white chocolate as possible would seem to be the logical answer, but in practice this does not work. It produced an overfatted ice cream which registers as a sandy texture on the tongue, which for our money (and white chocolate is too expensive to waste) was distinctly unpleasant.

So do not be seduced into making any of the many recipes around that use more than 15 per cent white chocolate to 85 per cent custard/cream. The problem is that most White Chocolate Ice Creams taste sandy and the secret is to get the ratio of white chocolate to cream correct. All in all we think it comes off best when used as a background or vehicle for other, stronger flavours. So try our recipes here and use them as a basis for your own experiments.

NOTE: *Some brands of white chocolate are so low in cocoa butter/solids that they will not melt, so please use a brand that contains a minimum of 25 per cent cocoa butter/solids. This information is given on the back of the packet. If it is not specified,* do not buy that brand. *We always use Lindt Swiss white chocolate as it is so readily available. For more information on white chocolate see Ingredients page 35.*

This recipe comes from the American Chocolatier *Magazine's book* Glorious Chocolate. *It is the best recipe for white chocolate ice cream that we have ever come across.*

INGREDIENTS

	Metric	U.S.	Imperial
Swiss white chocolate bars	2×85 g	2×3¼ oz	2×3¼ oz
Egg yolks	4	4	4
Granulated sugar	150 g	¾ cup	5¼ oz
Whipping/heavy cream (36 per cent fat)	750 ml	3 cups	24 fl oz
Milk	250 ml	1 cup	8 fl oz
Makes about	1.25 litres	5 cups	40 fl oz

Finely chop the chocolate and heat it in a double saucepan or in a heatproof glass bowl over hot, *not* boiling, water, stirring constantly, until smooth.

In a large bowl, combine the egg yolks with the sugar and beat, preferably with an electric hand mixer, until the mixture is pale and thick enough to hold the shape when a ribbon of the mix is trailed across the surface.

In a heavy non-reactive pan, bring the cream and milk to just below boiling point. Pour about half of the milk and cream into the egg and sugar mixture, whisking constantly. Next pour the remainder of the milk and cream mixture into the melted chocolate, whisking constantly until well blended. Return both these mixtures to the saucepan and continue heating slowly, stirring constantly, with the saucepan on a heat-diffuser mat, until the custard is thickened and the temperature has reached 85°C/185°F. As soon as the custard has reached the right temperature, plunge the base of the pan into a few inches of cold water. On no account should the custard be allowed to overheat or boil as the mixture will curdle. (For how to deal with an overheated custard see page 52.) Leave to cool, stirring occasionally. Strain the custard into a jug, and cover the surface of the custard with buttered greaseproof paper. Chill in the refrigerator for at least 4 hours or overnight. Then proceed according to the method for making French Vanilla Ice Cream (see page 51).

White Chocolate Ice Cream with Toasted Almonds

INGREDIENTS

	Metric	U.S.	Imperial
One recipe White Chocolate Ice Cream (see page 78)			
Whole skinned almonds	180 g	1 cup	6½ oz
Makes about	1.5 litres	6 cups	48 fl oz

Toast the almonds on a baking tray for 3–5 minutes until light golden brown. When ready, transfer the nuts to another baking tray to stop cooking; cool completely. Chop coarsely. When the ice cream is ready for freezing add the nuts and stir or process briefly to ensure even distribution. Then proceed according to the method for making French Vanilla Ice Cream (see page 51).

White Chocolate Ice Cream with Sour Cherries

INGREDIENTS

	Metric	U.S.	Imperial
One recipe White Chocolate Ice Cream (see page 78)			
Sour Morello cherries★	110 g	½ cup	3¾ oz
Makes about	1.5 litres	6 cups	48 fl oz

★ These are Polish sour cherries and are obtainable in glass jars from delicatessens. See also Morello Cherry Ice Cream, page 68.

Drain the cherries completely and coarsely chop them. When the ice cream is ready for freezing, add the cherries and stir or process briefly to ensure even distribution. Then proceed according to the method for making French Vanilla Ice Cream (see page 51).

Christmas Cake Ice Cream

Surprisingly successful, this really does have the flavour of Christmas about it. We use standard Christmas cake, including the marzipan, but not the sugar icing.

INGREDIENTS

	Metric	U.S.	Imperial
Milk	375 ml	1½ cups	12 fl oz
Soft light brown sugar	100 g	½ cup	3½ oz
Egg yolks	3	3	3
Whipping/heavy cream (36 per cent fat)	185 ml	¾ cup	6 fl oz
Brandy	1 Tbsp	1 Tbsp	1 Tbsp
Christmas cake, diced	175 g	1¼ cups	6¼ oz
Makes about	1 litre	4 cups	32 fl oz

Using the above quantities of milk, soft light brown sugar, egg yolks and cream, prepare and cook a custard according to the method for making French Vanilla Ice Cream (see page 51). Continue up to the stage when the chilled custard is combined with the cream. At this point stir in the brandy. Still freeze (see page 48) or start the ice-cream machine and freeze until the ice cream is the consistency of softly whipped cream. Now sprinkle in the diced cake, and stir it or leave to churn for about 5 more seconds than switch off. Quickly scrape the ice cream into plastic freezer boxes, giving the ice cream a final stir once or twice to make sure the cake is evenly distributed. Level the surface, and cover with waxed or greaseproof paper and a lid. Then label, and freeze for a minimum of 1 hour, and serve. If frozen solid, allow about 20 minutes in the fridge to soften sufficiently to serve.

Variation
This can be used to make a bombe. See Christmas Cake Ice Cream with Brandy Parfait Bombe page 171.

(left) Water colour of Christmas Cake Ice Cream by Judith Cheek.

Cider Sorbet

This is an ideal store-cupboard sorbet. It can be produced at little notice, provided cider is to hand, and always impresses. We prefer to use a very dry cider as it gives much more flavour in a sorbet. However, sweet cider lovers can use the sweet variety, and the result is very good. It is wonderful served with an apple ice cream.

INGREDIENTS

	Metric	U.S.	Imperial
Dry cider	600 ml	2½ cups	20 fl oz
Sugar syrup (see page 47)	375 ml	1½ cups	12 fl oz
Lemon juice	1 Tbsp	1 Tbsp	1 Tbsp
Egg white	1	1	1
Makes about	1 litre	4 cups	32 fl oz

Chill the cider, add the syrup and lemon juice to taste. When ready still freeze (see page 48) or start the ice-cream machine. Pour in the mixture and churn for about 10 minutes until just beginning to freeze very softly. Beat the egg white in a small bowl with a fork until loosened. Pour into the sorbet as it churns and leave the machine in motion until the ice is firm enough to serve.

If it is to be stored, quickly scrape the ice into plastic freezer boxes, and cover with a piece of waxed or greaseproof paper and a lid. Finally label, then freeze. Once the ice becomes solid it will need about 20 minutes in the fridge before it is soft enough to serve.

Serving
Good served with Bramley Apple Ice Cream (see page 54).

A mould for making an ice water cup in which to serve sorbets.

Cinnamon Ice Cream

Cinnamon is one of those spices that die quickly, the powder form inevitably losing fragrance and flavour faster than the cinnamon sticks or quills. If the aroma does not hit you when you take the lid off the jar, throw it out and buy some fresh.

INGREDIENTS

	Metric	U.S.	Imperial
Milk	600 ml	2½ cups	20 fl oz
Vanilla bean	1	1	1
Granulated sugar	250 g	1¼ cups	7¾ oz
Egg yolks	6	6	6
Cinnamon sticks	30 cm	12 inches	12 inches
Whipping/heavy cream (36 per cent fat)	300 ml	1¼ cups	10½ fl oz
Makes about	1 litre	4 cups	32 fl oz

Using the above quantities of milk, vanilla bean, sugar and egg yolks, prepare and cook a custard according to the method for making French Vanilla Ice Cream (see page 51), adding the cinnamon stick, broken into short lengths, at the same time as the vanilla bean. Cool the custard, then cover and chill in the fridge overnight to allow the cinnamon flavour to develop. When ready, strain the custard and add the cream. Then either still freeze (see page 48) or start the ice-cream machine. Pour in the custard and churn for 15–20 minutes. Serve at once; or to store, quickly scrape into plastic freezer boxes, and cover with waxed or greaseproof paper and a lid. Finally label, then freeze. Allow about 30 minutes in the fridge to soften sufficiently to serve.

My advice to you is not to inquire why or whither but just enjoy your ice cream while it's on your plate – that's my philosophy.

Thornton Wilder (1897–1975),
The Skin of Our Teeth, Act 1

Citrus Sorbet

Given the strong sweet/sharp flavours of citrus fruit it is almost impossible to make an indifferent citrus sorbet. However, it is important to get the sugar balance correct as the many different varieties of each fruit vary considerably in acidity. Taste, taste and taste again to get the balance right for this sorbet. It should be slightly tart.

INGREDIENTS

	Metric	U.S.	Imperial
Granulated sugar	100 g	½ cup	3½ oz
Water	125 ml	½ cup	4 fl oz
Oranges	6	6	6
Grapefruit	1	1	1
Lemons	2	2	2
Limes	2	2	2
Makes about	750 ml	3 cups	24 fl oz

In a small saucepan combine the sugar and water. Bring slowly to the boil, stirring frequently until the sugar dissolves. Once the syrup boils adjust the heat and leave to boil gently, uncovered, for 5 minutes. Then leave to cool.

Meanwhile, put 1 orange, the grapefruit, 1 lemon and 1 lime into warm soapy water. Scrub the fruit; then rinse thoroughly and dry. Use a zester to remove strips of coloured rind from each fruit. If necessary, chop the strips into shortish (1.25 cm/½ inch) lengths, otherwise they pose problems with the making, stirring and eating of the sorbet. Transfer the strips to a sieve, pour a kettle full of boiling water over them, then leave to drain on a pad of kitchen paper.

Squeeze and strain the juice from all the fruit into a bowl, and combine with the cooled syrup and strips of zest. Cover and chill in the fridge.

When ready still freeze (see page 48) or start the ice-cream machine. Pour in the liquid and leave to churn and freeze for about 20 minutes or until the mixture is a soft ice. Then quickly scrape into plastic freezer boxes, level the surface and cover with greaseproof or waxed paper and a lid. Finally label, then freeze. Serve within 1 hour. If frozen, allow about 20–25 minutes in the fridge to soften before serving.

Clementine Sorbet

With the bewildering variety of citrus fruits available, we decided to keep things simple. We aimed for a flavour that was clearly not lemon, lime, orange or grapefruit, and found that the flavour of clementines came through clean, clear, direct and unmistakable. Just make sure, though, that what you buy really are clementines!

INGREDIENTS

	Metric	U.S.	Imperial
Clementines	10	10	10
Sugar syrup (see page 47)	250 ml	1 cup	8 fl oz
Lemon juice	1 Tbsp	1 Tbsp	1 Tbsp
Makes about	750 ml	3 cups	24 fl oz

Scrub the clementines in soapy water then rinse and dry them. Using a zester, remove only the coloured part of the zest from 5 of the clementines. Put the zest in a non-reactive saucepan with the sugar syrup, bring to the boil, then lower the heat and simmer for 1 minute. Cover and leave aside to cool. Remove the zest from 1 more clementine, cover and set aside to add to the finished sorbet. When cooled, strain the sugar syrup and discard the zest. Squeeze the clementines and add the strained juice and the lemon juice to the flavoured sugar syrup. Chill in the fridge.

When ready still freeze (see page 48) or start the ice-cream machine. Pour in the liquid and leave to churn and freeze until the mixture is a soft ice. At this point add the reserved, uncooked zest from the 1 clementine and continue to churn for 10 seconds more. Then either serve or, if freezing, quickly scrape into plastic freezer boxes, level the surface and cover with greaseproof or waxed paper and a lid. Finally label, then freeze. Serve within 1 hour. If frozen solid, allow about 20–25 minutes in the fridge to soften before serving.

Clove Ice Cream

This is tailor-made for those who prefer to have ice cream served on top of puddings. Try this one with apple pie or rhubarb crumble.

INGREDIENTS

	Metric	U.S.	Imperial
Milk	250 ml	1 cup	8 fl oz
Whipping/heavy cream			
(36 per cent fat)	500 ml	2 cups	16 fl oz
Cloves	18	18	18
Egg yolks	6	6	6
Granulated sugar	70 g	⅓ cup	2½ oz
Makes about	875 ml	3½ cups	28 fl oz

Combine the milk, cream and cloves (yes, 18) in the top half of a non-reactive double saucepan. Sit this over a base pan of simmering water and allow the cream to reach just below boiling point. Turn off the heat, cover and leave the cream to keep hot and infuse for about 20 minutes. Taste regularly to assess the strength of the clove flavour, bearing in mind that when frozen the taste will be milder. Also consider the other puddings or ice creams this is to be served with; e.g. apple pie and rhubarb crumble will take a stronger flavour; a milder flavour is better if you are serving it with other ice creams or sorbets.

Strain the cream to remove the cloves and pour it back into the top half of the double pan. In a bowl whisk the egg yolks and sugar until foamy, and stiff enough to support a trail of mix. Pour half the hot cream into the bowl in a thin stream, whisking constantly. Return the blend to the rest of the cream and heat over a base pan of barely simmering water until the custard is thick enough to coat the back of a spoon. Strain the mixture into a bowl and cover with a sheet of buttered greaseproof paper to prevent a skin forming. Leave to cool, then chill in the fridge. When ready still freeze (see page 48) or start the ice-cream machine. Pour in the liquid and churn for about 15–20 minutes. Serve within 1 hour. If frozen solid, allow about 20–25 minutes in the fridge to soften.

Toasted Coconut Ice Cream

This recipe is based on using fresh coconut. For those who have never dealt with a coconut it can seem a problem, prompting people to reach for ice picks, sledge-hammers and electric drills. Our technique is not so dramatic. Since it is simpler and safer than most advice we have read on the subject, we pass it on.

First though, when buying a coconut, shake it; it should have an unmistakable, generously sloshing sound. Then check the three "eyes"; none of these should be mouldy or show any sign of damage. To open the coconut you first need to drain off the water inside. (It is called water, not milk.) A few experimental jabs will establish that one eye is softer than the other two. (This is the eye through which the coconut would have sprouted.) We find it easiest to use a corkscrew to make the first hole in this eye and then enlarge it with a kebab-type skewer. Use the corkscrew to make a second hole in another eye to avoid an air lock. Leave the coconut upside down to drain into a large glass or mug.

To open the shell, cover the coconut with a towel, place it on a stone or concrete floor and hit it with a hammer. This usually both cracks the shell and frees the meat at one and the same time. Try using a sharp potato peeler to pare off the thin brown skin, as this has proved to be safer than a knife. Any coconut meat left over keeps best immersed in coconut water, in the fridge.

INGREDIENTS

	Metric	U.S.	Imperial
Fresh coconut	1	1	1
Milk	560 ml	2¼ cups	18 fl oz
Egg yolks	6	6	6
Granulated sugar	150 g	¾ cup	5¼ oz
Whipping/heavy cream			
(36 per cent fat)	375 ml	1½ cups	12 fl oz
Vanilla extract		a few drops	
Makes about	1 litre	4 cups	32 fl oz

Preheat the oven to 160°C/325°F/Gas Mark 3. Prepare the coconut as outlined above. Coarsely grate the white meat either by putting it through the coarse grater disc of a good processor or by hand. Spread evenly over a large baking tray and bake for about 15 minutes or until the coconut is golden. Stir occasionally so that the coconut pieces brown evenly.

Measure 80 g/1¼ cups/2¾ oz of the toasted coconut into a saucepan, reserving the remainder in a sealed container. Add the milk and heat gently until the first bubbles appear. Remove the pan from the heat, cover and leave to infuse for about 30 minutes. Strain the milk, pressing the coconut firmly to extract all the juices. Measure the coconut milk and make it up to 375 ml/1½ cups/12 fl oz with fresh milk if necessary. Return the coconut milk to the saucepan and bring back to boiling point.

Meanwhile, whisk the egg yolks and sugar together in a heatproof bowl.

Pour the milk into the yolks and sugar in a thin steady stream, beating constantly, then either position the bowl over a pan of barely simmering water or pour the custard into the top half of a double saucepan. Continue to cook over hot water, stirring frequently, until the custard thickens and reaches 85°C/185°F (see page 51). Remove the bowl (or pan) to sit in cold water. When the custard is cool, cover and chill in the fridge.

When ready, stir the cream and vanilla into the custard, then either still freeze (see page 48) or start the ice-cream machine. Pour in the mixture. Leave to churn and freeze for about 20 minutes or until the consistency of thick cream. Quickly scrape into plastic storage boxes, level the surface and cover with greaseproof paper or waxed paper and a lid. Finally label, then freeze. Serve within 1 hour. If frozen, allow about 20–25 minutes in the fridge to soften sufficiently to serve.

Serving
Scoops of the ice cream can be served with a sprinkling of the remaining toasted coconut.

Easy Coconut Ice Cream

Having one recipe with fresh coconut, we thought it would be useful also to include a very quick, easy one made with canned coconut milk or desiccated, or creamed coconut. However, these ingredients could not produce anything like a satisfactory result, until, in desperation, we tried using dried coconut milk powder. This comes in a sealed foil pack in a box and looks like any other fine milk powder. Ordinary milk powder is not a flavour we welcome in ice cream, but coconut milk powder proved quite the opposite. The hard work is confined to opening the box and packet; the flavour of the ice cream is amazingly good! Which all goes to prove a good cookery maxim; keep an open mind.

INGREDIENTS

	Metric	U.S.	Imperial
One recipe Soft Scoop Vanilla Ice Cream (see page 154)			
Coconut milk powder	6 Tbsp	6 Tbsp	6 Tbsp
Makes about	875 ml	3½ cups	28 fl oz

Make the ice cream according to the method for making Soft Scoop Vanilla Ice Cream (see page 154), whisking in the coconut milk powder following the addition of the hot milk to the beaten sugar and egg. Cook, freeze and serve as directed in the recipe for Soft Scoop Vanilla Ice Cream.

Espresso Coffee Ice Cream

Quite simply the best coffee ice cream we have ever tasted.

INGREDIENTS

	Metric	U.S.	Imperial
Fresh espresso beans	40 g	½ cup	1½ oz
Milk	375 ml	1½ cups	12 fl oz
Whipping/heavy cream (36 per cent fat)	250 ml	1 cup	8 fl oz
Egg yolks	5	5	5
Granulated sugar	150 g	¾ cup	5¼ oz
Makes about	1 litre	4 cups	32 fl oz

Put the coffee beans in a food processor or blender and grind for 10 seconds.

Combine them in a saucepan with the milk and cream and heat gently, stirring occasionally, until bubbles start to appear around the edge. Then remove the pan from the heat, cover and leave until cold. In a heatproof bowl combine the egg yolks and sugar and beat until they take on a pale yellow colour and lighter consistency. Bring the coffee infusion back to just below boiling point then pour in stages through a fine strainer on to the egg yolks and sugar, whisking between each addition. The bowl can now be placed over a pan of simmering water, or the custard can be returned to the saucepan which is then put on top of a heat-diffuser mat so that it is not in direct contact with the heat. Only if you are confident that you will not overheat the custard should you put the saucepan on a gentle, direct heat. Stir the custard until it reaches 85°C/185°F or until it has thickened sufficiently to coat the back of a spoon. As soon as the custard reaches this stage, plunge the base of the pan into cold water. On no account should the custard be allowed to overheat or boil as the mixture will curdle. (For how to deal with an overheated custard see page 52.) Once cold, cover and chill in the fridge.

When ready, still freeze (see page 48) or start the ice-cream machine. Pour in the coffee mixture and churn for about 15 minutes or until the ice cream is the consistency of softly whipped cream. Quickly scrape into plastic freezer boxes, level the surface and cover with greaseproof or waxed paper and a lid. Finally label, then freeze. Serve within 1 hour. If fully frozen, allow about 20 minutes in a fridge to soften sufficiently to serve.

Coffee Fudge Ripple

See page 165.

Coffee Granita

INGREDIENTS

	Metric	U.S.	Imperial
Water	875 ml	3½ cups	28 fl oz
Granulated sugar	210 g	1 cup	7½ oz
Strips of lemon peel	3×2.5×1.25 cm	3×1×½ inch	3×1×½ inch
Instant coffee	5 Tbsp	5 Tbsp	5 Tbsp
Kahlua®★	2 Tbsp	2 Tbsp	2 Tbsp
Makes about	500 ml	2 cups	16 fl oz

Measure 250 ml/1 cup/8 fl oz of the water into a small pan and add the sugar and strips of lemon peel. Bring to the boil. Boil for 30 seconds, then remove the pan from the heat. Stir in the coffee and a further 625 ml/2½ cups/20 fl oz of cold water. Add the Kahlua and chill the liquid in the fridge. Discard the lemon strips.

For detailed instructions on how to prepare the perfect granita see page 49.

★ Mexican coffee liqueur.

Granita di Caffè Espresso

The Gelateria Tirreno, in Formia, Italy, makes an excellent coffee granita. In fact it is their speciality, and their method of serving is a good one to copy. Spoon the freshly made coffee granita into a tall, chilled glass. Push the handle of a spoon through the centre down to the base of the glass and wind it round to create a conical cavity; fill with whipped cream. Serve pronto!

INGREDIENTS

	Metric	U.S.	Imperial
Water	500 ml	2 cups	16 fl oz
Ground espresso coffee	40 g	½ cup	1½ oz
Lemon zest	2 tsp	2 tsp	2 tsp
Sugar syrup (see page 47)	250 ml	1 cup	8 fl oz
Lemon juice	1 Tbsp	1 Tbsp	1 Tbsp
Makes about	750 ml	3 cups	24 fl oz

Put the water in a pan, add the ground espresso coffee and bring to the boil. Immediately turn off the heat, add the lemon zest and allow to infuse for 5 minutes. Strain through a coffee filter to remove the grounds. Then add the sugar syrup and the lemon juice and leave to cool. Cover and leave to chill in the fridge.

For detailed instructions on how to prepare the perfect granita see page 49.

Coffee Parfait

Traditionally, parfaits were an iced dessert, flavoured with coffee. True parfaits have almost died out as they are difficult to make in large quantities while maintaining the lightness. However, they have the advantage of not needing an ice-cream maker as they are frozen and not even stirred. Parfaits are particularly suited to flavouring with fortified wines and liqueurs (see page 49). Fruits and flavourings that increase the solid content of the ice really spoil the light character of the parfait. For this reason, the only one we have included is Chocolate Parfait (see page 73), which has neither the texture nor lightness of a parfait but has a delightful chewy chocolate character all of its own.
NOTE: *This recipe is precise in order to get a perfect result.*

INGREDIENTS

	Metric	U.S.	Imperial
Egg yolks	4	4	4
Instant coffee	1 Tbsp	1 Tbsp	1 Tbsp
Sugar syrup (see page 47)	185 ml plus 2 Tbsp	¾ cup plus 2 Tbsp	6 fl oz plus 2 Tbsp
Whipping/heavy cream (36 per cent fat)	250 ml	1 cup	8 fl oz
Makes about	1.1 litres	4½ cups	36 fl oz

For this recipe you will need a thermometer, a good quality, three-speed electric hand mixer and, preferably, a double saucepan. Failing this, select a large heatproof bowl which will sit snugly into a saucepan. Into the bowl put the yolks and use the electric mixer to whisk them until light and pale.

Dissolve the instant coffee in the 2 Tbsp of sugar syrup by warming it slightly, then add the rest of the syrup and warm the coffee syrup to 30–40°C/86–104°F (around blood heat), then whisk this, a few tablespoons at a time, into the egg yolks. Now either position the bowl over, not in, a saucepan of barely simmering water, or pour the mixture into the top of a double saucepan positioned over, but not in, scarcely simmering water. Now proceed exactly according to the method for making parfaits (see page 50).

Cointreau Parfait

See page 49.

GRANITI. These beverages are considered most deliciously grateful drinks at evening parties in the summer season.

J. E. Tilton,
The Art of Confectionery, Boston, Mass, 1866

Cornish Clotted Cream Ice Cream

It is surprising how emphatically the flavour of clotted cream comes through in this ice cream, considering the comparatively small amount used in the recipe. For lovers of rich ice cream this is the ultimate.

INGREDIENTS

	Metric	U.S.	Imperial
Milk	375 ml	1½ cups	12 fl oz
Granulated sugar	125 g	½ cup plus 2 Tbsp	4½ oz
Egg yolks	5	5	5
Clotted cream (55 per cent fat)	125 ml	½ cup	4 fl oz
Makes about	1 litre	4 cups	32 fl oz

Combine the milk and half the sugar in a medium-sized saucepan and bring to just below boiling point. Now proceed according to the method for making French Vanilla Ice Cream (see page 51). Continue up to the stage where the custard has reached the right temperature and/or has thickened sufficiently and the pan has been removed from the heat and the base plunged in a few inches of cold water. At this point immediately stir in the clotted cream and leave until cold before covering and transferring to the fridge to chill. When ready, still freeze (see page 48) or start the ice-cream machine and pour in the custard.

CAUTION

Because of the high fat content this ice cream will not need churning for as long as most other ices; it will only need a maximum of 10 minutes to churn to the stage when it is very softly frozen and thickened. If it is churned past this stage it is very likely to become buttery.

Quickly scrape into plastic freezer boxes, level the surface and cover with greaseproof or waxed paper and a lid. Finally label, then freeze. Serve within 1 hour. If frozen solid, allow about 15 minutes in the fridge to soften before serving.

Cranberry Granita

For a long time the cranberry was scarcely more than a condiment for the Thanksgiving turkey and something of a rarity outside the U.S.A. Now, due to aggressive marketing by the producers, cranberries are cropping up everywhere on the menu, all the year round. Our feelings about this fruit are slightly less than enthusiastic because the flavour is not only sour but bitter, and all too often the reaction is to swamp the fruit with sugar to overcome the bitterness. With cranberry ices this is not such a problem because freezing seems to have a mellowing effect on the bitterness. Bear this in mind when you taste the mix before freezing, and do not feel daunted. A civilised ice of good colour and flavour will emerge.

INGREDIENTS

	Metric	U.S.	Imperial
Cranberries, fresh, or frozen and thawed	225 g	8 oz	8 oz
Water	625 ml plus 3 Tbsp	2½ cups plus 3 Tbsp	20 fl oz plus 3 Tbsp
Sugar syrup (see page 47)	300 ml	1¼ cups	10½ fl oz
Orange	1	1	1
Lemon	1	1	1
Makes about	1 litre	4 cups	32 fl oz

In a non-reactive saucepan, gently simmer the cranberries in the 3 Tbsp of water until they burst. Then pour the contents of the pan into a food processor or liquidiser. Add the 625 ml/2½ cups/20 fl oz of water and liquidise until it is a purée. Rub through a plastic sieve and add the sugar syrup and the strained juice of the orange and the lemon. Cover and chill thoroughly in the fridge.

For detailed instructions on how to prepare the perfect granita see page 49.

Serving
Serve the granita in a tall glass with some crème fraîche flavoured with Cointreau.

Cranberry Sorbet

INGREDIENTS

	Metric	U.S.	Imperial
Cranberries, fresh, or frozen and thawed	175 g	6 oz	6 oz
Water	165 ml plus 3 Tbsp	⅔ cup plus 3 Tbsp	5½ fl oz plus 3 Tbsp
Sugar syrup (see page 47) up to (see recipe)	750 ml	3 cups	24 fl oz
Juice of orange	1	1	1
Juice of lemons	2	2	2
Makes about	1 litre	4 cups	32 fl oz

In a non-reactive saucepan, gently simmer the cranberries in the 3 Tbsp of water until they burst. Then pour the contents of the pan into a food processor or liquidiser. Add the 165 ml/⅔ cup/5½ fl oz of water and liquidise until it is a purée. Rub this through a plastic sieve. This will produce between 315 and 375 ml/1⅓–1½ cups/10½ –12 fl oz of purée.

Take the purée and add exactly twice this volume of sugar syrup and the strained juice of 1 orange and of the 2 lemons. Check the flavour; more lemon may be needed as cranberries should be slightly tart or they taste unidentifiably jammy. Cover and chill in the refrigerator.

When ready, still freeze (see page 48) or start the ice-cream machine. Pour in the liquid and leave to churn and freeze for about 20 minutes or until the mixture becomes a soft ice. Quickly scrape into plastic freezer boxes, level the surface and cover with greaseproof or waxed paper and a lid. Finally label, then freeze. Serve within 1 hour. If frozen solid, allow about 20–25 minutes in the fridge to soften before serving.

Crème Fraîche Ice Cream

As the finale to a wonderful meal we ate at Postrio in San Francisco, the waiter persuaded the kitchen to give us a sample of all the ice creams and fresh fruit sorbets on their dessert menu. Out of some sublime ices the crème fraîche ice cream was so good it defied description. Modestly, we claim our version to be as near as dammit.

INGREDIENTS

	Metric	U.S.	Imperial
Eggs	3	3	3
Vanilla sugar (see page 36)	250 g	1¼ cups	8¾ oz
Milk	500 ml	2 cups	16 fl oz
Crème fraîche★	750 ml	3 cups	24 fl oz
Lemon juice	1 tsp	1 tsp	1 tsp
Makes about	1.5 litres	6 cups	48 fl oz

★ See Ingredients page 27.

In a heatproof bowl combine the eggs and half the sugar and whisk until pale and light. Bring the milk and the remaining sugar to boiling point then pour on to the eggs and sugar, whisking all the while. The bowl can now be placed over a pan of simmering water, or the custard can be returned to the saucepan which is then put on top of a heat–diffuser mat so that it is not in direct contact with the heat. Only if you have an accurate thermometer and/or are confident that you will not overheat the custard, should you put the saucepan over a gentle direct heat. Stir the custard until it reaches 85°C/185°F or has thickened sufficiently to coat the back of a spoon.

As soon as the custard has thickened plunge the base of the pan into cold water. On no account should the custard be allowed to overheat or boil as the mixture will curdle. (For how to deal with an overheated custard see page 52.) Once the custard has cooled, cover and chill in the fridge. When ready, start the ice-cream machine. Gradually beat the chilled crème fraîche and the lemon juice into the custard then either still freeze (see page 48) or pour into the machine. Churn until the mixture is the consistency of thick cream. Quickly scrape into plastic freezer boxes, level the surface and cover with greaseproof or waxed paper and a lid. Finally label, then freeze. Serve within 1 hour. If frozen, allow about 20–25 minutes in the fridge to soften before serving.

Cucumber, White Wine and Mint Sorbet

Although it may be difficult to adjust to the idea of cucumbers in a sweet sorbet, this combination is very successful.

INGREDIENTS

	Metric	U.S.	Imperial
Large cucumbers	2	2	2
Dry white wine	4 Tbsp	4 Tbsp	4 Tbsp
Granulated sugar	200 g	1 cup	7 oz
Juice of lemon	1	1	1
Fresh mint leaves	6	6	6
Egg white	1	1	1
Makes about	750 ml	3 cups	24 fl oz

Top, tail and peel the cucumbers. Then cut into chunks and put in a food processor or blender with the dry white wine and sugar. Blend until smooth. Position a fine mesh sieve over a bowl. Pour in the cucumber purée and lemon juice and leave to drain for a minute or two. Then press the residue left in the sieve until the maximum juice has been extracted. Do not be tempted to rub the pulp through the sieve as this gives the sorbet a slightly distracting sandy texture. Rinse and dry the mint leaves, finely chop and add to the cucumber liquid. Cover and chill in the fridge.

When ready still freeze (see page 48) or start the ice-cream machine. Pour in the liquid and leave to churn and freeze until the mixture starts to form an icy slush. Using a fork, beat the egg white until loosened and add to the sorbet with the machine still running. Continue to churn and freeze for about 10 minutes or until firm enough to serve. To store, quickly scrape into plastic storage boxes, level the surface and cover with greaseproof or waxed paper and a lid. Finally label, then freeze. Serve within 1 hour. If frozen, allow about 20–25 minutes in the fridge to soften before serving.

Damson and Sour Cream Ice Cream

Sourness and intensity of flavour are a virtue when making ices. They come through the blanket of cream and cold in just the right measure to produce a memorable and unusual home-made ice cream. A flavour we have never seen commercially.

INGREDIENTS

	Metric	U.S.	Imperial
Damsons/Damson plums	350 g	¾ lb	¾ lb
Water	2 Tbsp	2 Tbsp	2 Tbsp
Egg yolks	4	4	4
Granulated sugar	200 g	1 cup	7 oz
Whipping/heavy cream (36 per cent fat)	250 ml	1 cup	8 fl oz
Sour cream	250 ml	1 cup	8 fl oz
Makes about	1.1 litres	4½ cups	36 fl oz

Carefully sort through the damsons, discarding any that are damaged. Rinse the remaining fruit and drain thoroughly then transfer to a saucepan. Add the 2 Tbsp of water and bring to the boil. Cover and cook gently for 5–10 minutes or until the damsons are soft. Remove from the heat and leave to cool before rubbing through a plastic sieve until only the stones remain. Cover the purée and chill in the fridge.

In a heatproof bowl combine the egg yolks and half the sugar, and whisk until pale and light. Bring the whipping/heavy cream and remaining sugar to boiling point then pour on to the egg yolks and sugar, whisking all the while. The bowl can now be placed over a pan of simmering water, or the custard can be returned to the saucepan which is then put on top of a heat-diffuser mat so that it is not in direct contact with the heat. Only if you have an accurate thermometer and/or are confident that you will not overheat the custard, should you put the saucepan over a gentle direct heat. Stir the custard until it reaches 85°C/185°F or until it has thickened sufficiently to coat the back of a spoon. As soon as the custard reaches this stage, plunge the base of the pan into cold water. On no account should the custard be allowed to overheat or boil as the mixture will curdle. (For how to deal with an overheated custard see page 52). Once cold, cover and chill in the fridge.

When ready, still freeze (see page 48) or start the ice-cream machine. Combine the chilled sour cream, damson purée and custard and pour into the ice-cream machine. Churn until the mixture is the consistency of thick cream. Quickly scrape into plastic freezer boxes, level the surface and cover with greaseproof or waxed paper and a lid. Finally label, then freeze. Serve within 1 hour. If frozen, allow about 25–30 minutes in the fridge to soften before serving.

Dulche de Leche Ice Cream

Some twenty years ago there was a particular fad which involved the prolonged boiling of cans of condensed milk. This turned the contents into a toffee-like mixture which was then spread in a baked pastry case, sprinkled with nuts or whatever, and as such became the dinner party dessert. *While searching for this in old recipe files, it popped out of the pages of Nathalie Hambro's book,* Particular Delights.

She describes boiling the cans of condensed milk and spreading the contents on toast; a habit she discovered in South America. But we thought it would make a wonderful flavouring for an ice cream – and so it proved to be, something that is between butterscotch and toffee and something else besides. With her permission, we have used Nathalie Hambro's delightful recipe title for our ice cream.

INGREDIENTS

	Metric	U.S.	Imperial
One can full cream sweetened condensed milk	397 g	14 oz	14 oz
Milk	375 ml	1½ cups	12 fl oz
Light brown soft sugar	50 g	¼ cup	1¾ oz
Whipping/heavy cream (36 per cent fat)	250 ml	1 cup	8 fl oz
Makes about	1 litre	4 cups	32 fl oz

Boiling the condensed milk will take some 3 hours, so you will need to allow for this if the ice cream is to be served at a particular time. This is something of a drawback, so we usually boil at least two cans at a time in order to save both time and heat. Put the unopened tin(s) in a saucepan on a bed of folded kitchen paper. (This is to stop the incessant rattling of the cans as they boil.) Pour in sufficient cold water to cover and bring to the boil. Reduce the heat to give a simmer, prop a lid at a slight angle over the pan and continue to cook in this manner for 2–3 hours.

NOTE: Check the water level during this time, topping up with boiling water if necessary. Obviously the longer the cans are boiled, the more caramelised the contents will become, but we would not advise taking it much beyond the 3-hour mark. Leave the cans to cool in the water for 15 minutes before removing. CAUTION: Wait until the cans are cold before opening.

Now remove, open and put the contents of one can into a medium-sized saucepan with the milk and brown sugar. Bring slowly to the boil, and once the mixture gets hot whisk lightly to break down the condensed milk – it will need this bit of persuasion. When fully dissolved remove the pan from the heat and leave until cold before covering and transferring to the fridge to chill.

When ready, still freeze (see page 48) or start the ice-cream machine. Combine the chilled condensed milk mixture with the cream and pour into the machine. Continue to churn until the mixture is the consistency of softly whipped cream. Quickly scrape into plastic freezer boxes, level the surface and cover with greaseproof or waxed paper and a lid. Finally label, then freeze. Serve within 1 hour. If frozen, allow about 25–30 minutes in the fridge to soften before serving.

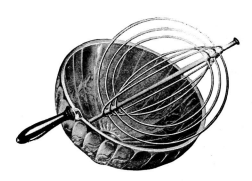

A cream whipper, *c.* 1890.

Elderberry Sorbet

In September the hedges in Britain are full of elderberries that can be picked and frozen for the winter. However, the season is short and you have to compete with the birds and wine-makers when picking them. Make sure that the berries are dark and fully ripe and avoid any greenish ones. Pick bunches and take them home, washing them very well in cold water. Then de-stalk them carefully, using a fork. Persuade all the family to join in; it is a thankless, finger-staining task. This process will lose about 30 per cent of the weight.

It is best to cook them and freeze the berries before the addition of any sugar. They make a wonderful winter sorbet for a dinner party.

INGREDIENTS

	Metric	U.S.	Imperial
Elderberries, de-stalked and washed	435 g	3 cups	15 oz
Water	165 ml	⅔ cup	5½ fl oz
Sugar syrup (see page 47)	250 ml	1 cup	8 fl oz
Salt	pinch	pinch	pinch
Water	185 ml	¾ cup	6 fl oz
Egg white	1	1	1
Makes about	750 ml	3 cups	24 fl oz

Put the elderberries in a non-reactive saucepan with the 165 ml/⅔ cup/5½ fl oz of water and bring to the boil. Then simmer for 5 minutes, stirring regularly. Sieve while hot through a fine plastic sieve to extract all the seeds. This should produce about 1 cup of purée which can either be frozen for later use or used immediately for the sorbet.

Take the cup of purée and add the syrup, the salt and the 185 ml/¾ cup/6 fl oz of water. Cover and chill in the fridge.

When ready, still freeze (see page 48) or start the ice-cream machine and churn for about 10 minutes until the mixture becomes a soft slush. Now, using a fork, beat the egg white until loosened and add to the sorbet with the machine still running. Continue to churn until firm enough to serve. Or, to store, quickly scrape into plastic freezer boxes, and cover with waxed or greaseproof paper and a lid. Finally label, then freeze. If frozen, allow about 30 minutes in the fridge before serving.

There were many minor culinary heresies, however, which he [Escoffier] deplored but had to accept because of the clients who knew no better and insisted on hors d'oeuvre and soup at the same meal instead of hors d'oeuvre *or* soup; or that abomination called a sorbet, a melting water ice, highly scented, served halfway through a meal with its horrid attendant, a cigarette.

André L. Simon in the introduction to *George Auguste Escoffier* by Eugène Herbodeau and Paul Thalamas, English translation, Practical Press, 1955

This may well be an example of André Simon's prejudices rather than Escoffier's as the Fondation Auguste Escoffier have no record of Escoffier's ever having written this about sorbets.

Elderflower Sorbet

Franco Taruschio who owns the Walnut Tree Inn near Abergavenny in Wales has probably the largest range of home-made ices of any restaurant in the British Isles. Even if it isn't the largest, it certainly is the best we have ever come across. Well worth the effort to go there just for the selection of ices. For twenty-seven years his Italian-born ice-cream maker, Anna, has been making ice creams, sorbets and granitas. Franco and Anna introduced us to elderflower cordial. This is our edition of their recipe that you can enjoy all year round.

INGREDIENTS

	Metric	U.S.	Imperial
Sugar syrup (see page 47)	500 ml	2 cups	16 fl oz
Water	250 ml	1 cup	8 fl oz
Elderflower cordial	1 Tbsp	1 Tbsp	1 Tbsp
Lemon juice, strained, about	3 Tbsp	3 Tbsp	3 Tbsp
Makes about	750 ml	3 cups	24 fl oz

Combine the measured sugar syrup with the water, elderflower cordial and strained lemon juice. Chill in the fridge.

When ready, still freeze (see page 48) or start the ice-cream machine and pour in the liquid. Continue to churn and freeze for 12–15 minutes or until the sorbet is firm enough to serve. Or to store, quickly scrape into plastic freezer containers, cover with waxed or greaseproof paper and a lid. Finally label, then freeze. If frozen, allow about 15–20 minutes in the fridge to soften.

Fresh Fig and Fig Leaf Ice Cream

The idea of infusing fig leaves to intensify the flavour of a fig ice cream was prompted by reading Geraldene Holt's French Country Kitchen. *She, in her turn, made a fig leaf custard as a result of reading the American cookery writer Diana Kennedy. As a way of making the most of imported figs it works beautifully. Of course, if fully ripened, flavourful figs are available the leaves need not be used.*

INGREDIENTS

	Metric	U.S.	Imperial
Ripe, fresh figs	450 g	1 lb	1 lb
Water	3 Tbsp	3 Tbsp	3 Tbsp
Egg yolks	3	3	3
Granulated sugar	100 g	½ cup	3½ oz
Whipping/heavy cream (36 per cent fat)	375 ml	1½ cups	12 fl oz
Lemon juice	squeeze	squeeze	squeeze
Fig leaves (about 10 cm/4 inches across)	10	10	10
Makes about	1 litre	4 cups	32 fl oz

Wash the figs, trim away the stem ends and cut into quarters. Select a saucepan that will accommodate the fruit in a single layer and add the water. Bring to simmering point, then cover and cook gently for about 15 minutes or until the figs are perfectly tender. Cool and blend briefly in a food processor or blender so that the fruit retains a definite and uneven texture. Transfer to a bowl, cover and chill in the fridge.

In a medium-sized heatproof bowl whisk together the egg yolks and the sugar until they take on a paler colour and lighter consistency. Bring the cream to just below boiling point and pour on to the egg yolks and sugar, whisking all the while. The bowl can now be placed over a pan of simmering water, or the custard can be returned to the saucepan which is then put on top of a heat-diffuser mat, so it is not in direct contact with the heat. Only if you have an accurate thermometer and/or are confident that you will not overheat the custard, should you put the saucepan over a gentle direct heat. Stir the custard until it reaches 85°C/185°F or has thickened sufficiently to coat the back of a spoon. As soon as the custard has thickened plunge the base of the pan into cold water. On no account should the custard be allowed to overheat or boil as the mixture will curdle. (For how to deal with an overheated custard see page 52.) Rinse and dry the fig leaves and submerge them in the hot custard. As soon as it is cool, cover and chill overnight in the fridge.

When ready, start the ice-cream machine, strain the custard and stir in the fig pulp. Add a squeeze of lemon juice (this will make the mixture go noticeably pinker) then either still freeze (see page 48) or pour into the ice-cream machine. Churn until the mixture is the consistency of softly whipped cream. Quickly scrape into plastic freezer boxes, level the surface and cover with greaseproof or waxed paper and a lid. Finally label, then freeze. Serve within 1 hour. If frozen, allow about 20–25 minutes in a fridge to soften before serving.

English ice cream glasses (penny licks), 1928,

No. 9
20 to pint
3/6 doz.

No. 14
6/- doz.

No. 15
6/- doz.

No. 10
25 to pint
2/9 doz.

Deep Fried Ice Cream

The contrast of hot and cold is very compelling to young and old alike. We were therefore very interested in any recipes that were based on this combination. Well, we have coated, crumbed and rolled ice cream in pancakes; we have dipped ice cream in egg and all manner of batters, then chilled and fried through a very wide temperature range, and our conclusion is that you cannot better our recipe below. Stick to our measurements, temperatures and timings and you will find this recipe reliable. Our tasters' verdict was "delicious" and "great fun".

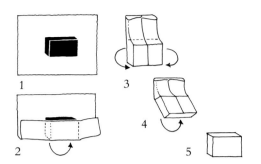

INGREDIENTS

	Metric	U.S.	Imperial
One recipe French Vanilla Ice Cream (see page 51), chilled but not frozen			
Butter	100 g	4 oz	4 oz
Filo pastry leaves	16	16	16
Groundnut/peanut oil for deep-frying			
Makes 8 parcels			

Churn, then freeze the ice cream in an 850 ml/3½ cup/ 30 fl oz loaf tin.

About 2 hours before serving, transfer the ice cream to the fridge for 15 minutes to soften slightly. Dip the tin briefly in hand-hot water then invert on to a plate or chopping board. Quickly cut into 8 (2 cm/¾ inch thick) slices and lay these on a baking sheet lined with silicone baking or greaseproof paper. Then replace immediately in the freezer for a minimum of 30 minutes.

Meanwhile warm the butter until melted, then remove from the heat.

Separate 1 sheet of filo pastry; trim, if necessary, to approximately 18×28 cm/7×11 inches. Brush all over with melted butter then lay a second (trimmed) sheet directly on top. Prepare the other sheets in the same manner. To accommodate them all on the work surface, stack the sheets, interleaving each pair with either sheets of plastic or greaseproof paper. This also prevents the pastry from drying out.

When completely ready, remove the ice cream slices from the freezer and wrap up as illustrated (see opposite). As soon as the first 4 have been wrapped, refrigerate them (they need not be covered) before continuing to wrap the remaining 4 slices. Then freeze the parcels for a minimum of 1 hour.

Just before serving, heat the oil in a deep-fat fryer or in a pan no more than two-thirds full to 195°C/383°F. (You *must* use a thermometer to accurately measure the temperature.) As soon as the oil is hot enough remove 2 parcels from the freezer and lower them into the oil. Time them carefully to fry for 50 seconds. Try to hold them under the surface of the oil with the aid of a wide frying slice, so that they brown all over. Remove immediately to a plate lined with kitchen paper. Flip backwards and forwards on the paper to mop up any excess oil, then serve immediately. Continue frying the remaining parcels, 2 at a time (any more lowers the temperature of the oil too much).

Serving

Very good with Light Lemon and Sultana Sauce (see page 165) or a thin, slightly sharp-flavoured fruit purée such as apple or apricot.

Variation

Deep Fried Marmalade Ice Cream (see page 115) is something really special.

FRIED ICE CREAM

In *The Times* on Saturday 9 June 1990 we were interested to read an article by Frances Bissell on the possible origins of deep fried ice cream. She relates having seen a so-called *new product* earlier that year, which consisted of a slice of ice cream, dipped in egg white and cake crumbs, ready to be deep fried from frozen. A few months later, she discovered a hand-written copy of a recipe for Surprise Caprice (which was none other than deep fried ice cream slices), between the pages of a 1954 edition of *La Cuisine Français*, which itself did not give this recipe. This posed the question – who invented fried ice cream?

Deep fried ice cream has recently found a home on the menu of many Mexican restaurant chains but there is no evidence of it having origins in Mexico; it just seems to have been adopted.

The earliest reference we have been able to find is in a 1915 copy of *The Soda Fountain*, the monthly magazine for the "Druggist, Confectioner and all Operators of Soda Fountains" which refers to "fried ice cream" being sold at the Chicago

World's Fair in 1893, where it was known as *Alaska Pie* and *Alaska Fritters*. Unfortunately, other than these names, there is no description or recipe. So *perhaps* it is a first for Chicago. Any other bids?

BAKED ALASKA
Baked Alaska has become whatever is the opposite of trendy, but it still excites curiosity.

Baron Brisse writing in 1866 attributed it to a French chef who learned it from a Chinese colleague who came to Paris with a Chinese mission. However, the Chinese version used *pastry* rather than meringue.

Delmonico's chef, Charles Ranhofer, is reputed to have named it Baked Alaska for a banquet held at Delmonico's to celebrate the purchase of Alaska from Russia in 1867, but the Delmonico version was covered in meringue, and it was probably adapted from Omelette Norvegienne.

Scented Geranium Leaf Ice Cream

Scented leaf geraniums (strictly pelargoniums) on the whole have rather insignificant flowers, but they are fascinating to grow for the variety of attractive leaves and their different scents. The predominant odour is citrus, but there are also varieties with leaves smelling of orange, apple, roses, lime, balsam/pine and various spices. For flavouring ice cream the balsam/pine is not good. The following varieties will give a better flavour: Attar of Roses, Odoratissimum (apple-scented), Radula (rose-lemon), Lady Plymouth (rose-scented). These varieties and much helpful advice are available from the Pelargonium Society (see Useful Addresses page 184).

INGREDIENTS

	Metric	U.S.	Imperial
One recipe Rose Petal Ice Cream (see page 140), omitting the rose petals and substituting			
Geranium leaves★	8	8	8
Makes about	500 ml	2 cups	16 fl oz

★NOTE: Only use unsprayed leaves.

Rinse the geranium leaves in cold water and pat dry with kitchen paper. Put the leaves in a saucepan with the milk and cream and follow the method for making and freezing Rose Petal Ice Cream (see page 140).

Gin and Tonic Sorbet

Rather unusual, and surprisingly good; wonderful made with gin infused with juniper berries. This very cold sorbet is delicious on hot summer days served before a meal in place of drinks. It is simplicity itself to make.

INGREDIENTS

	Metric	U.S.	Imperial
Gin	8 Tbsp	8 Tbsp	8 Tbsp
Sugar syrup (see page 47)	500 ml	2 cups	16 fl oz
Tonic water	375 ml	1½ cup	12 fl oz
Juice of lemon, strained	1	1	1
Egg white	1	1	1
Makes about	1 litre	4 cups	32 fl oz

Combine the gin, sugar syrup, tonic water and strained lemon juice. Stir, taste and add a little additional lemon juice, if preferred. Cover and chill in the fridge.

When ready, still freeze (see page 48) or start the ice-cream machine and pour in the liquid.

Because of the amount of gin in this mixture it will be impossible to churn it to the point at which it can be immediately eaten; the sorbet will need the lower temperature of the freezer to become firm enough to serve (see alcohol in ices page 183). After 15 minutes' churning, beat the egg white with a fork until loosened and add to the sorbet with the machine running. Churn for another 10 minutes by which time the sorbet will be slushy and runny. Quickly pour into plastic freezer containers, cover with waxed or greaseproof paper and freeze overnight. Serve straight from the freezer.

Note: Vodka can be substituted for gin.

Gin and Tonic Lollies

Perfect for a barbecue.

For lollies you need a harder ice so only use 6 Tbsp of gin in the above recipe. Put into lolly moulds and freeze hard. Serve straight from the freezer.

NOTE: Vodka can be substituted for gin.

Fresh Ginger Ice Cream

We found fresh ginger gives a good, positive, clean and clear flavour to ice cream. The method we use to extract the ginger flavour might seem a little laborious – why not simply infuse the chopped fresh ginger in the milk? Don't even think of trying it. The acidity in fresh ginger is so high they clean copper with it in South Africa, we are told. So, of course, it will curdle milk instantly. Also the flavour is unpleasantly bitter if the fresh ginger is not cooked in the way described in the recipe below.

INGREDIENTS

	Metric	U.S.	Imperial
Fresh ginger, peeled and finely chopped	4 Tbsp	4 Tbsp	4 Tbsp
Sugar syrup (see page 47)	250 ml	1 cup	8 fl oz
Milk	375 ml	1½ cups	12 fl oz
Egg yolks	3	3	3
Whipping/heavy cream (36 per cent fat), chilled	185 ml	¾ cup	6 fl oz
Vanilla extract	¼ tsp	¼ tsp	¼ tsp
Makes about	900 ml	3¾ cups	30 fl oz

Measure the chopped ginger into a small saucepan and add the sugar syrup. Bring to the boil, then simmer uncovered for 5 minutes before removing the pan from the heat. In a separate small pan bring the milk to just below boiling point then remove this from the heat. Pour the ginger syrup into the milk, cover and leave aside for a minimum of 30 minutes.

In a medium-sized heatproof bowl beat the egg yolks to break them up. Re-heat the syrup and milk to just below boiling point and pour on to the egg yolks, whisking vigorously all the while. The bowl can now be placed over a pan of simmering water, or the custard can be returned to the saucepan which is then put on top of a heat-diffuser mat so that it is not in direct contact with the heat. Only if you have an accurate thermometer and are confident that you will not overheat the sauce, should you put the saucepan over a gentle, direct heat. Stir the custard until it reaches 85°C/185°F or until it has thickened sufficiently to coat the back of a spoon. As soon as the custard has thickened, plunge the base of the pan into cold water. On no account should the pan be allowed to overheat or boil or the mixture will curdle. (For how to deal with an overheated custard see page 52.) Once the custard has cooled, cover and chill in the fridge.

When ready, strain the custard, allowing it simply to drain through the sieve. Add the chilled cream and vanilla extract, stir and taste. If a more intense flavour is preferred, firmly press the ginger left in the sieve until you arrive at an intensity of flavour that pleases you. Still freeze (see page 48) or start the ice-cream machine, and pour in the custard. Churn for about 15 minutes, or until the ice cream is the consistency of softly whipped cream. Quickly pour into plastic freezer containers, and cover with waxed or greaseproof paper and a lid. Finally label, then freeze overnight. Allow about 25–30 minutes in the fridge before serving.

Ginger and Lime Granita

Excellent flavour, both fresh-tasting and very refreshing.

INGREDIENTS

	Metric	U.S.	Imperial
Fresh ginger, peeled	50 g	2 oz	2 oz
Sugar syrup (see page 47)	250 ml	1 cup	8 fl oz
Water	500 ml	2 cups	16 fl oz
Zest of lime	1	1	1
Juice of limes	2	2	2
Makes about	750 ml	3 cups	24 fl oz

Chop the peeled ginger into small chunks, put in a food processor or blender and process until chopped as finely as possible. Add the syrup and process briefly again. Bring to the boil, then remove from the heat, cover, then chill and leave overnight to infuse.

Stir in the water then strain if you do not want the small pieces of ginger in the granita. Leave to cool. Carefully scrub 1 of the limes and dry the skin. Remove the zest with a zester and cut it in pieces no longer then 5 mm/¼ inch. Add the zest and then the strained juice of up to 2 limes, according to taste.

For detailed instructions on how to prepare the perfect granita see page 49.

Stem Ginger and Syrup Ice Cream

If fresh ginger is not available, this is a very acceptable alternative for an ice cream, and probably better if a more gentle ginger flavour is preferred. The recipe is in the quick and simple no-cook style.

INGREDIENTS

	Metric	U.S.	Imperial
One recipe Easy No-Cook Philadelphia Vanilla Ice Cream (see page 153), omitting the vanilla bean and substituting			
Vanilla extract	¼ tsp	¼ tsp	¼ tsp
Stem ginger (walnut-sized pieces)	3	3	3
Stem ginger syrup	1 Tbsp	1 Tbsp	1 Tbsp
Makes about	1 litre	4 cups	32 fl oz

Mix together the ingredients for Easy No-Cook Philadelphia Vanilla Ice Cream (see page 153), substituting the vanilla extract for the vanilla bean.

Then finely chop the stem ginger and stir into the ice cream mixture with the stem ginger syrup. Cover and chill in the fridge and proceed as described in the recipe for making Easy No-Cook Philadelphia Ice Cream.

**There was a young lady of Michigan,
To see her I never could wish again.
She would eat of ice cream
Till with pain she would scream,
Then order another big dish again.**

The Complete Limerick Book,
Jarrolds, London, 1924

Goat's Milk Ice Cream

There are people who dislike the flavour of anything derived from the goat. This ice cream is for them; it retains just enough flavour to be recognised by those who enjoy it, but not enough to be noticed by those who do not. We count this as one of our top ten favourites. Excellent served with fresh red berry fruits.

INGREDIENTS

	Metric	U.S.	Imperial
Goat's milk	375 ml	1½ cups	12 fl oz
Granulated sugar	100 g	½ cup	3½ oz
Egg yolks	3	3	3
Whipping/heavy cream (36 per cent fat)	185 ml	¾ cup	6 fl oz
Makes about	750 ml	3 cups	24 fl oz

Using the above quantities of goat's milk, sugar, egg yolks and cream prepare, cook and freeze the ice cream according to the method for making French Vanilla Ice Cream but omitting the vanilla bean (see page 51).

Moulds for ice puddings, *c.* 1894.

GOOSEBERRIES

Surely the essential element of a gooseberry is its sourness? And yet in an effort to revitalise the market and bring the fruit back into public favour, the growers seem bent on producing that strange enigma, the dessert gooseberry. It is to be hoped that they know what they are doing . . . All the recipes here require sour, cooking gooseberries.

Gooseberry Ice Cream

Gooseberry is a difficult flavour to retain but this recipe preserves the flavour. The ice cream is dense due to the high fibre content of the gooseberry, but delicious. It is best eaten freshly made.

INGREDIENTS

	Metric	U.S.	Imperial
Gooseberries	500 g	Generous 1 lb	Generous 1 lb
Water	2 Tbsp	2 Tbsp	2 Tbsp
Granulated sugar	150 g	¾ cup	5¼ oz
Whipping/heavy cream (36 per cent fat)	250 ml	1 cup	8 fl oz
Makes about	625 ml	2½ cups	20 fl oz

Top and tail the gooseberries and wash carefully. Then halve the gooseberries, add the water and cook gently for 5 minutes. Add the sugar and liquidise while hot in a food processor. Sieve to remove the skins and large seeds and chill in the fridge.

When ready, add the cream. Still freeze (see page 48) or start the ice-cream machine. Churn the ice cream for 8–10 minutes only as it is a very thick consistency. Scrape into plastic freezer boxes, cover with waxed or greaseproof paper and a lid. Label and freeze for at least 1 hour before serving. If frozen, allow at least 30 minutes to soften this rather dense ice cream before serving.

Gooseberry and Rosemary Sorbet

INGREDIENTS

	Metric	U.S.	Imperial
Gooseberries	500 g	Generous 1 lb	Generous 1 lb
Sprigs of rosemary	4×8 cm	4×3 inch	4×3 inch
Sugar syrup (see page 47)	375 ml	1½ cups	12 fl oz
Lemon juice	3 Tbsp	3 Tbsp	3 Tbsp
Makes about	1 litre	4 cups	32 fl oz

Top and tail the gooseberries and put them into a colander or sieve. Rinse with cold water, drain and put into a non-reactive saucepan with the rinsed and dried sprigs of rosemary. Pour in the sugar syrup and bring to simmering point. Cover and continue to simmer gently for 5 minutes. By this time, the gooseberries should be soft. Remove the pan from the heat and leave to cool for a few minutes. Discard the rosemary before briefly processing the fruit in a food processor or blender, then rub the pulp through a nylon sieve. Cover and chill in the fridge.

When ready, stir the strained lemon juice into the purée, then still freeze (see page 48) or start the ice-cream machine.

NOTE: This is quite a thick mixture due to the high fibre content of gooseberries, so the churned sorbet is correspondingly thicker than normal.

When firm enough, serve at once, or quickly scrape into plastic freezer boxes and cover with greaseproof or waxed paper and a lid. Finally label, then freeze. Serve within 1 hour. Or, if frozen solid, the sorbet, due to its density, may need as much as 30 minutes in a fridge to soften before serving.

Fresh Muscat Grape and Wine Sorbet

Ignore all recipes that call for carton, canned or bottled grape juice, and any recipe that merely calls for "seedless white grapes". When frozen, the flavour of commercial grape juice is frankly ersatz, and any old white grapes will give, well, any old flavour grape sorbet. But if you use muscat grapes *and* muscat wine *you will taste heaven here on earth.*

INGREDIENTS

	Metric	U.S.	Imperial
Muscat grapes	500 g	Generous 1 lb	Generous 1 lb
Sugar syrup (see page 47)	500 ml	2 cups	16 fl oz
Muscat sweet wine	250 ml	1 cup	8 fl oz
Lemon juice	2–3 Tbsp	2–3 Tbsp	2–3 Tbsp
Egg white	1	1	1
Makes about	1 litre	4 cups	32 fl oz

Separate the grapes from the bunch, wash and dry carefully. Then liquidise the sugar syrup with the grapes very briefly (about 3 seconds, no longer, or the pips will break up and the flavour will be bitter). Strain through a fine nylon sieve to remove the pips and the skins, making sure that most of the flesh of the grapes is pushed through. Immediately add the wine and lemon juice to stop the grape juice discolouring. Mix thoroughly and chill in the fridge.

When ready, still freeze (see page 48) or start the ice-cream machine and churn for about 10 minutes until the mix becomes a soft slush. Now, using a fork, beat the egg white until loosened and add to the sorbet with the machine still running. Continue to churn until firm enough to serve. Or to store, quickly scrape into plastic freezer boxes and cover with waxed or greaseproof paper and a lid. Finally label, then freeze. If frozen, allow about 10 minutes in the fridge before serving.

Grapefruit Sorbet

Any kind of grapefruit can be used for this recipe, from the pale yellow through to the almost blood red of the "pink" varieties. But the darker the flesh the sweeter the taste, so slightly less syrup will give a better flavour. The strips of grapefruit zest, which are added to this sorbet, should be cut very fine and short as they tend to wind around the paddle/ dasher during churning. If this happens, scrape them free and stir evenly into the sorbet before freezing.

INGREDIENTS

	Metric	U.S.	Imperial
Grapefruit	2	2	2
Sugar syrup (see page 47)	500 ml	2 cups	16 fl oz
Juice of lemons, strained	2	2	2
Egg white	1	1	1
Makes about	1 litre	4 cups	32 fl oz

Thoroughly scrub and dry the grapefruit. Use a zester to remove short strips of peel from the 2 grapefruit. The alternative is the more laborious process of removing strips of zest with a sharp potato-peeler. Pare away any white pith then cut into short, hair-like strips. Put the strips in a medium-sized non-reactive pan with the strained grapefruit juice and sugar syrup. Bring to the boil and continue to boil gently for about 10 minutes or until the zest is tender. Remove the pan from the heat and add the strained lemon juice. Cool, then chill in the fridge.

When ready, still freeze (see page 48) or start the ice-cream machine. Pour in the liquid and churn for 5–10 minutes or until it starts to freeze and becomes opaque. Using a fork, beat the egg white until loosened and add to the sorbet with the machine still running. Continue churning until the sorbet is firm enough to serve. Or to store, quickly scrape into plastic freezer containers and cover with waxed or greaseproof paper and a lid. Finally label, then freeze. Once the sorbet becomes solid, it will need about 30 minutes in the fridge before it is soft enough to serve.

Grapefruit and Campari® Sorbet

This is strongly flavoured with a definite "bitters" taste and therefore would probably not appeal to children. A sorbet best teamed up with ice cream rather than other sorbets.

INGREDIENTS

	Metric	U.S.	Imperial
Grapefruit	3	3	3
Granulated sugar	100 g	½ cup	3½ oz
Campari®	3–4 Tbsp	3–4 Tbsp	3–4 Tbsp
Egg white	1	1	1
Makes about	750 ml	3 cups	24 fl oz

Thoroughly scrub the grapefruit in warm soapy water, rinse and dry. Use a sharp potato peeler to remove the zest from 1 grapefruit. Shave off any white pith and roughly chop the zest. Put into a food processor or blender with the sugar and process until the zest and the sugar are of a uniform size. Transfer this into a large measuring jug then add sufficient strained grapefruit juice to measure 500 ml/2 cups/16 fl oz. Stir in 3 Tbsp of Campari®, adding a further Tbsp, if preferred. Cover and chill in the fridge.

When ready, still freeze (see page 48) or start the ice-cream machine. Pour in the liquid and churn until it starts to form a slush. Using a fork, beat the egg white until loosened and add to the sorbet with the machine still running. Continue churning until the sorbet is firm enough to serve. Or to store, quickly scrape into plastic freezer boxes and cover with greaseproof or waxed paper and a lid. Finally label, then freeze. If frozen, allow about 15–20 minutes in the fridge to soften sufficiently to serve.

Grapefruit, Pimms® and Fresh Mint Sorbet

The marriage of grapefruit and Pimms is a highly successful one.

INGREDIENTS

	Metric	U.S.	Imperial
Granulated sugar	100 g	½ cup	3½ oz
Pimms No 1®	8 Tbsp	8 Tbsp	8 Tbsp
Fresh grapefruit juice	500 ml	2 cups	16 fl oz
Lemon juice	1 Tbsp	1 Tbsp	1 Tbsp
Water	125 ml	½ cup	4 fl oz
Mint leaves	8	8	8
Egg white	1	1	1
Makes about	875 ml	3½ cups	28 fl oz

Dissolve the sugar in the measured Pimms® – it will do this without heating, albeit rather slowly. Stir in the strained grapefruit and lemon juice, then the water. Wash and pat the mint leaves dry, roll them up together and cut across to give very thin strips. Add these to the liquid and chill in the fridge.

When ready, still freeze (see page 48) or start the ice-cream machine. Pour in the liquid and leave to churn until firm enough to serve. Make sure all the strips of mint leaves are removed from the paddle/dasher and mixed back into the sorbet before serving. If the sorbet is to be stored, quickly transfer to freezer storage containers and cover with waxed or greaseproof paper and a lid. Finally, label then freeze.

Serving
The sorbet can be served with some fresh raspberries and decorated with sprigs of crystallised mint leaves.

A sundae set. An ice-cream sundae was usually accompanied by a drink of either iced water, ginger ale or a flavoured aerated drink.

Guava and Lime Sorbet

Walking into our supermarket one day, a heady aroma hit us of what could only be some perfectly ripe exotic fruit. We followed our noses to the fruit section where the source proved to be guavas, which were indeed absolutely, perfectly ripe. We snatched them up, ran home and made this superb sorbet.

INGREDIENTS

	Metric	U.S.	Imperial
Guavas, ripe (about 3)	450 g	1 lb	1 lb
Sugar syrup (see page 47)	250 ml	1 cup	8 fl oz
Water	4 Tbsp	4 Tbsp	4 Tbsp
Limes	2–3	2–3	2–3
Makes about	750 ml	3 cups	24 fl oz

Peel the guavas as you would apples, then quarter and put in a food processor or blender with the syrup. Blend until smooth, then rub through a sieve until only the fragments of seeds remain. Into the guava purée stir the water, the grated rind of 1 lime and the strained juice of 2–3 limes, according to taste. Cover and chill in the fridge.

When ready, still freeze (see page 47) or start the ice-cream machine. Pour in the guava mixture and churn until the sorbet is firm enough to serve. To store, quickly scrape into plastic freezer boxes and cover with waxed or greaseproof paper and a lid. Finally label, then freeze. Once the sorbet has frozen solid, it will need about 15 minutes in the fridge before it is soft enough to serve.

Halva Ice Cream

The commercial version of this Middle Eastern confection, which is a blend of crushed sesame seeds, sugar, glucose syrup, vegetable oil and flavouring, can be bought in most delicatessens. Some shops stock small packs of approximately 250 g (½ lb) or it can be bought by weight, cut from a long slab.
NOTE: *This is one of the few recipes in the book that uses single (light) cream 18–19 per cent fat content. This is due to the high fat content of the halva.*

INGREDIENTS

	Metric	U.S.	Imperial
Milk	375 ml	1½ cups	12 fl oz
Vanilla bean	1	1	1
Granulated sugar	150 g	¾ cup	5¼ oz
Egg yolks	6	6	6
Single/light cream (18–19 per cent fat)	375 ml	1½ cups	12 fl oz
Halva (plain vanilla)	200 g	7 oz	7 oz
Makes about	1 litre	4 cups	32 fl oz

Using the above quantities of milk, vanilla, sugar and egg yolks, prepare and cook a custard according to the method for making French Vanilla Ice Cream (see page 51).

Once the thickened custard has cooled and chilled it is ready to churn. Add the cream and still freeze (see page 48) or start the ice-cream machine. Pour in the custard and allow it to churn and freeze to the consistency of softly whipped cream. Quickly scrape the ice cream into plastic freezer boxes. Cut the halva into 5 mm/¼ inch dice and fold into the softly frozen ice cream. Smooth the surface flat, cover with a piece of waxed or greaseproof paper and a lid and freeze. Serve within 1 hour. Or if frozen solid, allow 30 minutes in the refrigerator to soften sufficiently for serving.

Serving
Very good with Chocolate Fudge Sauce (see page 165).

Variations
Halva comes in a number of flavour variations: marbled chocolate and vanilla (Polish variety is best), vanilla, walnut, almond and pistachio. The ice cream can be made with any of these but it is particularly good made with pistachio halva to which an additional 25 g/1 oz of skinned pistachio nuts can be added.

Herb Granitas

To make a herb granita add 560 ml/2¼ cups/18 fl oz of chilled water to any of the herb sorbets (see below).

For detailed instructions on how to prepare the perfect granita see page 49.

Herb Sorbets

Until we wrote this book we had never entertained the idea of herb sorbets. Their clean, clear flavour comes as a revelation. Make with fresh herbs only.
Do not attempt with dried herbs.
This recipe, although written for basil, mint, rosemary, pineapple sage or thyme, can be used for most herbs provided you take care with the amount and strength of the herb.

TABLE OF HERBS AND LEMON JUICE

	Quantity	Lemon juice
Basil	15 g or 10 leaves	3 Tbsp
Mint	6×10 cm/4 inch sprigs	2 Tbsp
Rosemary	4×15 cm/6 inch sprigs	3–4 Tbsp
Pineapple Sage	15 g or 25 leaves	2 Tbsp
Thyme	10 g or 4×5 cm/2 inch sprigs	2 Tbsp

INGREDIENTS

	Metric	U.S.	Imperial
Herb (see table)			
Sugar syrup (see page 47)	500 ml	2 cups	16 fl oz
Water	250 ml	1 cup	8 fl oz
Dry white wine	250 ml	1 cup	8 fl oz
Lemon juice (see table)			
Makes about	1 litre	4 cups	32 fl oz

Rinse and dry the herbs, and put in a non-reactive saucepan with the sugar syrup and the water. Bring slowly to the boil. Remove the pan from the heat and add the wine. Cover and leave to cool. Chill overnight in the fridge. Add lemon juice to taste, then strain.

When ready, still freeze (see page 48) or start the ice-cream machine. Pour in the liquid and leave to churn for about 20 minutes or until the mixture freezes to a soft slush. Then quickly scrape into plastic freezer boxes and cover with waxed or greaseproof paper and a lid. Finally label, then freeze for about 1–2 hours before serving. It takes longer to freeze because of the alcohol in the wine. Once the sorbet has frozen solid, it will need about 10–15 minutes in the fridge to soften sufficiently to serve.

Honey Ice Cream

Since the flavour of this ice cream directly reflects the flavour of honey used, avoid the blander, blended varieties. Instead search out orange-blossom honey, Greek honey or, best of all, Scottish heather honey.

INGREDIENTS

	Metric	U.S.	Imperial
Whipping/heavy cream (36 per cent fat)	500 ml	2 cups	16 fl oz
Vanilla bean	½	½	½
Egg yolks	4	4	4
Honey	175 g	½ cup	6 oz
Makes about	750 ml	3 cups	24 fl oz

Make the custard following the method given for French Vanilla Ice Cream on page 51, omitting the addition of any sugar to the egg yolks. Whisk these on their own, then add the cream as directed. As soon as the custard has been cooked and put in cold water to cool, stir in the honey. When completely cold, cover and chill in the fridge.

When ready, still freeze (see page 48) or start the ice-cream machine and pour in the custard. Leave to churn and freeze for 15–20 minutes or until the ice cream has the consistency of softly whipped cream. Quickly scrape into plastic freezer boxes and cover with waxed or greaseproof paper and a lid. Finally label, then freeze. Eat in about 1–2 hours, Or, if frozen solid, leave the ice cream in the fridge for about 20 minutes so that it becomes soft enough to serve.

Serving
Serve with Light Lemon and Sultana Sauce (see page 165).

Should I, after tea and cakes and ices,
Have the strength to force the moment to its crisis.

T. S. Eliot (1888–1965),
"Macavity: The Mystery Cat", *Old Possum's Book of Practical Cats*

Honey and Toasted Walnut Ice Cream

INGREDIENTS

	Metric	U.S.	Imperial
One recipe Honey Ice Cream (see page 100)			
Walnut pieces	70 g	⅔ cup	2½ oz
Makes about	875 ml	3½ cups	28 fl oz

About 30 minutes before the nuts are needed preheat the oven to 180°C/350°F, Gas Mark 4. Make the Honey Ice Cream as directed (see page 100). As soon as it has been left to churn put the walnuts on a baking tray and bake for 6–8 minutes. Remove and leave to cool slightly, then chop – not too finely. As the ice cream is scraped into the plastic freezer boxes, sprinkle with the chopped nuts. Stir well, before covering and freezing as directed in the recipe for Honey Ice Cream.

Variations
Hazelnuts or almonds can be used instead of walnuts. Quantity, temperature and timing are the same but preparation varies a little.

The hazelnuts will need toasting then rubbing in a tea towel to skin them.

If using unblanched almonds, pour boiling water over them and leave for a few minutes before squeezing the nuts out of their skins and toasting in the manner of the walnuts.

Honey and Lavender Ice Cream

Use a lavender honey and instead of infusing the cream with vanilla pod, use a sprig of lavender. (Remember lavender is very pungent and just one sprig is sufficient.) If lavender is out of season a sprig of thyme can be used.

A most delicious ice!
From a print, London, *c.* 1825.

Jackfruit Sherbet

Jackfruit (breadfruit) is imported mainly from Thailand, Indonesia and Kenya and is usually more readily available canned than fresh. It is one of those fruits that has a dual personality; green, that is unripened, it is served as a vegetable; yellow and ripened, it is a sweet fruit that is delightful when made into a delicate sherbet. Both yellow and green jackfruit are sold in cans, so read the label carefully and buy the yellow for this recipe.

This sherbet is particularly suitable for serving after Chinese or Thai food, on its own or in combination with Easy, or Toasted, Coconut Ice Cream (see pages 82 and 83) or Mango Sorbet (see page 113) or Lychee and Lime Sorbet (see page 112).

INGREDIENTS

	Metric	U.S.	Imperial
One can yellow jackfruit/ breadfruit, whole in syrup, net wt.	565 g	1 lb 4 oz	1 lb 4 oz
Granulated sugar	90 g	½ cup minus 1 Tbsp	3¼ oz
Juice of lemon, strained	1	1	1
Milk, chilled	250 ml	1 cup	8 fl oz
Makes about	500 ml	2 cups	16 fl oz

Drain the syrup from the can of jackfruit and measure 150 ml/½ cup plus 2 Tbsp/5 fl oz into a saucepan. Add the sugar, and warm gently until the sugar is dissolved before removing from the heat. Liquidise the drained jackfruit with the strained lemon juice; add the warm syrup and liquidise again. Strain, then allow to cool. When cold, add the chilled milk.

As soon as you are ready, still freeze (see page 48) or start the ice-cream machine and churn for about 15–20 minutes or until frozen sufficiently to serve. To store, scrape quickly into plastic freezer boxes and cover with waxed or greaseproof paper and a lid. Finally label, then freeze. Eat in about 1–2 hours. Or, if frozen solid, leave the sherbet in the fridge for about 20 minutes so that it becomes soft enough to serve.

Junket Ice Cream

Hidden away in The Dispenser's Formulary or Soda Water Guide *we found junket ice cream. First published (circa 1913) by the staff of an American magazine called* The Soda Fountain, *this book contains over 2,000 formulae and was the bible of the ice-cream parlour.*

This formidable recipe started with 18 quarts of sweet new milk and 6 quarts of rich cream and 10 pounds of sugar. However, the fascination lay in the final sentence of the recipe: "A good formula of its kind but only a low grade fountain would use it."

We tried it a number of ways and it was cold and icy as there simply wasn't sufficient butterfat in it. We have redressed the balance by increasing the amount of cream and reducing the sugar. It is now an interesting ice cream, with a curious old-fashioned flavour.

NOTE: *Rennet can be bought in liquid or tablet form; either can be used for this recipe. But, whichever you buy, be sure it is plain and* not *flavoured.*

INGREDIENTS

	Metric	U.S.	Imperial
Whipping/heavy cream (36 per cent fat)	375 ml	1½ cups	12 fl oz
Milk	125 ml	½ cup	4 fl oz
Granulated sugar	100 g	½ cup	3½ oz
Rennet – liquid	1 tsp	1 tsp	1 tsp
OR			
– tablet	1	1	1
Vanilla extract	½ tsp	½ tsp	½ tsp
Makes about	750 ml	3 cups	24 fl oz

Combine the cream and milk with the sugar and stirring, heat very gently until the temperature reaches blood heat: 37°C/98°F. Use a thermometer to confirm this.

Immediately remove the pan from the heat, stir in the rennet (if using a tablet, dissolve in a small amount of the milk), then the vanilla extract and pour into a shallow dish. Leave to set at room temperature completely undisturbed. Once set, transfer to the fridge to chill. As soon as it is chilled, the junket is ready to be made into ice cream.

Still freeze (see page 48), after stirring the set junket, or start the ice-cream machine and pour in the junket complete. Churn for about 15 minutes until it is the consistency of whipped cream, then quickly scrape into plastic freezer boxes, smooth flat, cover with waxed or greaseproof paper and a lid. Finally label, then freeze for at least 1 hour before serving. If frozen overnight, allow about 20–25 minutes in the fridge to soften sufficiently to serve.

Kir Sorbet

The classic Kir is made from two-thirds Burgundian white Aligoté and one-third cassis★, but most people find this too strong so a lighter combination is usually served. Certainly when it comes to making a sorbet any dry white wine will do and only a small amount of cassis is needed.
NOTE: *The amount of alcohol in this sorbet requires a longer time to freeze at a lower temperature in order to solidify, so it is best made the day before.*

INGREDIENTS

	Metric	U.S.	Imperial
Dry white wine, chilled	375 ml	1½ cups	12 fl oz
Sugar syrup (see page 47)	250 ml	1 cup	8 fl oz
Cassis★	1½ Tbsp	1½ Tbsp	1½ Tbsp
Lemon juice	1½ Tbsp	1½ Tbsp	1½ Tbsp
Egg white	1	1	1
Makes about	750 ml	3 cups	24 fl oz

★ Blackcurrant liqueur, preferably from Dijon where they make the best blackcurrant liqueur in the world.

Combine the first four ingredients in a jug. If the wine is sufficiently chilled at the outset, then there is no necessity to chill the mixture before churning.

When ready, still freeze (see page 48) or start the ice-cream machine. Pour in the liquid and leave to churn until the mixture freezes to a soft slush. At this stage, use a fork to beat the egg white to loosen it and add to the sorbet with the machine still running. Continue until the sorbet is firm enough to serve. To store, quickly scrape into plastic freezer boxes and cover with waxed or greaseproof paper and a lid. Finally label, then freeze overnight. Once the sorbet has frozen solid, it will need about 15–20 minutes in the fridge to soften sufficiently to serve.

We dare not trust our wit for making our house pleasant to our friends so we buy ice cream.

Ralph Waldo Emerson (1803–82), 1841

Kiwi Sorbet

Such a good all-rounder as kiwi fruit is now something of a fruit cliché. But no one will sneer at this sorbet – it is as good as it is simple. As with all ice creams and sorbets the best results are obtained from well ripened fruit. Kiwis can be made to ripen in a day if they are sealed in a plastic bag with another ripe fruit e.g. an apple or a banana. The ethylene gas given off by the ripe fruit accelerates the ripening of the kiwi fruit.

INGREDIENTS

	Metric	U.S.	Imperial
Kiwi fruit	450 g	1 lb	1 lb
Sugar syrup (see page 47)	250 ml	1 cup	8 fl oz
Juice of lemons, strained	2	2	2
Makes about	1 litre	4 cups	32 fl oz

The simplest way to prepare the kiwi fruit is to cut them in half around the equator, cradle the half in a cupped hand and scoop out the fruit with a teaspoon, avoiding the hard white core at each end. Put the fruit into a food processor or blender with the sugar syrup and the strained lemon juice. Blend until smooth, then chill in the fridge.

When ready, still freeze (see page 48) or start the ice-cream machine. Pour in the liquid and leave until it has formed a sorbet firm enough to scoop. Or, to store, quickly scrape it into plastic freezer containers and cover with waxed or greaseproof paper and a lid. Finally label, then freeze. It will need about 20 minutes in the fridge before it is soft enough to scoop.

Variation
An even simpler form of frozen kiwi fruit purée can be made by thinly slicing the same quantity of peeled kiwi fruit and arranging them in overlapping rows on baking trays lined with silicone paper. Freeze the fruit solid. Immediately before serving, purée them in a food processor or liquidiser with the rind and juice of 1 lime and sufficient sugar to taste. That's it! Serve immediately.

KULFI

Kulfi is the traditional Indian ice cream and has a strongly characteristic cooked-milk flavour and dense icy texture. The original way of making it is time-consuming and tedious, but it really is worth the effort as short-cut versions do not have the same flavour and texture. For those with less time or patience we have a Quick Kulfi (see page 105), but once you have tasted the real thing we are sure you will find the time to make it the long way.

The basis of making kulfi is to reduce a large volume of milk down to a very small concentrated amount of "condensed milk". This can take anything between 2 and 4 hours. Kulfi was traditionally frozen in small conical moulds, 12–15 cm/5–6 inches long (see Equipment), with screw tops that were sealed with dough to prevent leakage and were then immersed in earthenware pots in a brine and crushed ice solution to freeze. They were removed from the moulds by rolling in the palms of the hands and then turned out on to a dish and were stood on their base.

The consistency of the kulfi mixture is much thicker than ordinary ice cream but it melts quickly.

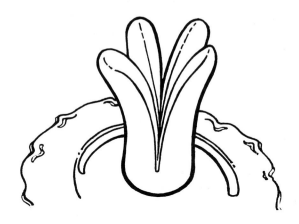

Usually, when served, they are stood on their base and cut twice across the top in the shape of a cross to make them easier to eat with a spoon. On special festive occasions they are decorated with a small piece of silver or gold leaf on the top (see Useful Addresses page 184).

Pistachio Kulfi

INGREDIENTS

	Metric	U.S.	Imperial
Milk	2.5 litres	84 fl oz (4⅕ pints U.S.)	84 fl oz
Granulated sugar	125 g	½ cup plus 2 Tbsp	4½ oz
Pistachio nuts, skinned and chopped coarsely	35 g	⅓ cup	1¼ oz
Rosewater	1 tsp	1 tsp	1 tsp
Makes about	12×10 cm/4 inch kulfi		

In a large-diameter saucepan, sauté pan or non-stick wok, standing on a heat-diffuser mat, raise the milk to boiling point, stirring constantly. Then gently simmer, stirring frequently, until the milk is reduced to a thick liquid of about 750 ml/3 cups/24 fl oz. This can take anything up to 4 hours, depending on the pan. When reduced, remove from the heat and pour the kulfi into a jug, adding the sugar, nuts and rosewater. Stir slowly until the sugar has dissolved, then cool. Chill in the fridge.

When ready, stir to ensure the nuts are evenly distributed in the kulfi, then pour into about 12 kulfi moulds. Cover and store at once, pointed end down, in the freezer.

To unmould: either partially immerse in cold or cool water or place in the fridge for a few minutes. Do not immerse in warm or hot water as kulfi are fragile and defrost very fast. Warm or hot water will make the outside liquefy and the inside will remain frozen.

Variations
With the basic kulfi recipe above it is easy to develop other recipes using spices, e.g. ground cardamom, cinnamon, other nuts like almonds, or other flavours such as mango or orange flower water.

Quick Kulfi

Although not as good as the real thing, this is a really quick kulfi that is very easy to make and is a very acceptable impromptu dessert to follow a curry meal at home. This recipe is flavoured with cardamom and rosewater but many other flavours can be used as long as they can be mixed into the liquid without precipitating. Ingredients such as nuts are best sprinkled over the kulfi just before being served as, even finely chopped, they fall to the base of the kulfi mix before freezing can take place.

INGREDIENTS

	Metric	U.S.	Imperial
Cardamom pods	4–5	4–5	4–5
Milk	250 ml	1 cup	8 fl oz
Caster/Ultra fine sugar	235 g	1¼ cup	8¼ oz
Rosewater	1 Tbsp	1 Tbsp	1 Tbsp
Evaporated milk, chilled	250 ml	1 cup	8 fl oz
Whipping/heavy cream (36 per cent fat), chilled	250 ml	1 cup	8 fl oz
Makes about or 6 kulfi moulds	1 litre	4 cups	32 fl oz

Remove the cardamom seeds from the pods, discard the pods and grind the black seeds in a mortar and pestle until they are a fine powder. Do not use ready-ground cardamom from a bottle, as some manufacturers grind up the pods as well as the seeds and the result has little flavour.

Combine the milk, sugar and rosewater in a large jug and stir occasionally until the sugar has dissolved. Stir in the chilled evaporated milk and cream.

Pour into kulfi moulds (see page 42) or into a plastic freezer box. Cover with greaseproof paper, freezer tissue or waxed paper, and a lid. Finally label, then freeze for at least 6 hours. Once frozen, allow about 10 minutes in the refrigerator before serving.

Quick Mango Kulfi

Good ripe mangoes are hard to find. Since this is a quick mango kulfi we have used tinned mangoes, which, sadly, are often of a far more reliable quality than fresh. This makes it an ideal store-cupboard ice.

INGREDIENTS

	Metric	U.S.	Imperial
One can of mango slices in syrup approx gross weight	850 g	30 oz	30 oz
Caster/Ultra fine sugar	235 g	1¼ cup	8¼ oz
Evaporated milk	250 ml	1 cup	8 fl oz
Whipping/heavy cream (36 per cent fat)	250 ml	1 cup	8 fl oz
Lemon juice	1 Tbsp	1 Tbsp	1 Tbsp
Makes about or 6 kulfi moulds	1 litre	4 cups	32 fl oz

Drain the mangoes, discarding the syrup, and purée the flesh in a food processor or blender until smooth. Measure 250 ml/1 cup/8 fl oz of the purée and combine with the sugar in the food processor or blender. Process until the sugar is completely dissolved. Chill.

When ready, mix the sweetened mango purée with the evaporated milk and the cream. Add lemon juice, half a tablespoonful at a time, to taste. You can add a pinch of ground cardamom, if liked.

Pour into kulfi moulds (see page 42) or into a plastic freezer box and cover with a piece of waxed or greaseproof paper and a lid. Finally label, then freeze. Once frozen allow about 10 minutes in the fridge before serving.

**When water turns to ice does it remember one time it was water?
When it turns back into water does it remember it was ice?**

Carl Sandburg (1878–1967),
Metamorphosis in Honey and Salt,
Harcourt Brace and World, New York, 1963

Lavender Sorbet

The amount of lavender used in this sorbet sounds very little, but in fact four heads of lavender flowers are all that is needed to achieve a delicately pink sorbet with an intriguing flavour. Do not use the dried lavender that is sold for flower arranging as it may have been sprayed with insecticides. If flowers are unavailable, use one teaspoon of lavender tea.

INGREDIENTS

	Metric	U.S.	Imperial
Sugar syrup (see page 47)	250 ml	1 cup	8 fl oz
Lavender heads	4	4	4
Juice of lemon, strained	1	1	1
Water	375 ml	1½ cups	12 fl oz
Makes about	750 ml	3 cups	24 fl oz

Pour the measured syrup into a pan, add the lavender flowers and bring slowly to the boil. Remove the pan from the heat, add the strained juice of half a lemon, then cover and leave to cool. Strain the syrup to remove the lavender and add the cold water. Taste, and add the remaining strained lemon juice, if it seems too sweet.

Still freeze (see page 48) or start the ice-cream machine and pour in the liquid. Leave to churn for 8–10 minutes or until the sorbet is firm enough to serve. To store, quickly scrape into plastic freezer boxes and cover with waxed or greaseproof paper and a lid. Finally label, then freeze. Allow 10–15 minutes in the fridge to soften sufficiently before serving.

See also Honey and Lavender Ice Cream page 101.

**A Palma de Majorque
Tout le monde est heureux
On mange dans la rue
Des sorbets au citron
Racontez-moi encore
Palma des Baléares
Je ne connais qu'une île
Au milieu de la Marne.**

Jean Cocteau (1891–1963)
Iles

LEMONS

As much as lemons vary in size, so do they vary in acidity. We have tried to deal with this by giving a weight of lemons, and the number of average-sized fruit that would comprise the weight. However, the degree of acidity is unpredictable so our quantities of juice can only act as a guideline.

With both these versions of lemon ice cream we have looked for a balanced flavour of lemon that is positive and without any acidic/bitter back-taste. Removing all the white pith from the zest goes more than halfway to achieving this. Adjusting the amount of lemon juice sees to the rest. Of course it is a matter of taste but our advice is to flirt with danger and push the acidity a fraction more than you think.

Lemon Ice Cream – Cooked

This cooked version is a fuller, rounder, more unctuous ice cream than the uncooked one (see page 108), and is best served to accompany puddings from the ranks of pies, tarts and crumbles. The flavour verges on that of home-made lemon curd but has a bit more refinement.

INGREDIENTS

	Metric	U.S.	Imperial
Lemons, about 3	350 g	12 oz	12 oz
Whipping/heavy cream (36 per cent fat)	625 ml	2½ cups	20 fl oz
Egg yolks	5	5	5
Vanilla sugar (see page 36)	200 g	1 cup	7 oz
Makes about	1 litre	4 cups	32 fl oz

Thoroughly scrub the lemons in warm, soapy water, then rinse and dry. Using a sharp potato-peeler, remove only the coloured part of the zest from 1 lemon. If some of the white pith is removed with the zest, this should be shaved off, using a sharp knife angled almost flat against the peel. Put the strips of zest in a small saucepan with the cream and heat gently until just below boiling point, then cover and leave aside to infuse for 30 minutes.

In a heatproof bowl combine the egg yolks and sugar and beat until they take on a pale yellow colour and

lighter consistency. Re-heat the lemon and cream infusion to just below boiling point then pour, in stages, through a sieve on to the egg yolks, whisking between each addition. The bowl can now be placed over a pan of simmering water, or the custard can now be returned to the saucepan which is then put on top of a heat-diffuser mat so that it is not in direct contact with the heat. Only if you have an accurate thermometer and/or you are confident you will not overheat the custard should you put the saucepan on a gentle direct heat. Stir the custard until it reaches 85°C/185°F or until it has thickened sufficiently to coat the back of a spoon. As soon as the custard reaches this stage plunge the base of the pan or bowl momentarily into cold water to arrest the cooking and cool the base quickly, then leave aside on a work surface to continue cooling at room temperature. On no account should the custard be allowed to overheat or boil as the mixture will curdle. (For how to deal with an overheated custard see page 52.)

Immediately, and while the custard cools, finely grate only the lemon-coloured zest from the remaining 2 lemons and add to the custard. When it has cooled to room temperature, cover the surface of the custard with a circle of lightly buttered greaseproof paper and transfer to the fridge to chill.

When ready, squeeze the juice from all the lemons and gradually add to the chilled custard via a plastic sieve. Once 6 Tbsp of lemon juice have been stirred in, start tasting, and add a little more lemon juice at a time until the flavour is to your liking. Now either still freeze (see page 48) or start the ice-cream machine. Pour in the flavoured custard and churn until the ice cream has the consistency of softly whipped cream. Then quickly scrape into plastic freezer boxes and cover with waxed or greaseproof paper and a lid. Finally label, then freeze for a minimum of 1 hour before serving. If frozen solid, leave the ice cream in the fridge for about 20–25 minutes to soften sufficiently to serve.

Lemon Ice Cream – Uncooked

Quick, fresh-tasting and light (it contains no eggs), this version is better served as part of a selection of other ice creams and/or sorbets. Eat within three days. (We say this not because something dreadful happens to the ice cream at the 73rd hour, but just because the bright edge of freshness is all but gone from the flavour by then.
NOTE: *Use very fresh cream for this recipe or there is a danger that the lemon juice will curdle it.*

INGREDIENTS

	Metric	U.S.	Imperial
Lemons, about 3	350 g	12 oz	12 oz
Granulated sugar	200 g	1 cup	7 oz
Whipping/heavy cream (36 per cent fat), chilled	500 ml	2 cups	16 fl oz
Salt	good pinch	good pinch	good pinch
Makes about	875 ml	3½ cups	28 fl oz

Prepare and remove the peel from all 3 lemons as outlined in the recipe for Lemon Ice Cream – Cooked (see page 107), making sure all the white pith is removed from the zest. Put the peel and sugar into a food processor or blender and blend for about 4 minutes, or until the peel is so fine it "disappears" into the sugar. Squeeze the juice from the lemons and measure 6 Tbsp into the food processor. Keep the remaining juice. Blend again for 30 seconds then stir slowly and steadily into a jug containing the chilled cream. Cover and chill again for about 1 hour.

When ready, taste the mixture and add more lemon juice if preferred; a further tablespoon will usually suffice. Now either still freeze (see page 48) or start the ice-cream machine. Pour in the flavoured cream via a plastic sieve. Churn until the cream has the consistency of softly whipped cream. Then quickly scrape into plastic freezer boxes and cover with waxed or greaseproof paper and a lid. Finally label, then freeze. Eat in about 1 hour. Or, if frozen solid, leave the ice cream in the fridge for about 20–25 minutes so that it becomes soft enough to serve.

Fresh-Tasting Lemon Yoghurt Ice Cream

This ice is light, clean and quite honestly rather sharp. Taste the mixture just before freezing and add an additional tablespoonful or two of sugar, if you really must. But, if you add too much, the ice cream is in danger of tasting like a shop-bought, sweetened yoghurt.

INGREDIENTS

	Metric	U.S.	Imperial
Juice of lemons, strained	2	2	2
Granulated sugar	100 g	½ cup	3½ oz
Whipping/heavy cream (36 per cent fat), chilled	150 ml	½ cup plus 2 Tbsp	5 fl oz
Greek/Russian style yoghurt, chilled	420 g	1¾ cups	14¾ oz
Makes about	875 ml	3½ cups	28 fl oz

The ice cream mix takes scarcely 5 minutes to make, so if using an electric ice-cream machine with a built-in compressor, start by switching it on so it can be cold enough to churn the ice-cream mix as soon as it is made.

Scrub 1 lemon in warm, soapy water. Rinse, dry and use a potato peeler to remove 3 strips (approximately 1.25 cm/½ inch wide) of zest from stem to stern of the lemon. Put the lemon strips in a food processor or blender with the sugar, and liquidise until the lemon is so fine it "disappears" into the sugar. Add the cream and yoghurt and the strained juice of both lemons and process just long enough to mix thoroughly.

Still freeze (see page 48) or set the ice-cream machine in motion and pour in the mixture. Freeze until it has the consistency of softly whipped cream. Then quickly scrape into plastic freezer boxes and cover with waxed or greaseproof paper and a lid. Finally label, then freeze. Eat in about 2 hours. Or, if frozen solid, leave the ice cream in the fridge for about 20 minutes so that it becomes soft enough to serve.

Lemon Sorbet

Beside the other exotic recipes, this sorbet still has a place because when made well it is superb. However, it is often abused. Frequently, even in expensive restaurants, we have enquired if the sorbets are made on the premises and the question usually prompts an offended affirmative. Then our imagination conjures up chefs in tall white hats squeezing a pile of lemons. Not a bit of it. In many cases they are shaking a packet of ready-mix white crystals into a bowl, adding water and making the restaurant's "own home-made lemon sorbet". Who do they think they are fooling? Because when it isn't the real McCoy it is instantly detectable. Citric acid, lemon essence, lemon juice from a bottle or the stuff from squeezy plastic lemons do not work either. Simply taste the sorbet made from this recipe and you will know what we are talking about and it will save us a thousand words of text.

INGREDIENTS

	Metric	U.S.	Imperial
Lemons	5	5	5
Sugar syrup (see page 47)	375 ml	1½ cups	12 fl oz
Water	125 ml	½ cup	4 fl oz
Egg white	1	1	1
Makes about	750 ml	3 cups	24 fl oz

Thoroughly scrub the lemons in warm soapy water, then rinse and dry. Use a sharp potato peeler to remove the zest from 3 lemons. If some white pith comes away with the zest, this should be shaved off, using a sharp knife angled almost flat against the peel. If the white pith is not removed, the sorbet is likely to have an underlying bitterness.

Put the strips of zest in a small saucepan with the syrup, bring to the boil, then remove, cover and leave to cool. Add the water and the strained juice from all 5 lemons then re-cover and chill overnight in the fridge.

The next day, when ready, start the ice-cream machine and pour in the lemon mixture via a plastic sieve to remove the lemon strips. Still freeze (see page 48) or start the ice-cream machine and churn for about 10 minutes or until the mixture starts to become opaque and icy. Using a fork, beat the egg white until loosened and add to the sorbet with the machine still running. Continue until the sorbet is firm enough to serve. To store, quickly scrape into plastic freezer boxes and cover with waxed or greaseproof paper and a lid. Finally label, then freeze. Once the sorbet becomes solid it will need about 20 minutes in the fridge to soften sufficiently to serve.

Variation
A Colonel is a lemon sorbet that has vodka poured over it just before it is served.

Basil-Flavoured Lemon Sorbet
Sorbetto di Limone al Sapor di Basilico

Over the last ten years or so basil has risen from anonymity to become one of the favourite culinary herbs. Witness the popularity in its presence, fresh, all year round, cheek by jowl with mint and parsley in most supermarkets. Basil marries so well with tomato that the combination is in danger of becoming a tired culinary cliché. What is surprising is how slow people have been to recognise its potential with fruit. Only one herb book, admittedly written over fifteen years ago, timorously suggests adding a pinch (a measurement so small it can serve no purpose) to stewed fruit. This, however, is Anna del Conte's recipe, which comes from her new book Entertaining all'Italiana. *It combines basil, oranges and lemons in a sorbet with typical Italian vigour and the result is excellent.*

INGREDIENTS

	Metric	U.S.	Imperial
Lemons	8	8	8
Oranges	2	2	2
Water	625 ml	2½ cups	20 fl oz
Granulated sugar	350 g	1¾ cups	12 oz
Basil leaves	24×	24×	24×
	2.5 cm	1 inch	1 inch
Makes about	1 litre	4 cups	32 fl oz

Scrub the fruit in warm, soapy water; rinse and dry. Use a sharp potato peeler to remove the peel from the oranges and lemons, without chipping the white pith, and put this into a non-reactive saucepan. Add the water and the sugar. Bring slowly to the boil and boil rapidly for 3–4 minutes to reduce slightly the amount of liquid. Remove from the heat, cover and allow to cool. When cool, strain into a bowl. Meanwhile squeeze the lemons and oranges, strain, and add this to the syrup. Tear up the basil leaves into very small pieces and add these as well. Chill overnight.

When ready still freeze (see page 48) or start the ice-cream machine and pour in the liquid. Leave to churn for 10–15 minutes or until the sorbet is firm enough to serve. To store, quickly scrape into plastic freezer boxes (give a good stir to mix the basil leaves evenly as they have a habit of getting wound round the paddles). Cover with waxed or greaseproof paper and a lid. Finally label, then freeze. Allow 10–15 minutes in the fridge to soften sufficiently before serving.

Lemon Grass Ice Cream

Lemon grass is a flavour used extensively in the cooking of Thailand, Malaysia, Indonesia and Sri Lanka. Lemon grass contributes a perfume to a dish, something akin to lemon verbena, with no notion of sourness. It can be bought from most shops specialising in Asian foods; and fresh, which is preferable to either the dried or certainly the powdered form, it usually comes in bundles of six or eight stalks, about 30 cm/12 inches long. Looking like a somewhat drier, woodier version of a spring onion or scallion, they are prepared in much the same way, using only about 13 cm/5 inches of the bulb-like base. Having discarded the top, trim the base and peel off the tough outer leaves (about eight stalks will suffice for this recipe) and you are ready to go. Any remaining lemon grass will keep for about three weeks if stored in a plastic bag in the fridge, and can be used to flavour all manner of rice, soups, fish and chicken dishes.

INGREDIENTS

	Metric	U.S.	Imperial
Lemon grass, trimmed stalks (see above)	110 g	4 oz	4 oz
Milk	250 ml	1 cup	8 fl oz
Whipping/heavy cream (36 per cent fat)	250 ml	1 cup	8 fl oz
Egg yolks	3	3	3
Granulated sugar	100 g	½ cup	3½ oz
Makes about	750 ml	3 cups	24 fl oz

Thinly slice the lemon grass and put this into a saucepan with the milk and cream. Bring to just below boiling point then remove the pan from the heat, cover and leave to infuse for a minimum of 30 minutes.

In a medium-sized, heatproof bowl whisk together the egg yolks and sugar until they take on a pale yellow colour and lighter consistency. Bring the lemon grass infusion back to just below boiling point and pour on to the egg yolks, whisking all the while. The bowl can now be placed over a pan of simmering water, or the custard can be returned to the saucepan which is then put on top of a heat-diffuser mat so that it is not in direct contact with the heat. Only if you have an accurate thermometer and/or are confident that you will not overheat the sauce, should you put the saucepan on a gentle direct heat. Stir the custard until it reaches 85°C/185°F or until it has thickened sufficiently to coat the back of a spoon. As soon as the custard reaches this stage plunge the base of the pan into cold water. On no account should the custard be allowed to overheat or boil or it will curdle. (For how to deal with an overheated custard see page 52.) When the custard has cooled, cover and transfer to the fridge to chill.

When ready, still freeze (see page 48) or start the ice-cream machine. Then strain the custard allowing it simply to drain through the sieve. Taste, then if a more intense flavour is preferred, firmly press the lemon grass left in the sieve until you arrive at the flavour you like. Pour the custard into the ice-cream machine and churn for about 15 minutes, or until the custard is the consistency of softly whipped cream. Quickly scrape into plastic freezer boxes and cover with waxed or greaseproof paper and a lid. Finally label, then freeze. Eat in about 1 hour. Or if frozen solid, leave the ice cream in the fridge for about 20 minutes so that it becomes soft enough to serve.

Lime Sorbet

A wonderfully refreshing, delightfully tart sorbet. To us limes always seem to have more than a hint of coconut about them, so teaming this sorbet with Easy Coconut Ice Cream (see page 83) works well. In fact, if you think about all the other fruits that grow in a similar climate and base your ideas on combinations of these, you can't go far wrong.

INGREDIENTS

	Metric	U.S.	Imperial
Limes	5	5	5
Sugar syrup (see page 47)	375 ml	1½ cups	12 fl oz
Lemon juice, strained	1 Tbsp	1 Tbsp	1 Tbsp
Water	250 ml	1 cup	8 fl oz
Egg white	1	1	1
Makes about	800 ml	3¼ cups	26 fl oz

Since the zest of only 1 lime is needed, it is only necessary to wash one. Use a zester and remove the coloured peel only from this one. Cover and keep to add to the sorbet when frozen. Squeeze the limes, strain, and mix the juice with the sugar syrup, strained lemon juice and water. Chill in the refrigerator, preferably overnight.

When ready, still freeze (see page 48) or start the ice-cream machine and pour in the lime mixture. Churn for about 10 minutes or until the mixture starts to become opaque and icy. Using a fork, beat the egg white until loosened and add to the sorbet with the machine still running. Continue until the sorbet is firm enough to serve; fork in the reserved lime zest.

NOTE: We prefer putting in the lime zest at this stage; added earlier, the tendrils of peel tend to get wound around the dasher of the machine and time spent removing them allows the sorbet to melt.

To store, quickly scrape into plastic freezer boxes and cover with waxed or greaseproof paper and a lid. Finally label, then freeze. Once the sorbet becomes solid it will need about 20 minutes in the fridge to soften sufficiently to serve.

Lychee and Lime Sorbet

Lychees are a fruit that take to canning very well. In fact, they are often better from the can than the fresh ones we buy, so they make an ideal store-cupboard type of sorbet which fits the Western need for a dessert to follow a Far Eastern meal. The flavour is light, fresh, fragrant; an exquisite sorbet which people eat in embarrassing amounts. Fresh lime leaves are available from Thai or Oriental greengrocers.

INGREDIENTS

	Metric	U.S.	Imperial
One can lychees in natural juice	425 g	15 oz	15 oz
Granulated sugar	150 g	¾ cup	5¼ oz
Fresh lime leaves	9	9	9
Juice of lime, strained	1	1	1
Egg white	1	1	1
Makes about	750 ml	3 cups	24 fl oz

Drain the juice from the can into a small saucepan and add the sugar and 6 rinsed and dried lime leaves. Bring slowly to the boil then remove the pan from the heat, cover and leave aside to infuse for a minimum of 30 minutes. Liquidise the lychees for about 30 seconds then stop the machine and pour in the strained lime juice and syrup; blend for a further 30 seconds. Strain the pulp, pressing hard on the debris left in the sieve to extract the maximum juices. Slice the remaining 3 lime leaves as finely as possible then chop about 6 times with the knife. Mix into the strained liquid, cover and chill in the fridge.

When ready, still freeze (see page 48) or start the ice-cream machine. Pour in the lychee and lime leaf mixture and churn for about 10 minutes or until it is just beginning to become icy. Using a fork, beat the egg white until loosened then add to the sorbet with the machine running. Continue churning until the sorbet is firm enough to serve. Or to store, quickly scrape into plastic freezer boxes and cover with a piece of waxed or greaseproof paper and a lid. Finally label, then freeze. Once the sorbet becomes solid it will need about 25 minutes in the fridge before it is soft enough to serve.

Mai Tai Sorbet

Mai Tai is a cocktail invented in 1944 by Victor Bergeron, the founder of Trader Vic's in Oakland, California. The name, Mai Tai, is Tahitian and means "Out of this World" which this sorbet really is. For absolute authenticity the cocktail must be made with Trader Vic's Mai Tai Rum, but for the sorbet a good matured dark rum will do.

NOTE: *Because of the amount of alcohol in this sorbet it will probably not freeze sufficiently in a machine to serve immediately – it depends on the type of machine. So we would not recommend it, say, as an impromptu ice on a hot summer's day. Much better to consult a weather forecast and make it the previous day.*

INGREDIENTS

	Metric	U.S.	Imperial
Matured Dark Rum	4 Tbsp	4 Tbsp	4 Tbsp
Curaçao	2 Tbsp	2 Tbsp	2 Tbsp
Orgeat (see page 53)	2 Tbsp	2 Tbsp	2 Tbsp
Lime juice	2 Tbsp	2 Tbsp	2 Tbsp
Caster/Ultra fine sugar	2 tsp	2 tsp	2 tsp
Lemon juice	4 Tbsp	4 Tbsp	4 Tbsp
Sugar syrup (see page 47)	375 ml	1½ cups	12 fl oz
Water	375 ml	1½ cups	12 fl oz
Egg white	1	1	1
Makes about	875 ml	3½ cups	28 fl oz

Mix all the ingredients together except the egg white. Stir until the sugar is completely dissolved, then cover and chill in the fridge.

When ready, still freeze (see page 48) or start the ice-cream machine. Pour in the Mai Tai mixture and churn for about 10 minutes or until it is just beginning to become icy. Using a fork, beat the egg white until loosened and add to the sorbet with the machine running. Continue churning until the sorbet is thick and slushy, then quickly scrape into plastic freezer boxes and cover with a piece of waxed or greaseproof paper and a lid. Finally label, then freeze. Once the sorbet becomes solid it will only need about 5 minutes in the fridge before it is soft enough to serve.

Serving
Serve with a sprig of fresh mint before or after a meal.

Quick Mango Kulfi

See page 106.

Mango Sorbet

There is no doubt a good mango is hard to find. In fact it can be so long between one good mango and the next you can forget how plain perfect a ripe mango can be. But there are six varieties to look for: Alfonse from India; Haden, Keitt, Kent and Tommy Atkins from Puerto Rico; and from the West Indies, Julie.

INGREDIENTS

	Metric	U.S.	Imperial
Fresh mango	675 g	1½ lb	1½ lb
Sugar syrup (see page 47)		see recipe	
Juice of lemon	1	1	1
Salt	pinch	pinch	pinch
Egg white	1	1	1
Makes about	625 ml	2½ cups	20 fl oz

Remove the flesh and skin from the mango and purée in a food processor or blender until smooth. Pour into a measuring jug; there will be about 400 ml/1¾ cups/14 fl oz. Now add half this volume of syrup, i.e. 200 ml/⅞ cup/7 fl oz. Strain the lemon juice and add with the salt. Mix well, taste and add a little more lemon juice, if preferred. Cover and chill in the fridge.

When ready, still freeze (see page 48) or start the ice-cream machine. Pour in the liquid and churn until the mixture starts to form an ice slush. Using a fork, beat the egg white until loosened and add to the sorbet with the machine still running. Continue running until the sorbet is firm enough to serve. Or to store, quickly scrape into plastic freezer boxes and cover with a piece of waxed or greaseproof paper and a lid. Finally label, then freeze. Once the sorbet becomes solid it will need about 20 minutes in the fridge before it is soft enough to serve.

Maple Syrup Ice Cream

This is of course using genuine maple syrup and not maple-flavoured syrup; the real stuff has a maple leaf motif on the label. A slightly different cooking technique is used for the custard; it is baked in individual ramekins in a water bath. Nothing can go wrong with this method; the custard is simply left to bake, then once cooled, the contents of the ramekins can be emptied into a jug and left to chill in the fridge until you are ready to churn it. That is all. The flavour of the ice cream is A.1.

INGREDIENTS

	Metric	U.S.	Imperial
Whipping/heavy cream (36 per cent fat)	500 ml	2 cups	16 fl oz
Egg yolks	6	6	6
Maple syrup	125 ml	½ cup	4 fl oz
Light soft brown sugar	3 Tbsp	3 Tbsp	3 Tbsp
Makes about	750 ml	3 cups	24 fl oz

You will need 6×185 ml/¾ cup/6 fl oz capacity ramekins and a roasting tin large enough to accommodate them. Preheat the oven to 160°C/325°F/Gas Mark 3. Warm the cream in a saucepan until hand-hot. Meanwhile put the egg yolks into a bowl and beat for 1–2 minutes, then continue beating and pour in the maple syrup and soft brown sugar. Beat for a further minute before pouring the hot cream on to the egg yolk mix in a thin stream, still whisking all the while.

continued overleaf

"Don't care syrup,"
for people who when asked what flavour they required in an ice cream soda said, "I don't care"

Pineapple syrup	4 fl oz
Strawberry syrup	**4 fl oz**
Vanilla syrup	**4 fl oz**
Port wine	**2 fl oz**
Sugar syrup	**32 fl oz**

A. Emil Hiss,
Standard Manual of Soda and other Beverages,
Engelhardt, Chicago, 1897

Pour an equal quantity of the mixture into each ramekin via a sieve. Put the ramekins in a roasting tin, then into the oven before pouring sufficient tap-hot water into the roasting tin to the same depth as the mixture inside the pots. Lay a sheet of foil over the top to prevent the surface of the custards forming a crust. Bake for about 60–75 minutes or until the custards are just set.

Carefully remove the roasting tin from the oven then the ramekins from the water bath. Leave to cool. It takes up less space in the fridge if the custards are now emptied into a jug before transferring to the fridge to chill.

When ready, still freeze (see page 48) or start the ice-cream machine. Pour in the mixture and churn until the ice cream is the consistency of softly whipped cream. Quickly scrape into plastic freezer boxes and cover with a piece of waxed or greaseproof paper and a lid. Finally label, then freeze. Serve within 1 hour. Or, if frozen, the ice will need about 20 minutes in the fridge before it is soft enough to serve.

Maple Syrup and Pecan Ice Cream

INGREDIENTS

	Metric	U.S.	Imperial
One recipe Maple Syrup Ice Cream (see page 113)			
Pecans, shelled and chopped	40–60 g	½ to ⅔ cup	1½ to 2¼ oz
Makes about	875 ml	3½ cups	28 fl oz

Make the Maple Syrup Ice Cream according to the recipe (see page 113). Add the chopped pecans, sprinkling them into the ice cream as it is spooned into the plastic freezer boxes. Stir well to mix, then cover and store according to the method for making Maple Syrup Ice Cream.

Marguerita Sorbet

Because of the amount of alcohol in this sorbet it is almost impossible to chill sufficiently in a machine to serve immediately; so allow overnight in the freezer to solidify.

INGREDIENTS

	Metric	U.S.	Imperial
Sugar syrup (see page 47)	500 ml	2 cups	16 fl oz
Water	375 ml	1½ cups	12 fl oz
Cointreau®	4 Tbsp	4 Tbsp	4 Tbsp
Tequila	4 Tbsp	4 Tbsp	4 Tbsp
Juice of lemons, strained	2–3	2–3	2–3
Egg white	1	1	1
Makes about	1 litre	4 cups	32 fl oz

Mix the sugar syrup, water, alcohol and the strained juice of 2 lemons. Then taste, and add more lemon juice, if liked. Chill the mixture in the fridge.

When ready, still freeze (see page 48) or start the ice-cream machine. Pour in the Marguerita mixture and churn for about 10 minutes or until it is just beginning to become icy. Using a fork, beat the egg white until loosened and add to the sorbet with the machine running. Continue churning until the sorbet is thick and slushy. Then quickly scrape into plastic freezer boxes and cover with a piece of waxed or greaseproof paper and a lid. Finally label, then freeze overnight. Once the sorbet becomes solid it will only need about 5 minutes in the fridge before it is soft enough to serve.

A cone of ice cream turned out from an early ice-cream disher.

Marmalade Ice Cream

This ice cream may have a modern ring about it, but in fact harks back to a recipe in Mrs Marshall's Book of Ices *(1885). Her recipe is a little more complicated than ours, which is sensationally quick, simple and delicious. Just be sure to use a good quality Seville orange marmalade – extra thick-cut and home-made preferred. Mrs Marshall strains her marmalade ice cream, but we like to keep the character of the peel. The recipe might well work with other types of marmalade (e.g. ginger, lime, orange and whisky) but we have not tried these yet . . .*

INGREDIENTS

	Metric	U.S.	Imperial
Seville orange marmalade	310 g	1 cup	11 oz
Whipping/heavy cream (36 per cent fat), chilled	500 ml	2 cups	16 fl oz
Caster/Ultra fine sugar	30 g	⅛ cup	1 oz
Orange juice	1–2 tsp	1–2 tsp	1–2 tsp
Makes about	1 litre	4 cups	32 fl oz

Combine the marmalade, cream and sugar in a food processor or blender and blend briefly so that the peel remains in discernible pieces. Taste and add the orange juice to your liking. Either still freeze (see page 48) or start the ice-cream machine. Pour in the marmalade mix, and churn until the ice cream is the consistency of softly whipped cream. Quickly scrape into plastic freezer boxes and cover with a piece of waxed or greaseproof paper and a lid. Finally label, then freeze. Serve within 1 hour, or if frozen the ice will need about 20 minutes in the fridge before it is soft enough to serve.

Notes: This is really special served as Deep Fried Ice Cream (see page 92).

Ginger marmalade or any other jam or marmalade makes delicious ice cream.

MELONS

The variety, size and flavour of melons varies so greatly there are no recipes that will cover all types. Don't even bother with water melon unless you are going to use it for decoration. Although the colour would seem ideal for sorbets, which it is, the flavour simply isn't there. As a general rule don't attempt a melon sorbet unless the melon is really ripe, or you will be disappointed. Stick to the most strongly flavoured of the melon varieties: Cantaloupe, Charentais or Galia.

Cantaloupe Melon Sorbet

INGREDIENTS

	Metric	U.S.	Imperial
Cantaloupe melon, about	750 g	1½ lb	1½ lb
Sugar syrup (see page 47)	250 ml	1 cup	8 fl oz
Lemon juice	1 Tbsp	1 Tbsp	1 Tbsp
Egg white (see recipe)	1	1	1
Makes about	750 ml	3 cups	24 fl oz

Halve the melon and scoop out the seeds. Remove the flesh from the melon rind and put it in a food processor or blender with the sugar syrup. Blend until smooth. There are then two possibilities:

1. There is quite a lot of fibre in a Cantaloupe melon. If you like a very firm sorbet, with a Cantaloupe melon texture, that will melt slowly, do not sieve and do not add an egg white to the frozen mixture.

2. If you do not like the texture and thickness that the fibre gives, rub through a fine sieve and add an egg white during freezing.

So, then sieve or do not sieve, as the case may be, and add the lemon juice. Taste, and add more, if necessary. Then transfer to a large jug, cover and chill in the fridge.

When ready, still freeze (see page 48) or start the ice-cream machine. Pour in the chilled melon purée and churn for 5–10 minutes or until the mixture begins to freeze and is a fairly liquid slush. (If you have sieved the purée: using a fork, beat the egg white until loosened and add to the sorbet with the machine still running.)

With both methods, continue to churn for a further 10 minutes or until the sorbet is firm enough to serve. Or to store, quickly scrape into plastic freezer containers and cover with a piece of waxed or greaseproof paper and a lid. Finally label, then freeze. Once the sorbet becomes solid, it will need about 20 minutes in the fridge before it is soft enough to scoop.

"She was a butterscotch sundae of a woman, as beautiful as a tulip of beer with a high white collar," wrote A. J. Liebling of Lillian Russell. **"If a western millionaire, one of the Hearst or Mackay kind, could have given an architect a carte blanche to design him a woman, she would have looked like Lillian. She was San Simeon in corsets."** She also ate a fourteen-course dinner almost every night for years, and a popular dessert called after her consisted of half a cantaloupe holding nearly a quart of ice cream.

A. J. Liebling (1904–1963)

She: I think I should like ice-creams better if they were not so cold.
He: Should you my dear? Then I'd recommend you to have the chill taken off in future.

From a print *c.* 1830.

Charentais Melon Sorbet

A bold and full-flavoured sorbet of an almost unreal pastel orange. As usual, for the best results, use a melon that is so ripe that the aroma hits you when you walk into the kitchen.

INGREDIENTS

	Metric	U.S.	Imperial
Charentais/musk melon, about	900 g	2 lb	2 lb
Granulated sugar	300 g	1½ cups	10½ oz
Juice of lemons, strained	2	2	2
White port	3 Tbsp	3 Tbsp	3 Tbsp
Egg white	1	1	1
Makes about	1 litre	4 cups	32 fl oz

Halve the melon and scoop out the seeds. Remove the flesh from the melon rind and put in a food processor or blender with the sugar, strained lemon juice and port. Blend until smooth, then transfer to a large jug. Cover and chill in the fridge.

When ready, still freeze (see page 48) or start the ice-cream machine. Pour in the chilled melon purée and churn for 5–10 minutes or until the mixture begins to freeze and is a fairly liquid slush. Using a fork, beat the egg white until loosened and add to the sorbet with the machine still running. Continue to churn for a further 10 minutes or until the sorbet is firm enough to serve. To store, quickly scrape into plastic freezer containers and cover with a piece of waxed or greaseproof paper and a lid. Finally label, then freeze. Once the sorbet becomes solid it will need about 20 minutes in the fridge before it is soft enough to scoop.

Galia Melon Sorbet

Follow the instructions for making a Charentais Melon Sorbet (see above), omitting the white port.

Fresh Mint Ice Cream

A wonderful flavour that only the fresh herb will generate. It has a delicate green colour.

INGREDIENTS

	Metric	U.S.	Imperial
One recipe French Vanilla Ice Cream (see page 51), omitting the vanilla bean and substituting			
Vanilla sugar (see page 36)	90 g	½ cup minus 1 Tbsp	3¼ oz
Sprigs of fresh mint	4×10 cm	4×4 inch	4×4 inch
Makes about	800 ml	3¼ cups	26 fl oz

Make the French Vanilla Ice Cream, omitting the vanilla bean and substituting the less strong vanilla sugar. (If this is not easily to hand, ¼ tsp vanilla extract can be used with ordinary sugar.)

Continue up to the stage where the custard has thickened sufficiently and reached 85°C/185°F. Have the sprigs of mint ready, rinsed and patted dry, and put them into a 1 litre/4 cup/32 fl oz measuring jug. As soon as the custard is ready, remove it from the heat and pour it into the measuring jug on top of the sprigs of mint. Leave to cool to room temperature and transfer to the fridge.

When ready, stir in the cream, then still freeze (see page 48) or start the ice-cream machine and pour in the contents of the measuring jug via a sieve, pressing the mint firmly to extract the flavour. Leave to churn until the ice cream is the consistency of softly whipped cream. Quickly scrape into plastic freezer boxes, level, then cover with waxed or greaseproof paper and a lid. Finally label, then freeze. If frozen solid, allow 15–20 minutes in the fridge to soften sufficiently to serve.

Chocolate and Fresh Mint Ice Cream

See page 74.

Mint Granita/Sorbet

See Herb Granitas/Sorbets pages 99 to 100.

Mint Ice Cream with Blackcurrant Ripple

Blackcurrant being such a strong flavour, it is difficult to find another that will match yet alone marry with it, but mint is one that does.
Here the ratio of blackcurrant purée to mint ice cream, and the manner in which they are mingled, go to make an admirable balance.

INGREDIENTS

	Metric	U.S.	Imperial
One recipe Fresh Mint Ice Cream (see page 117)			
Blackcurrants	115 g	1 scant cup (4 oz)	4 oz
Granulated sugar	60 g	¼ cup plus 1 Tbsp	2¼ oz
Makes about	1.1 litres	4½ cups	36 fl oz

Following the ingredients and method given for making Fresh Mint Ice Cream (see page 117), prepare a mint-flavoured custard. Then cover and put in the fridge to chill.

To prepare the blackcurrants work over a colander or sieve and use a fork to strip the blackcurrants from the stalks, discarding all damaged and underripe berries.

Rinse and drain the blackcurrants. Then, if you have a microwave, tip into a microwave-safe casserole so that the fruit forms a shallow layer. It will need no additional water other than that left clinging to the berries. Cover and microwave at full power for 2 minutes. Stop, uncover and stir. Re-cover and microwave for a further 2 minutes. By this time the berries should be soft.

Alternatively, tip the drained berries into a small saucepan, add 1 Tbsp of water, cover and heat gently until the berries are soft.

Empty the berries and juices into a food processor or blender and add the sugar. Blend for 10 seconds, then rub the pulp through a nylon sieve into a bowl. Cover and chill in the fridge.

When ready, still freeze (see page 48) or start the ice-cream machine and make the ice cream as directed in the method for making Fresh Mint Ice Cream. Whilst the ice cream is churning have ready the chilled blackcurrant purée and a plastic freezer box, minimum 1 litre/4 cups/ 32 fl oz capacity. When the ice cream has reached the consistency of softly whipped cream, stop the machine and quickly spoon one-third of the mixture into the container. Cover this with a layer of half the blackcurrant purée; repeat the layering, finishing with the ice cream. Using a large spoon, turn and fold the mixture twice, making sure the spoon goes right to the base. More than this is not necessary and in fact will start to mix the ice cream and the purée. Cover with waxed or greaseproof paper and a lid. Finally label, then freeze for a minimum of 1 hour before eating. If frozen solid, allow 20 minutes in the fridge to soften sufficiently to serve.

Mint Julep Ice Cream

The julep, often assumed to be American, is in fact of Persian origin. In The Legendary Cuisine of Persia, *Margaret Shaida traces it back to the Persian word "golab". ("Gol" means flower, "ab" means water. "Golab" meant rose-water.) However, the Arabs do not have a hard "g" and pronounced it "jolab" and this was turned into the English julep. The meaning of the word changed in England to denote a diluted sweetened drink – the julep cordial. It was further changed in America where the alcoholic mint julep is a popular, delicious and refreshing summer drink in the South.*

The texture of this mint julep is on the icy side which is a result of adding sufficient alcohol to get the flavour right and holding the sugar down so as not to drown the mint.

INGREDIENTS

	Metric	U.S.	Imperial
Milk	500 ml	2 cups	16 fl oz
Vanilla bean	1	1	1
Granulated sugar	100 g	½ cup	3½ oz
Egg yolks	4	4	4
Fresh mint leaves	6	6	6
Whipping/heavy cream (36 per cent fat), chilled	500 ml	2 cups	16 fl oz
Bourbon whisky	125 ml	½ cup	4 oz
Makes about	1.25 litres	5 cups	40 fl oz

Using the above quantities of milk, vanilla, sugar and egg yolks, prepare and cook a custard according to the method for making French Vanilla Ice Cream (see page 51). Continue up to the stage where the cooked custard is transferred from the heat to sit in a few inches of cold water. At this point add the rinsed, dried mint leaves to the hot custard, then leave to cool. Cover and chill in the fridge overnight.

When ready strain the custard and stir in the chilled cream and the bourbon. Then, either still freeze (see page 48) or start the ice-cream machine. Pour in the custard mix and churn until the ice cream is the consistency of thick pouring cream, about 25 minutes.

NOTE: In the machine this mixture will be unable to reach a low enough temperature to freeze to a firm enough consistency to serve, because of the high alcohol content.

Quickly scrape into plastic freezer boxes, level the surface and cover with waxed or greaseproof paper and a lid. Finally label, then freeze. Leave the ice cream overnight in the freezer. Allow some 15–20 minutes in the fridge for the ice cream to soften sufficiently to serve.

Muscat Sorbet

See page 157.

Nectarine

See also peach pages 125 and 126.

Winston Churchill to Lord Woolton. 22 September 1942 *PROHIBITION OF THE MANUFACTURE AND SALE OF ICE CREAM* **Without definite information as to the saving in transport and manpower, I cannot judge whether the destruction of this amenity was worth while.**

I suppose the large numbers of American troops in this country will have their own arrangements made for them. They are great addicts of ice cream, which is said to be a rival to alcoholic drinks.

The step should not have been taken without the Cabinet having an opportunity to express an opinion.

Nectarine and Amaretti Ice

Rich, creamy and not too sweet.

INGREDIENTS

	Metric	U.S.	Imperial
Eggs	2	2	2
Granulated sugar	100 g	½ cup	3½ oz
Whipping/heavy cream (36 per cent fat)	250 ml	1 cup	8 fl oz
Nectarines	4	4	4
Greek/Russian style yoghurt	120 g	½ cup	4¼ oz
Almond extract	few drops	few drops	few drops
Amaretti biscuits	50 g	2 oz	2 oz
Makes about	750 ml	3 cups	24 fl oz

In a medium-sized heatproof bowl beat the eggs with half the sugar until thoroughly mixed. Bring the cream and remaining sugar to the boil and pour on to the eggs and sugar, whisking steadily. Then either sit the bowl over a pan of simmering water or return the mixture to the saucepan, positioning the saucepan on a heat-diffuser mat and not in direct contact with the heat. Gently cook the custard, stirring frequently until the mixture coats the back of a spoon or the temperature reaches 85°C/185°F. The custard will be quite a thick one. Immediately remove the pan from the heat and cool by sitting it in a few inches of cold water. On no account should the custard be allowed to overheat or boil as the mixture will curdle. (For how to deal with an overheated custard see page 52.) Leave to become cold, stirring occasionally.

Meanwhile peel the nectarines by immersing them in boiling water for about 1 minute. Slip off the skins and quarter 3 of them. Put these in a food processor or blender and blend briefly so that the flesh remains in smallish pieces and is not reduced to a uniform purée. Fold these into the custard with the yoghurt and 1–2 drops of almond extract. Chill in the fridge.

When ready, still freeze (see page 48) or start the ice-cream machine. Pour in the fruit and custard mixture. Churn for about 15 minutes or until the consistency of whipped cream.

While the ice is churning, dice the remaining nectarine and roughly crumble the biscuits by hand. When the ice cream is ready, quickly scrape into a plastic freezer box, folding in the diced nectarine and crumbled biscuit at the same time. Smooth the surface and cover with a piece of waxed or greaseproof paper and a lid. Finally label, then freeze. Serve after about 1½ hours or, if frozen solid, allow about 20 minutes in the fridge to soften sufficiently to serve.

Variations
Other almond-flavoured biscuits can be used instead of amaretti e.g. ratafias or macaroons.

Serving
Serve with a sweetened fresh raspberry sauce scattered with additional crumbled biscuits, if liked.

Extraordinary ice cream confections, from Fred T. Vine, *Ices, Plain and Decorated*, 1890.

PLATE 3

NO. 77. ICED PUDDING A LA MILLEFRUIT ON FROZEN MARBLE STAND NO. I.

NO. 93. ICED TROPHYA L'AUTOMNE.

NO. 96. ICED COMPOTE OF GREENGAGES.

NO. 95. ICED COMPOTE OF PEARS.

NO. 97. ICED COMPOTE A LA PRINCESSES.

Nougat Ice Cream

The flavour of this ice has everything you look for in the conventional sweet but rarely seem to find; i.e. a good honey flavour forming a background for nuts (toasted almonds and hazelnuts, untoasted pistachio or walnuts) and candied fruits. All individually identifiable but forming a pleasing whole that certainly will not break your teeth. The ratio of nuts to crystallised fruits is a matter of personal preference. We prefer crystallised fruits that retain their flavour rather than those which are just sweet. So our selection would contain a preponderance of crystallised pineapple, oranges or clementines and angelica, but not too many crystallised cherries or apricots. This recipe makes sufficient to fill 2×1.5 litre/6 cup/48 fl oz loaf tins, which may seem a bit excessive but we have left it this way because to halve the ingredients makes them awkward to deal with and the results can be unreliable. Our alternative was to leave the recipe out of the book, but it is too good to do that. Far better to freeze the second loaf tin. We use a loaf tin as this ice cream must be served sliced; it cannot be served in scoops.

INGREDIENTS

	Metric	U.S.	Imperial
Mixed finely diced crystallised fruits and slivered nuts (see intro)	400 g	2½ cups	14 oz
Sugar syrup (see page 47)	500 ml	2 cups	16 fl oz
Clear mild honey e.g. acacia	325 g	1 cup	11½ oz
Dextrose Monohydrate (see page 154)	2 Tbsp	2 Tbsp	2 Tbsp
OR			
Light corn syrup	4 Tbsp	4 Tbsp	4 Tbsp
Egg whites	4	4	4
Whipping/heavy cream (36 per cent fat), chilled	500 ml	2 cups	16 fl oz
Icing sugar, sieved	6 Tbsp	6 Tbsp	6 Tbsp
Makes about	2.6 litres	10½ cups	84 fl oz

You will need 2×1.5 litre/6 cup/48 fl oz loaf tins, preferably non-stick. Brush with a tasteless oil.

Put the finely diced crystallised fruits in a small sauce-pan with the syrup. Bring to the boil then remove from the heat. Pour the contents of the pan into a sieve and leave the fruits to cool and drain. Have the egg whites ready in a large grease-free bowl, with a stand mixer if possible, otherwise have an electric hand mixer ready. Combine the honey with the dextrose or corn syrup in a small saucepan and bring to the boil. Boil gently until the mixture reaches 120°C/248°F. When the syrup is within 5 degrees of the correct temperature start whisking the egg whites so that they reach the soft peak stage as the syrup reaches 120°C/248°F. With the machine set at high speed whisking the egg whites, immediately pour in the syrup in a thin, slow stream, avoiding the beater(s).

When all the syrup has been added reduce the speed to medium and continue to beat until the mixture is almost cold; this will take about 10 minutes. Set aside for a few minutes while you beat the cream until very softly thickened. Set the mixer to the slowest speed and add the thoroughly cooled, drained crystallised fruits, slivered nuts and sieved icing sugar to the beaten cream. Finally, add the beaten egg whites and mix just sufficiently to combine thoroughly and evenly. Spoon the mixture into the 2 tins, level the surfaces and cover with waxed or greaseproof paper, cut to fit.

For a short term freeze (i.e. overnight), it can be put straight into the freezer.

It will freeze well for up to 1 month as long as it is carefully wrapped. To do this, cover it closely with freezer foil, then slip the tin into a plastic freezer bag. Evacuate as much air as possible using a straw, then seal well.

NOTE: Many nougat recipes contain orange flower water but we preferred the nougat ice without it. However, you might like to try serving this with Rose Pouchong Tea Syrup (see page 166). The method we use to make the syrup keeps it subtle, and we think it marries better with the nougat flavours than anything else we have tried.

Noyau Sherbet

Crème de Noyau or Noyaux is a peach-flavoured liqueur made from a selection of nuts and fruits kernels. Be careful not to get Crème de Noyeau which is a pink or white almond-flavoured liqueur. This sherbet is a very good foil for other flavours of ices and sorbets such as those of the plum family and soft fruit ice creams.

INGREDIENTS

	Metric	U.S.	Imperial
Sugar syrup (see page 47)	250 ml	1 cup	8 fl oz
Crème de Noyau *or* Noyaux	3 Tbsp	3 Tbsp	3 Tbsp
Lemon juice	2 Tbsp	2 Tbsp	2 Tbsp
Milk	1 cup	250 ml	8 fl oz
Bitter almond extract	1 drop	1 drop	1 drop
Egg white	1	1	1
Makes about	560 ml	2¼ cups	18 fl oz

Mix the sugar syrup, Noyau and lemon juice together and chill.

When ready, add the milk, stirring the mixture briskly. Finally add the bitter almond extract, using a fine metal skewer. Taste and, if liked, add another drop of extract. Either still freeze (see page 48) or start the ice-cream machine. Pour in the chilled Noyau mixture and churn for 5–10 minutes or until the mixture begins to freeze and is a fairly liquid slush. Using a fork, beat the egg white until loosened and add to the sorbet with the ⸺ ⸺ ⸺ ⸺ rn for a further
ntainers

Orange Ice Cream

The combination of orange juice, boiled to reduce and concentrate the flavour, and finely grated fresh orange zest added to the cooling custard gives an excellent balance of intensity with freshness of flavour. Rather a nifty trick if we do say it ourselves! One stage is tedious but important; remove all the white pith from the strips of orange zest, or the ice cream is likely to have an underlying bitterness.

INGREDIENTS

	Metric	U.S.	Imperial
Oranges	3	3	3
Milk	125 ml	½ cup	4 fl oz
Whipping/heavy cream (36 per cent fat)	500 ml	2 cups	16 fl oz
Egg yolks	5	5	5
Vanilla sugar (see page 36)	150 g	¾ cup	5¼ oz
Makes about	1 litre	4 cups	32 fl oz

Thoroughly scrub the oranges in warm soapy water, then rinse and dry. Using a sharp potato peeler, remove only the coloured part of the zest from 2 oranges. If some white pith comes away with the zest, this should be shaved off using a sharp knife almost flat against the peel. Put the strips of zest in a small saucepan with the milk and half the cream. Bring slowly to the boil then remove from the heat, cover and leave on one side for a minimum of 30 minutes.

In a heatproof bowl combine the egg yolks and sugar and beat until they take on a pale yellow colour and lighter consistency. Bring the orange peel infusion back just below boiling point then pour in stages through a strainer on to the egg yolks, whisking between each addition.

The bowl can now be placed over a pan of simmering water, or the custard can be returned to the saucepan which is then put on top of a heat-diffuser mat so that it is not in direct contact with the heat. Only if you have an accurate thermometer and/or you are confident that you will not overheat the custard should you put the saucepan on a gentle direct heat. Stir the custard until it reaches 85°C/185°F or until it has thickened sufficiently to coat the back of a spoon. As soon as the custard reaches this stage plunge the base of the pan into cold water. On no account should the custard be allowed to overheat or boil as the mixture will curdle. (For how to deal with an overheated custard see page 52.)

While the custard cools finely grate the orange coloured zest *only* from the remaining orange into the custard then squeeze the juice from all 3 (about 250 ml/ 1 cup/8 fl oz). Strain this into a small saucepan and boil until reduced by half. Stir this also into the cooling custard. When cold, cover with a circle of lightly buttered greaseproof paper and leave to chill in the fridge.

When ready, still freeze (see page 48) or start the ice-cream machine. Combine the chilled custard with the remaining cream and pour into the machine. Churn until the ice cream has the consistency of softly whipped cream. Quickly scrape into plastic freezer boxes and cover with a sheet of waxed or greaseproof paper and a lid. Finally label, then freeze. If frozen solid allow about 20 minutes in the fridge to soften sufficiently to serve.

Orange Ice Cream with Fresh Dates

Dates and oranges always have been perfect partners – it is the freshness of flavour of both that is remarkable in this ice cream.

INGREDIENTS

	Metric	U.S.	Imperial
One recipe Orange Ice Cream (see page 121)			
Fresh dates	12	12	12
Makes about	1 litre	4 cups	32 fl oz

Skin, halve and pit the dates. Quarter the fruit lengthways, then slice across finely. Sprinkle the pieces of date into the still-frozen or churning ice cream. Stir carefully or leave to churn for 3 or 4 revolutions until evenly distributed in the ice cream. Then stop the machine and box, label and store the ice cream as described in the recipe for making Orange Ice Cream.

Seville Orange Sorbet

One of our all-time favourites. Sadly, this is a very seasonal recipe.

INGREDIENTS

	Metric	U.S.	Imperial
Seville oranges	6	6	6
Sugar syrup (see page 47)	500 ml	2 cups	16 fl oz
Lemon	1	1	1
Makes about	1 litre	4 cups	32 fl oz

Thoroughly scrub and dry the oranges. Use a zester to remove short, thin strips of zest from 2 of the oranges; alternatively finely grate them.

Squeeze the juice from all the oranges and the lemon and strain through a plastic sieve into a measuring jug. Add the sugar syrup and make up to 750 ml/ 3 cups/24 fl oz with cold water. Chill in the refrigerator.

When ready, still freeze (see page 48) or start the ice-cream machine. Pour in the liquid and churn until the sorbet is firm enough to serve. If it is to be stored, quickly scrape the sorbet into plastic freezer containers, making sure all the strips of zest are removed from the paddle/ dasher and incorporated into the sorbet. Level the surface and cover with waxed or greaseproof paper and a lid. Finally label, then freeze. Once frozen allow 30 minutes in the fridge before serving.

ORANGE ICE

2 dozen Navel Oranges
15 pounds Granulated Sugar
1 ounce Orange Extract
4 gallons Water
Orange-Shade Color as required

A stone jar or enamel vessel should be used for mixing the following ingredients:

FIRST:—Grate the rind of 2 dozen Navel Oranges, using only the yellow part of the peel. Avoid the white inside, as it is bitter.

SECOND:—Mix the grated rind into 15 pounds Granulated Sugar.

THIRD:—Peel the Oranges and put through a grinder. (The pulp will be tender and juicy and will not be stringy when cut this way.)

FOURTH:—Then pour the Orange Juice and pulp over the Sugar mixture. Add 1 ounce Orange Extract.

FIFTH:—Now add the 4 gallons Water. Stir thoroughly and freeze as you would ice cream.

Add Orange-Shade Color to produce a rich Orange Shade.

NOTE:—When using Color, the Ice should be labeled "Artificially Colored."

From *Heller's Guide for Ice Cream Makers*, 1918.

Fresh-tasting Orange Yoghurt Ice Cream

Omit the lemons from the recipe for Fresh-Tasting Lemon Yoghurt Ice Cream (see page 108) and substitute the following.

INGREDIENTS

	Metric	U.S.	Imperial
Freshly squeezed orange juice	275 ml	1 cup plus 2 Tbsp	9 fl oz
Rind of oranges	3	3	3
Lemon juice	1 tsp	1 tsp	1 tsp
Makes about	875 ml	3½ cups	28 fl oz

Following the recipe for Fresh-Tasting Lemon Yoghurt Ice Cream (see page 108), prepare the oranges in the same manner and liquidise the peel with the sugar so that it becomes as fine as the sugar.

Squeeze the juice from the oranges, strain and put into a small non-reactive saucepan. Boil gently until reduced to just under half the quantity, about 6–7 Tbsp. Cool.

Follow the method for making Fresh-Tasting Lemon Yoghurt Ice Cream, stirring together the flavoured sugar, reduced orange juice, lemon juice and yoghurt to still freeze (see page 48) or churn.

Orange Blossom Sorbet

This is made with orange blossom (or flower) water which is the distillation of orange flowers. The smell is somewhat reminiscent of cheap boiled sweets but do not be put off, it does magic things to both sweet and savoury food. Avoid citrus flower water and look for the softer, more mellow varieties of orange flower water from Egypt, Morocco, Lebanon and the South of France.

INGREDIENTS

	Metric	U.S.	Imperial
Sugar syrup (see page 47)	375 ml	1½ cups	12 fl oz
Water	375 ml	1½ cups	12 fl oz
Orange flower water	1 Tbsp	1 Tbsp	1 Tbsp
Juice of lemon, strained	1	1	1
Egg white	1	1	1
Makes about	875 ml	3½ cups	28 fl oz

In a large measuring jug combine the sugar syrup, water, orange flower water and the strained juice of the lemon. Chill in the fridge.

When ready, still freeze (see page 48) or start the ice-cream machine. Pour in the liquid and churn for 5 minutes or until it becomes opaque. Using a fork, beat the egg white until loosened and add to the sorbet with the machine still running. Continue until the sorbet is firm enough to serve. To store, quickly scrape into plastic freezer containers, and cover with a piece of waxed or greaseproof paper and a lid. Finally label, then freeze. Once the sorbet becomes solid it will need about 30 minutes in the fridge before it is soft enough to scoop.

Passion Fruit Sorbet

A fruit with a fragrant, penetrating flavour which has no equal; it is superb. The only way to make a bad passion fruit sorbet is to make it too strong. If the sorbet is to be made almost immediately pass over the smooth-skinned passion fruit and go for the gently wrinkled as these will be riper, sweeter and more fragrant. Smooth fruit will ripen (i.e. wrinkle) if kept at room temperature for several days, or one to two weeks in a fridge. Serve this as part of a selection of tropical fruit sorbets e.g. Guava and Lime (see page 99) and Lychee and Lime (see page 112).

INGREDIENTS

	Metric	U.S.	Imperial
Ripe passion fruit	10	10	10
Sugar syrup (see page 47)	250 ml	1 cup	8 fl oz
Juice of lemons, strained	2	2	2
Egg white	1	1	1
Makes about	500 ml	2 cups	16 fl oz

Working over a food processor or blender cut each passion fruit in half and use a teaspoon to scoop out the seedy pulp into the bowl. Set the machine in motion and pour in the measured sugar syrup. Continue to blend for a further 15 seconds then switch off. Have a plastic sieve ready, positioned over a bowl. Pour the passion fruit purée into the sieve, then rub through until only the seeds remain. (Liquidising the pulp makes the flesh come apart more easily from the seeds so sieving is made simpler.) Stir in the strained lemon juice. The mixture can now be frozen, or covered and refrigerated until required.

When ready, still freeze (see page 48) or start the ice-cream machine. Pour in the passion fruit liquid and churn for about 10 minutes or until the mixture freezes to a soft slush. At this stage, use a fork to beat the egg white until loosened, and add to the sorbet with the machine still running. Continue until the sorbet is firm enough to serve. To store, quickly scrape into plastic freezer boxes and cover with waxed or greaseproof paper and a lid. Finally label, then freeze. Once the sorbet becomes solid it will need about 20–25 minutes in the fridge to soften.

Pea and Mint Savoury Ice Cream

One of our favourite savoury ice creams. The sweetness of the peas is to some extent offset by the lactic flavour of cream cheese and sharpened by lemon juice. If served with a dollop of salted fromage frais mixed with snipped chives, the balance is perfect. It also makes an excellent light lunch on a hot summer's day served as a garnish in chilled soup such as lettuce, tomato and buttermilk. Ladle the soup into large shallow soup dishes, put two or three quenelles (or scoops) of the savoury ice in the centre of each portion and top with the aforementioned fromage frais. Serve with hot home-made bread flavoured with onion seeds.

INGREDIENTS

	Metric	U.S.	Imperial
Frozen peas	225 g	½ lb	½ lb
Cream cheese, crumbled	115 g	4 oz	4 oz
Lemon juice	1 Tbsp	1 Tbsp	1 Tbsp
Fresh mint leaves, finely chopped	1 Tbsp	1 Tbsp	1 Tbsp
Salt	½ tsp	½ tsp	½ tsp
Granulated sugar	¼ tsp	¼ tsp	¼ tsp
Whipping/heavy cream (36 per cent fat)	150 ml	½ cup plus 2 Tbsp	5 fl oz
Makes about	500 ml	2 cups	16 fl oz

NOTE: The use of a liquidiser/blender is specified in the method as this will give a smoother consistency than a food processor. The best consistency is achieved by a combination of liquidising and sieving. But this is time-consuming, and the improvement is marginal, so the choice is yours. However, do sieve if you use just a food processor.

Put the peas into a small saucepan and pour in just sufficient boiling water to cover. Add a little salt and bring back to the boil; cook for 5 minutes then decant the contents of the pan into a sieve. Sluice with cold water and drain thoroughly before transferring the peas to a liquidiser or blender.

Blend in short bursts, stopping frequently to scrape down the sides of the liquidiser goblet. For a really smooth-textured ice cream the peas should be sieved at this point. If you decide against this rather finicky stage, make sure you liquidise the peas as thoroughly as you can before adding the crumbled cream cheese and lemon juice. Blend until smooth then finally add the chopped mint, salt and sugar and whipping cream. Liquidise just long enough to mix thoroughly, and no more, then pour into a plastic freezer box (21×16×6cm/8×6×2½ inches). Cover and freeze for 30 minutes. Use a fork to scrape the frozen mix from the base and sides of the container; beat into the rest of the mix until smooth, then cover and re-freeze for 1 further hour. Put into a food processor and process for about 10 seconds until smooth. Re-freeze until just sufficiently soft to serve, about 1 hour. If frozen solid, allow about 20 minutes in the fridge to soften before serving. Serve cut into slices.

Peach or Nectarine Ice Cream

The flavour of most fruit ice creams and sorbets relies heavily on the fruit being fully ripe. This is particularly so with peach ice cream. Sadly it is very difficult to get ripe peaches in Britain and in some parts of America. "Ready to eat" ones are often not and anyway are far too expensive a delicacy to be pulped in an ice cream. Furthermore if they are on the firm side, don't buy peaches in the hope that they will ripen. Experience has shown that they remain firm for up to two days then, very suddenly, they shrivel and rot. Nectarines generally have a better flavour, are cheaper and will ripen slightly if kept for a day or two. As far as ice creams and sorbets are concerned either fruit can be used, but nectarines seem to us a better choice.

INGREDIENTS

	Metric	U.S.	Imperial
Milk	250 ml	1 cup	8 fl oz
Granulated sugar	150 g	¾ cup	5¼ oz
Egg yolks	2	2	2
Peaches or nectarines	450 g	1 lb	1 lb
Juice of lemons	1	1	1
Vanilla extract	¼ tsp	¼ tsp	¼ tsp
Whipping/heavy cream (36 per cent fat), chilled	250 ml	1 cup	8 fl oz
Makes about	1 litre	4 cups	32 fl oz

Using the above quantities of milk, sugar and egg yolks (omitting the vanilla bean), prepare and cook a custard according to the method for making French Vanilla Ice Cream (see page 51).

While the custard is cooling, peel the peaches or nectarines by immersing in boiling water for about 1 minute. Slip off the skins, halve the peaches and discard the stones, then slice the fruit into a food processor or blender, add the lemon juice and blend very briefly so that the fruit remains in definite bits. Cover and chill the fruit pulp and custard. When ready, combine the two, and stir in the vanilla extract and chilled cream. Either still freeze (see page 48) or start the ice-cream machine. Pour in the custard, mix and churn for 15–20 minutes, or until the ice cream is the consistency of whipped cream. Serve at once; or to store, quickly scrape into plastic freezer boxes, level the surface and cover with waxed or greaseproof paper and a lid. Finally label, then freeze. If frozen, allow about 20 minutes in the fridge before serving.

Since the introduction of ice across the country the trade has been almost exclusively in the hands of foreigners, and the money which found its way into their pockets would to a great extent have been spent in other sweetmeats to the benefit of local shopkeepers; therefore it becomes necessary, for those who would hold their own against the stranger, to adopt the manufacture of ice cream.

Many moderate fortunes have been acquired within the last twenty or thirty years by adventurers, simply through making and selling ice creams during the summer months.

E. Skuse,
The Confectioner's Handbook, London, 1881

PEACH ICE

Peach and Hyssop Ice Cream

One of the lesser-known herbs but one that is attractive and easy to grow. However, on first inspection it is not inspiring. It has a strong, sour, spicy camphor-type smell; rather medicinal. The flavour is bitter and considered slightly minty. All in all, not the sort of herb to go with peaches, you would think, yet in a curious way it blends with these (and apricots) and boosts their flavour. Since it is also reputed to aid digestion of fat, what better way in which to use it than in an ice cream?

INGREDIENTS

	Metric	U.S.	Imperial
One recipe Peach or Nectarine Ice Cream (see page 125)			
Sprigs of hyssop	2	2	2
Makes about	1 litre	4 cups	32 fl oz

The herb can either be used to infuse the milk, or the leaves chopped and added to the custard before churning. For an infusion, bruise 2 sprigs of hyssop by rolling with a rolling pin. Bring to a boil in the milk then cover and leave aside for about 1 hour. Re-heat the milk and strain before using to make a custard. Or, add 1 tsp of chopped hyssop leaves to the custard before churning.

Peach and Praline Ice Cream

INGREDIENTS

	Metric	U.S.	Imperial
One recipe Peach or Nectarine Ice Cream (see page 125)			
Crushed almond praline (see page 163)	4 Tbsp	4 Tbsp	4 Tbsp
Makes about	1 litre	4 cups	32 fl oz

Crush the praline, not too finely, in a pestle and mortar or use a small bowl and the end of a rolling pin. Either method is more satisfactory than a food processor which tends to run away with you and reduce the praline to powder. Make the Peach or Nectarine Ice Cream according to the method (see page 125). As the churned ice cream is put into plastic freezer boxes, sprinkle with the praline, stir to distribute evenly, then cover and freeze.

A Wall's ice cream tricycle, *c.* 1900. The "Stop Me and Buy One" slogan became the butt of many jokes.

Bellini Sorbet

Harry's Bar in Venice is the home of the famous Bellini cocktail, a combination of peaches and Prosecco. Prosecco is not as easy to find as dry Champagne, so if you cannot find it use dry Champagne; but stick with Prosecco if you have a strong sense of tradition and/or a good wine merchant.

INGREDIENTS

	Metric	U.S.	Imperial
Peaches, large	4	4	4
Sugar syrup (see page 47)	250 ml	1 cup	8 fl oz
Juice of lemon	1	1	1
Prosecco			
OR			
Dry Champagne	375 ml	1½ cups	12 fl oz
Egg white	1	1	1
Makes about	1 litre	4 cups	32 fl oz

Skin the peaches by immersing them in boiling water for up to 1 minute, then drain and cool for a short while before slipping off the skins. Cut each fruit into 6 or 8, discarding the stone. Put the fruit in a food processor or blender with the sugar syrup and blend until smooth. Position a sieve over a bowl and strain the peach purée, then stir in the strained lemon juice. Cover and chill in the fridge.

When ready, stir in the chilled Champagne and the lightly beaten egg white. Either still freeze (see page 48) or start the ice-cream machine and churn until firm enough to serve. Or to store, quickly scrape into plastic freezer boxes and cover with waxed or greaseproof paper and a lid. Finally label, then freeze. Once frozen, allow about 15–20 minutes to soften in the fridge before serving.

Pear Ice Cream

You have to wait on the pears in order to make a good pear ice cream. Choose a flavourful variety, Williams/Bartlett and Comice are good because they have flavour without granulation. Get them home, then settle down to wait – there is no other way. For the best-flavoured ice cream they need to be caught at their peak, that stage when they are so juicy, the cut pears slip around like small wet fishes as you try to prepare them.

NOTE: *When pears are so perfectly ripe it may seem a shame to cook them, but it is necessary to make sure the pears are heated to boiling point throughout in order to destroy the enzyme (polypherioloxidase) which would cause them to brown. Chilling (i.e. below 4°C/39°F) only slows down the action of this enzyme; it does not destroy it as heat does. So the colour of the ice cream would continue to get browner, albeit very slowly, the longer the ice cream was stored.*

INGREDIENTS

	Metric	U.S.	Imperial
Pears, fully ripe	450 g	1 lb	1 lb
Water	3 Tbsp	3 Tbsp	3 Tbsp
Egg yolks	3	3	3
Granulated sugar	100 g	½ cup	3½ oz
Whipping/heavy cream (36 per cent fat)	250 ml	1 cup	8 fl oz
Makes about	750 ml	3 cups	24 fl oz

Select a pan large enough to take the sliced pears in a single layer. Put the water into the pan and have this heated, ready to take the pears directly they are prepared. Peel, quarter and core each pear then slice quickly into the hot pan. Transfer to the heat, cover and cook for 1–2 minutes or until the pears are piping hot throughout. Remove the pan from the heat and leave covered until cooled slightly. Transfer the contents of the pan to a food processor or blender and blend until smooth.

Pour the purée into a small bowl and push a piece of clingfilm down to lie directly on top of the purée. Seal the clingfilm to the edge and up the side of the bowl to cut out as much air as possible, then put in the fridge to chill.

In a heatproof bowl combine the egg yolks and half the sugar and whisk until pale and light. Bring the cream to the boil with the remaining sugar then pour on to the eggs and sugar, whisking all the while.

The bowl can now be placed over a pan of simmering water or the custard can be returned to the saucepan which is then put on a heat-diffuser mat so that it is not in direct contact with the heat. Only if you have an accurate thermometer and/or are confident that you will not overheat the custard should you put the saucepan over a gentle, direct heat. Stir the custard until it reaches 85°C/185°F or has thickened sufficiently to coat the back of a spoon. As soon as the custard has thickened plunge the base of the pan into cold water. On no account should the custard be allowed to overheat or boil or the mixture will curdle. (For how to deal with an overheated custard see page 52.) Once the custard has cooled, cover and chill in a fridge.

When ready, still freeze (see page 48) or start the ice-cream machine. Combine the chilled pear purée and custard then still freeze or pour into the machine. Churn for about 15 minutes or until the mixture is the consistency of thick cream. Quickly scrape into plastic freezer boxes and cover with waxed or greaseproof paper and a lid. Finally label, then freeze. Once frozen, allow about 20–25 minutes to soften in the fridge before serving.

Pear and Fudge Ripple

See page 165.

Pear Granita

Make exactly according to the instructions for making Pear Sorbet (see right) but add an additional 375 ml/1½ cups/12 fl oz of water. Chill thoroughly in the fridge.

For detailed instructions on how to prepare the perfect granita see page 49.

Pear Sorbet

INGREDIENTS

	Metric	U.S.	Imperial
Fully ripe pears	675 g	1½ lb	1½ lb
Sugar syrup (see page 47)	250 ml	1 cup	8 fl oz
Vanilla bean	1	1	1
Water	375 ml	1½ cups	12 fl oz
Juice of lemon, strained	1	1	1
Makes about	1.25 litres	5 cups	40 fl oz

Peel, core and slice pears and slip into simmering sugar syrup to which the vanilla bean has been added. Simmer for about 5–10 minutes very gently. Liquidize briefly and allow to cool. Add the water and the strained juice of 1 lemon. Chill in the fridge.

When chilled, either still freeze (see page 48) or start the ice-cream machine. Pour in the liquid and churn until the sorbet is firm enough to serve. If it is to be stored, quickly scrape the sorbet into plastic freezer containers, level the surface and cover with waxed or greaseproof paper and a lid. Finally label, then freeze. Once frozen, allow 30 minutes in the fridge before serving.

Red and Black Pepper Granita

This granita, a savoury one, is made with a purée of roasted red peppers, spiked with a generous amount of ground black pepper. To prepare the peppers, grill them whole until blackened all over, then leave to cool. Work over a bowl to catch the juices while skinning and seeding them. It is fiddly but try to pick out all the seeds without resorting to rinsing the peppers and washing away some of the flavour.

INGREDIENTS

	Metric	U.S.	Imperial
Red peppers	900 g	2 lb	2 lb
Granulated sugar	65 g	⅓ cup	2¼ oz
Water	500 ml	2 cups	16 fl oz
Juice of lemon	1	1	1
Salt and freshly milled black pepper			
Makes about	875 ml	3½ cups	28 fl oz

Prepare the peppers as described in the introduction. In a small saucepan combine the sugar and water. Bring slowly to the boil, stirring occasionally until the sugar has dissolved. Remove the pan from the heat and leave the syrup to cool. Put the skinned and seeded peppers in a food processor or blender with their juices and the syrup and blend until smooth. Pour the purée into a bowl and mix in the strained lemon juice, salt and a fairly generous amount of freshly milled black pepper. Taste and adjust the seasoning with the lemon juice, salt and pepper if necessary; cover and chill in the fridge.

For detailed instructions on how to prepare the perfect granita see page 49.

Serving
A good palate cleanser to serve between courses or as a summer starter with *fromage frais*.

Peppermint Rock Ice Cream

The idea of this ice cream met with some resistance, but in practice the flavour is delightful. Of course it is intended mainly for children but we find children of all ages enjoy it.

INGREDIENTS

	Metric	U.S.	Imperial
One recipe Easy No-Cook Philadelphia Vanilla Ice Cream (see page 153), omitting the vanilla bean			
Peppermint rock/mint candy cane	100 g	¼ lb	¼ lb
Makes about	1 litre	4 cups	32 fl oz

Make the Easy No-Cook Philadelphia Vanilla Ice Cream according to the recipe (see page 153), omitting the vanilla bean. When the liquid ice cream mix has chilled and is ready, either still freeze (see page 48) or to churn, start the ice-cream machine and pour it in. Whilst the ice cream is freezing, crush the peppermint rock/mint candy cane into pieces about the size of coarse sea salt crystals. (Don't do this too far ahead of time or the rock/candy will quickly go sticky and weld together if left out in the humid atmosphere of the kitchen.)

As soon as the ice cream has reached the consistency of softly whipped cream, stop the machine and quickly scrape it into plastic freezer boxes scattering with some of the crushed rock/candy between each spoonful. Give the mix 2–3 stirs with a spoon to distribute the crushed rock/candy evenly throughout the mix, then cover with waxed or greaseproof paper and a lid. Finally label, then freeze. Freeze for 1–2 hours before serving. Once frozen solid, allow 20 minutes to soften in the fridge before serving.

Pernod Parfait

See page 49.

Physalis Sorbet

This fruit is also known as Cape Gooseberry or Golden-berry. Normally it is sold as a small round orange fruit enclosed in a papery "lantern", but very recently we were surprised that a supermarket has taken to selling these fruits, minus the "lantern" in 225 g/8 oz packs. These fruits seem smaller than the usual whole type and they are certainly cheaper, so we used them to make a sorbet. The 225 g/8 oz quantity did not make much, but the flavour was exquisite. Definitely a sorbet for a small and special dinner party.

INGREDIENTS

	Metric	U.S.	Imperial
Physalis	225 g	8 oz	8 oz
Sugar syrup (see page 47)	250 ml	1 cup	8 fl oz
Lemon juice	1 Tbsp	1 Tbsp	1 Tbsp
Egg white	1	1	1
Makes about	400 ml	1⅔ cups	14 fl oz

Put the fruit into a sieve or colander and rinse with cold water, drain and dry on paper towels. Put the fruit into a food processor with the sugar syrup and lemon juice and process in short bursts of 5 seconds about 5 times. Strain through a fine sieve to remove the seeds; press the pulp to extract as much liquid as possible but avoid working the small seeds through the sieve, as their presence will spoil the consistency of the sorbet. Chill in the fridge.

When ready, still freeze (see page 48) or start the ice-cream machine. Pour in the mixture and churn for about 10 minutes. Beat the egg white until loosened, then add to the machine and churn for another 10 minutes or until the ice cream is the consistency of softly whipped cream. Quickly scrape into plastic freezer boxes, level the mixture and cover with waxed or greaseproof paper and a lid. Finally label, then freeze for about 1 hour before serving. If frozen solid, allow about 20 minutes in the fridge to soften sufficiently to serve.

Pineapple, Coconut and Banana Frozen Yoghurt

We prefer to use a full fat yoghurt for this ice. It gives a more rounded flavour to temper the fresh pineapple. It is important to use a fully ripe pineapple; then success is guaranteed.

INGREDIENTS

	Metric	U.S.	Imperial
Prepared fresh pineapple	370 g	2 cups	13 oz
Banana	1	1	1
Fresh grated coconut	20 g	¼ cup	4 Tbsp
Soft light brown sugar	100 g	½ cup	3½ oz
White rum	2 Tbsp	2 Tbsp	2 Tbsp
Natural yoghurt	240 g	1 cup	8½ oz
Freshly squeezed lime juice	1 Tbsp	1 Tbsp	1 Tbsp
Makes about	1 litre	4 cups	32 fl oz

Chop the pineapple in chunks and put them in a food processor or blender with the peeled, halved banana and remaining ingredients. Blend until almost smooth. Chill in the fridge.

When ready, still freeze (see page 48) or start the ice-cream machine. Pour in the yoghurt mixture and leave to churn until firm enough to serve. To store, quickly scrape into plastic freezer boxes and cover with waxed or greaseproof paper and a lid. Finally label, then freeze. Once frozen, allow about 20–25 minutes to soften in the fridge before serving.

Pineapple Sage Granita/Sorbet

See Herb Granitas/Sorbets pages 99 and 100.

Pistachio Ice Cream

You might detect from the following that feelings run high about pistachio ice cream in this household. More times than we wish to recall, from every sort of outlet we have eaten pistachio ice creams that are so bad they beggar description. Even up-market restaurants are no guarantee of a passable product. Time and time again we order in hope, even when just colour has told us there is none. It seems most purveyors rely on brainwashing and nothing else; they tell you it is pistachio, it arrives a sufficiently lurid green; ergo it is pistachio. Except the flavour . . . The flavour is often as far from pistachio as you can get.

Of course pistachios are expensive, and skinning the things can drive you to drink, but if you are going to call it pistachio ice cream let's throw away the bottles of flavouring and colour and let the pistachio speak for itself.

Our combination of toasted and untoasted nuts gives the maximum flavour and best appearance.

NOTE: *It is necessary to toast and grind the pistachios the day before making the ice cream.*

INGREDIENTS

	Metric	U.S.	Imperial
Shelled pistachios	115 g	Scant cup	4 oz
Whipping/heavy cream (36 per cent fat)	625 ml	2½ cups	20 fl oz
Vanilla sugar (see page 36)	150 g	¾ cup	5¼ oz
Makes about	750 ml	3 cups	24 fl oz

Preheat the oven to 180°C/350°F/Gas Mark 4. Take half the pistachios and toast them in the oven for 8 minutes. This is when they just begin to smell toasted, but are not coloured. Remove from the oven and leave to cool.

Put the toasted pistachios in a food processor or blender with the sugar and process in short bursts until the nuts are reduced to a fine meal; put this in a measuring jug. Heat the cream to just below boiling point. When it starts to bubble around the edge, immediately pour it on to the ground nuts and sugar in the measuring jug. Leave to cool, then stir, cover and refrigerate overnight.

The following day, put the remaining nuts in a very small pan, pour in boiling water and bring back to the boil; boil for 1 minute then remove the pan from the heat.

Drain the nuts in a sieve and leave to cool for 1 minute or so before slipping off the skins. Chop the nuts 2–3 times, so that they remain chunky – almost in halves. If the nuts are skinned much ahead in time they discolour, so leave this job until the ice cream is ready to freeze.

When ready, still freeze (see page 48) or start the ice-cream machine and pour in the chilled pistachio cream. Churn until the mixture is the consistency of whipped cream. Add the skinned nuts and continue to churn just long enough to mix in the nuts. Quickly transfer the ice cream to plastic freezer boxes, level and cover with waxed or greaseproof paper and a lid. Finally label, then freeze.

Serve within 2 hours. If frozen solid, allow about 20 minutes in the fridge to soften before serving.

Plum Granita

Make exactly as per the recipe for Plum Sorbet (see below). However, when you have made the mixture add 375 ml/1½ cups/12 fl oz of water. Mix well, cover and chill in the fridge.

For detailed instructions on how to prepare the perfect granita see page 49.

"I wish I weren't so cold." A Bonzo dog, popular in the early 1920s.

Plum Sorbet

When the market allows, or if you plan your freezing, it makes a pretty effect and interesting eating to serve a trilogy of plum sorbets; dark purple-skinned, yellow and green. If you confine yourself to one variety the sorbet can be served with a little plum brandy or eau de vie or with Noyau Sherbet (see page 121) and Almond Tuiles (see page 160) or macaroons.

INGREDIENTS

	Metric	U.S.	Imperial
Plums	675 g	1½ lb	1½ lb
Sugar syrup (see page 47)	250 ml	1 cup	8 fl oz
Lemon juice	2 tsp	2 tsp	2 tsp
Makes about	1 litre	4 cups	32 fl oz

Rinse, then halve and stone the plums and either microwave in a covered dish with 1 Tbsp of water until tender, or cook gently, covered, in a thick non-reactive saucepan until tender. When cool enough, remove the skins by simply picking them out; then liquidise the flesh with the sugar syrup, and add the lemon juice to taste. Transfer to a jug, then cover and chill in the fridge.

When ready, still freeze (see page 48) or start the machine. Pour in the plum purée and churn until the sorbet is firm enough to serve. If it is to be stored, quickly scrape the sorbet into plastic freezer containers. Level the surface and cover with waxed or greaseproof paper and a lid. Finally label, then freeze. Once frozen allow about 20 minutes in the fridge before serving.

Plum Blush Ice Cream

Recently it has been almost impossible to buy home-grown plums in Britain, so the dark/black skinned imported varieties have to do. Blush is a range of California wines based on the Zinfandel grape. For a brief time the white juice is left in contact with the black skin of the grapes to produce a rose-coloured wine. This is light and fresh with quite a berry fruit flavour – ideal for pairing with plums whose flavour can be elusive in ice cream.

INGREDIENTS

	Metric	U.S.	Imperial
Dark skinned plums	450 g	1 lb	1 lb
Medium dry California Blush	125 ml	½ cup	4 fl oz
Whipping/heavy cream (36 per cent fat)	250 ml	1 cup	8 fl oz
Egg yolks	2	2	2
Granulated sugar	100 g	½ cup	3½ oz
Vanilla extract	¼ tsp	¼ tsp	¼ tsp
Makes about	1 litre	4 cups	32 fl oz

Wash, halve, stone and cut each plum into 6 or 8. Put the fruit into a medium-sized pan, pour in the wine and bring to the boil. Lower the heat to give a gentle simmer then cover and cook gently for 10 minutes, stirring once or twice during this time. When cooked, remove the pan from the heat, cool a little then whirl to a rather coarse textured pulp in a food processor or blender. Cover and chill in the fridge.

Using the above quantities of cream, egg yolks, sugar and vanilla extract, make up a custard. Cook, cool and chill as outlined in the method for French Vanilla Ice Cream (see page 51).

When ready combine the chilled plum pulp and custard and stir together with the vanilla extract. Still freeze (see page 48) or start the ice-cream machine. Pour in the mixture and churn for about 20 minutes or until the ice cream is the consistency of whipped cream. Quickly scrape into plastic freezer boxes, level the mixture and cover with waxed or greaseproof paper and a lid. Finally label, then freeze. After about 1–1½ hours the ice cream will be firm enough to serve. Or, if frozen solid, allow about 20 minutes in the fridge to soften sufficiently to serve.

Pomegranate Sorbet

A remarkable flavour, and if you use the pomegranates that have a positive pink or crimson flesh, rather than those which are almost white, this sorbet will be a glorious fuchsia red. Frances Bissell, the Times *cookery writer who has a talent for marrying flavours, suggests serving a pomegranate sorbet with fresh figs. She is right; it is a very successful combination.*

INGREDIENTS

	Metric	U.S.	Imperial
Pomegranates	3 large or 4 small	3 large or 4 small	3 large or 4 small
Caster/Ultra fine sugar	150 g	¾ cup	5¼ oz
Lemon juice	3 Tbsp	3 Tbsp	3 Tbsp
Makes about	625 ml	2½ cups	20 fl oz

Halve and squeeze the juice from the pomegranates as you would a citrus fruit, using a lemon squeezer. Any debris retained in the lemon squeezer should be transferred into a plastic sieve positioned over a bowl; then, either manually squeeze the pulp or press it *hard* to extract the last of the juice; there should be about 500 ml/2 cups/16 fl oz. Stir the sugar and strained lemon juice into the pomegranate juice, then cover and chill in the fridge.

When ready, still freeze (see page 48) or start the ice-cream machine. Pour in the pomegranate juice and churn until the sorbet is firm enough to serve. Or to store, quickly scrape the sorbet into plastic freezer containers. Level the surface and cover with waxed or greaseproof paper and a lid. Finally label, then freeze. Once frozen, allow about 10 minutes in the fridge before serving.

(right) Cold Kitchen from Urbain Dubois, Cuisine Artistique 1872.

Spiced Pumpkin Ice Cream

If you like pumpkin pie you will like this ice cream. Do not worry about the type of pumpkin to use. Whatever the colour or shape of pumpkins, they all seem to taste the same, though be prepared for wastage. Cut a generous size wedge (about 700 to 900 g/1½ to 2 lbs). Scrape away all the seeds and woolly strands, slice into smaller wedges then into good-sized chunks, removing the rind as you go. Preferred method of cooking is steaming; simply steam over simmering water until tender then leave to cool a little before puréeing in a food processor or blender. The flavour is preferable to canned pumpkin.

Using the above quantities of milk, light brown soft sugar and egg yolks prepare and cook a custard according to the method for making French Vanilla Ice Cream (see page 51), whisking the vanilla extract and the spices into the yolks and sugar before adding the hot milk. Once the cooked custard has cooled in a cold water bath, beat in the cold pumpkin purée and cream. Taste and add the brandy and more spice if preferred, then cover and chill in the fridge.

When ready, still freeze (see page 48) or start the ice-cream machine and pour in the pumpkin custard via a sieve, as sometimes small pieces of pumpkin remain. Freeze until the ice cream is the consistency of softly whipped cream. Quickly scrape into plastic freezer boxes, level the surface and cover with waxed or greaseproof paper and a lid. Finally label, then freeze. Leave for a minimum of 1 hour before serving. If frozen solid, allow about 20 minutes in the fridge to soften the ice cream sufficiently to serve.

INGREDIENTS

	Metric	U.S.	Imperial
Milk	375 ml	1½ cups	12 fl oz
Light brown soft sugar	200 g	1 cup	7 oz
Egg yolks	3	3	3
Vanilla extract	½ tsp	½ tsp	½ tsp
Ground cloves	pinch	pinch	pinch
Ground ginger	½ tsp	½ tsp	½ tsp
Ground cinnamon	¼ tsp	¼ tsp	¼ tsp
Ground pepper	⅛ tsp	⅛ tsp	⅛ tsp
Pumpkin purée	250 ml	1 cup	8 fl oz
Whipping/heavy cream (36 per cent fat)	185 ml	¾ cup	6 fl oz
Brandy	2 tsp	2 tsp	2 tsp
Makes about	1 litre	4 cups	32 fl oz

(above) John Bull and his family in a London ice café. Drawn by J. J. Chalon, *c.* 1820.

Quince Sorbet

In his excellent book Cultivated Fruits of Britain, their Origins and History, *Frederick Roach writes that quinces were extensively cultivated in Britain during the sixteenth to eighteenth centuries when this wonderful fruit was fully appreciated, "No other fruit having so many uses both for meat dishes and sweet courses." He observes that "the decline of the quince seems to have coincided with the increase in cultivation of soft fruits, particularly the strawberry." Well, now the strawberry is ubiquitous and quinces are hard to find. Occasionally American or Cypriot imports appear in British shops but these are a pale shadow of the British quince varieties. If necessary, beg, borrow or steal your neighbours' quinces in order to get the exquisite aroma and remarkable taste that is unlike any other fruit. Serve the sorbet with pear and apple ice cream or sorbets.*

NOTE: To store quinces in the freezer; peel, quarter and remove the core, then blanch for 2 minutes in boiling water, allow to cool and dry on a wire rack, then freeze in tightly sealed plastic bags. These can be stored for up to 1 year in the freezer.

INGREDIENTS

	Metric	U.S.	Imperial
Quinces (6–8 small)	450 g	1 lb	1 lb
Sugar syrup (see page 47)	500 ml	2 cups	16 fl oz
Lemon juice	4½ Tbsp	4½ Tbsp	4½ Tbsp
Makes about	750 ml	3 cups	24 fl oz

Peel, quarter and core the quinces. Do not worry if they are discoloured or an uneven colour, this is normal. Put the quinces in an enamel saucepan with the sugar syrup, cover with a lid, heat to boiling point, then simmer gently for 15 minutes. Liquidise, hot, until a smooth pulp, then immediately sieve first through a medium sieve then afterwards through a fine one. This is to remove the coarse granular texture of the quince which we think spoils the finished texture of the sorbet. If you like a coarse texture in your sorbet omit the second sieving. Add the lemon juice to taste. Chill in the fridge.

When ready, still freeze (see page 48) or start the ice-cream machine and churn for about 20 minutes or until the sorbet is firm enough to serve. To store, quickly scrape into plastic freezer boxes and cover with a piece of waxed or greaseproof paper and a lid. Finally label, then freeze. Serve within 1 hour. If frozen hard, allow 10–15 minutes in the fridge to soften sufficiently to serve.

NOTE: Quinces contain a high proportion of pectin so there is no need to add egg whites to stabilise this sorbet.

Raspberry Ice Cream

This is one of the very few ices where we suggest adding gelatine. This is because there is a large amount of water in raspberries and gelatine improves the texture of the finished ice cream.

INGREDIENTS

	Metric	U.S.	Imperial
Raspberries	450 g	1 lb (3 cups)	1 lb
Granulated sugar	100 g	½ cup	3½ oz
Gelatine	2 tsp	2 tsp	2 tsp
Hot water	65 ml	¼ cup	2 fl oz
Lemon juice	1 Tbsp	1 Tbsp	1 Tbsp
Framboise★ (optional)	2 Tbsp	2 Tbsp	2 Tbsp
Whipping/heavy cream (36 per cent fat)	375 ml	1½ cups	12 fl oz
Makes about	1 litre	4 cups	32 fl oz

★ Raspberry-flavoured liqueur.

Liquidise the raspberries with the sugar and sieve to remove the pips (you can leave them in if you like the texture that the pips give the finished ice cream). Dissolve the gelatine in the hot water and add to the purée with the lemon juice and framboise, if used. The framboise is optional but sometimes helps the flavour of the raspberries, especially at the end of the season. Chill in the fridge.

When ready, still freeze (see page 48) or start the ice-cream machine. Combine the chilled purée and the cream, pour in the mixture and churn for about 20 minutes or until the ice cream is the consistency of whipped cream. Quickly scrape into plastic freezer boxes, level the mixture and cover with waxed or greaseproof paper and a lid. Finally label, then freeze. After about 1–1½ hours the ice cream will be firm enough to serve. Or if frozen solid allow about 20 minutes in the fridge to soften sufficiently to serve.

Raspberry Sorbet

This can be made with either fresh or frozen raspberries so keep some handy in the freezer in the winter.

INGREDIENTS

	Metric	U.S.	Imperial
Raspberries	450 g	1 lb	1 lb
Sugar syrup (see page 47)	375 ml	1½ cups	12 fl oz
Juice of lemons, strained	2	2	2
Makes about	1 litre	4 cups	32 fl oz

Pick over the raspberries, carefully discarding any suspect fruit. Even in these days of great concern over all manner of sprays, in our opinion raspberries are such a fragile fruit, they should never be washed. Transfer the berries to a food processor or blender, pour in the measured syrup and blend to a uniform pulp. Have ready a plastic sieve positioned over a bowl. Strain the pulp, rubbing the residue through until all that remains are the seeds. Add the strained lemon juice, stir, cover and chill in the fridge.

When ready, still freeze (see page 48) or start the ice-cream machine. Pour in the chilled raspberry purée and continue to freeze until the sorbet is firm enough to serve. Or to store, quickly scrape into plastic freezer boxes and cover with a piece of waxed or greaseproof paper and a lid. Finally label, then freeze. Serve within 1 hour, or if frozen hard, allow 20–25 minutes in the fridge to soften sufficiently to serve.

**A sallow waiter brings me beans and
   pork . . .
Outside there's fury in the firmament.
Ice cream, of course will follow; and I'm
   content.
O Babylon! O Carthage! O New York!**

Siegfried Sassoon (1886–1967),
"Storm on 5th Avenue"

Raspberry Spoom

This spoom can be made with either fresh or frozen raspberries, making it a wonderful stand-by dessert for the winter.

INGREDIENTS

	Metric	U.S.	Imperial
Raspberries (fresh)	250 g	2 cups	8¾ oz
or frozen	250 g	8¾ oz	8¾ oz
Sugar syrup (see page 47)	250 ml	1 cup	8 fl oz
Lemon juice	1–2 Tbsp	1–2 Tbsp	1–2 Tbsp
Egg whites	2	2	2
Granulated sugar	70 g	⅔ cup	2½ oz
Makes about	875 ml	3½ cups	28 fl oz

Liquidise the raspberries with the sugar syrup, then strain them through a fine nylon sieve to remove the pips. Add 1 Tbsp of lemon juice, taste and add more lemon juice, half a teaspoon at a time, until the purée is just sweet. Cover and chill thoroughly in the fridge.

In a large grease-free bowl beat the egg whites with a hand-held beater until they form soft peaks, then gradually add the sugar until it is absorbed and the egg whites are in a fairly stiff peaks. They need to be stiff enough to incorporate the purée but not so stiff that you cannot fold in the purée. Fold into the chilled purée making sure that the purée is completely mixed with the meringue, then transfer to a plastic freezer box and cover with a piece of greaseproof or waxed paper and a lid. Finally label, then freeze. Eat after about 2 hours, or if frozen solid, allow about 20 minutes in the fridge to soften sufficiently to serve.

(right) A Pashley motorised ice-cream tricycle, *c.* 1925.

Redcurrant Granita

There is something altogether clear and crystalline about the colour and taste of redcurrants, and so it is apt that they make a more satisfactory granita than ice cream or sorbet. Serve just on its own in a tall glass or in a shallow bowl. If you prefer, spoon over a little vodka or gin just before serving.

INGREDIENTS

	Metric	U.S.	Imperial
Redcurrants	450 g	1 lb	1 lb
Water	375 ml	1½ cups	12 fl oz
Sugar syrup (see page 47)	250 ml	1 cup	8 fl oz
Lemon juice, strained	1 Tbsp	1 Tbsp	1 Tbsp
Makes about	750 ml	3 cups	24 fl oz

Working over a colander or sieve strip the redcurrants from the stalks using the prongs of a fork, discarding all damaged or small, underripe berries. Rinse with cold water, drain and tip the redcurrants into a saucepan. Pour in the 375 ml/1½ cups/12 fl oz of water, and simmer gently, uncovered, until the berries have burst. Process briefly in a food processor or blender then rub through a plastic sieve to remove the pips. Stir the sugar syrup and strained lemon juice into the purée, cover and transfer to the fridge to chill.

For detailed instructions on how to prepare the perfect granita see page 49.

RHUBARB

Auberge de l'Ill, at Illhaeusern has a wonderful dessert that is eight different miniature rhubarb desserts on a plate. A brilliant idea for this humble and often forgotten fruit. Among the eight were both a rhubarb sorbet and a rhubarb ice cream.

Champagne Rhubarb Marbled Vanilla Ice Cream

Choose young pink/red stems, not too thin but no more than thumb-thick; never green. Marbling the ice cream with rhubarb has the effect of being able to taste the two flavours clearly at the same time.

INGREDIENTS

	Metric	U.S.	Imperial
One recipe French Vanilla Ice Cream (see page 51)			
Prepared rhubarb	225 g	8 oz	8 oz
Water	1 Tbsp	1 Tbsp	1 Tbsp
Granulated sugar	2 Tbsp	2 Tbsp	2 Tbsp
Makes about	1 litre	4 cups	32 fl oz

Cut the rhubarb into 2 cm/¾ inch lengths and put them in a small saucepan with the water. Bring to a simmer, cover and cook gently, stirring occasionally until the rhubarb is tender. Remove the pan from the heat and stir in the sugar. Process only briefly in a food processor or blender; it is better if the rhubarb keeps some texture. Transfer to a bowl, cover and chill. Make the French Vanilla Ice Cream (see page 51), churning until it is the consistency of softly whipped cream. Put alternative spoonfuls of ice cream and rhubarb pulp in a plastic freezer box then fold the two mixtures together briefly so that clear seams of rhubarb pulp are still discernible throughout the vanilla ice cream. Smooth the surface and cover with waxed or greaseproof paper and a lid. Finally label, then freeze until firm. If frozen hard, allow 20–30 minutes to soften in the fridge before serving.

Rhubarb Sorbet

INGREDIENTS

	Metric	U.S.	Imperial
Prepared rhubarb	500 g	1 lb 2 oz	1 lb 2 oz
Water	4 Tbsp	¼ cup	2 fl oz
Sugar syrup (see page 47)	500 ml	2 cups	16 fl oz
Juice of lemons	2	2	2
Makes about	1 litre	4 cups	32 fl oz

Cut the rhubarb into 2 cm/¾ inch lengths and put them in a small saucepan with the water. Bring to a simmer, cover and cook gently, stirring occasionally, until the rhubarb is tender. Leave to cool before transferring to a food processor or blender. Pour in the sugar syrup and blend until smooth. Sieve the purée into a bowl and add the lemon juice. Cover and chill in the fridge.

When ready, still freeze (see page 48) or start the ice-cream machine. Pour in the purée and continue to churn until the sorbet is firm enough to serve. Or to store, quickly scrape into plastic freezer boxes and cover with a piece of waxed or greaseproof paper and a lid. Finally label, then freeze. Serve within 1 hour, or if frozen hard, allow 20–25 minutes in the fridge to soften sufficiently to serve.

Serving
Serve with a little Ginger Wine drizzled over.

PROGRESS OF CIVILISATION.

Ramoneur (on Donkey). "FITCH US OUT ANOTHER PEN'NORTH O' STRAWBERRY ICE, WITH A DOLLOP OF LEMON WATER IN IT."

Punch, 1854.

Rice Ice Cream

Mrs Marshall in her Book of Ices *(1885) features a rice ice cream which contains bay leaves, cinnamon and lemon peel. In her book* Fancy Ices *(1894) flavourings for a rice ice cream become even more complicated with a recipe for Sicilian ice cream containing coriander, cinnamon, white rum, rosewater, citron peel, shredded ginger and dried cherries. Needless to say with all these additions the delicate flavour of the rice is lost, which is a great shame. In Italy, one of the countries where this ice cream is still regularly made, it occasionally has such additions as candied cherries and oranges, toasted almonds and rum, which you can add if you see fit. But you will also get rice ice cream served to you, unadorned save for a flavouring of vanilla and perhaps a chilled fruit sauce. This is to eat it at its best and enjoy the ice cream for what it is.*

INGREDIENTS

	Metric	U.S.	Imperial
Pudding (short grain) rice	110 g	½ cup	3¾ oz
Milk	500 ml	2 cups	16 fl oz
Vanilla sugar (see page 36)	170 g	1 cup minus 1 Tbsp	6 oz
Whipping/heavy cream (36 per cent fat), chilled	500 ml	2 cups	16 fl oz
Makes about	1.25 litres	5 cups	40 fl oz

Rinse the rice, drain and put in the top half of a double saucepan (or in a heatproof bowl over a saucepan of water) with the milk and the vanilla sugar. Bring to the boil, over direct heat, stirring constantly. Transfer to sit over the base pan of simmering water, cover and continue to cook for a further 40 minutes or until the rice is perfectly tender. Remove the top half of the pan from the heat and leave to cool, still covered, until the rice mixture reaches room temperature, then transfer to the fridge to chill.

When ready, still freeze (see page 48) or start the ice-cream machine, stir the chilled cream into the rice then pour into the machine. Churn for about 15 minutes or until the mixture is the consistency of thick cream. Quickly scrape into plastic freezer boxes and cover with a piece of waxed or greaseproof paper and a lid. Finally label, then freeze. Allow to freeze overnight.

NOTE: Because of the high starch content of this ice cream you must allow it about 1 hour in the fridge to soften sufficiently to serve. Do not try to thaw it at room temperature; the outside will melt while the centre remains rock solid.

Rice Ice Cream with Rum-Soaked Fruits

If you want to serve a plain rice ice cream, for the best flavour we recommend cooking the rice as outlined in the recipe above. But if you add crystallised fruits, nuts and rum the emphasis in flavour switches to these, so a can or carton of creamed rice pudding can be substituted very successfully. The flavour of the candied fruits will now come to the fore so, if possible, try to buy the caps of orange, lemon and citron, rather than the brands of ready chopped mixed peel.

INGREDIENTS

	Metric	U.S.	Imperial
Mixed crystallised cherries, orange, lemon and citron, finely diced	90 g	½ cup	3¼ oz
Dark rum	85 ml	⅓ cup	3 fl oz
Whipping/heavy cream (36 per cent fat)	250 ml	1 cup	8 fl oz
Vanilla sugar (see page 36)	100 g	½ cup	3½ oz
Toasted almonds, chopped	40 g	¼ cup	1½ oz
One can/carton creamed rice pudding	435 g	15 oz	15 oz
Makes about	1 litre	4 cups	32 fl oz

Put the finely diced crystallised fruits into a small saucepan with the rum and bring to simmering point. Cover and continue to simmer gently for 3–4 minutes, or until the peel is perfectly tender and only about 1 tablespoon of liquid remains. Leave to cool, covered. Combine with remaining ingredients, stir well, cover and chill in the fridge.

When ready, still freeze (see page 48) or start the ice-cream machine and pour in the mixture. Continue running until the ice cream is firm enough to serve; or to store, quickly scrape into plastic freezer boxes and cover with a piece of waxed or greaseproof paper and a lid. Finally label, then freeze. Once the ice cream becomes solid it will need about 20 minutes in the fridge before it is soft enough to scoop.

Ricotta Ice Cream

We had reservations about basing an ice cream on so delicate a flavour as ricotta, but were surprised how successful it proved to be. Both the flavour and the texture are clearly ricotta.

INGREDIENTS

	Metric	U.S.	Imperial
Milk	400 ml	1⅔ cups	13½ fl oz
Granulated sugar	220 g	1 cup plus 1 Tbsp	7¾ oz
Egg yolks	3	3	3
Ricotta	250 g	2¼ cups	8¾ oz
Whipping/heavy cream (36 per cent fat), chilled	150 ml	⅔ cup	5 fl oz
Dark rum	1 Tbsp	1 Tbsp	1 Tbsp
Makes about	900 ml	3¾ cups	30 fl oz

Using the above quantities of milk, granulated sugar and egg yolks, prepare and cook a custard according to the method for making French Vanilla Ice Cream (see page 51), omitting the vanilla bean. Continue up to the point when the custard has reached 85°C/185°F and is removed from the heat. Now gradually beat in pieces of the crumbled ricotta and continue to beat vigorously until the custard is almost smooth. (Do not worry if a few small lumps remain, these will be broken down in the churning process.) To cool the custard quickly the pan can now be put into a cold water bath. When cold, remove, cover and chill in the fridge.

When ready, still freeze (see page 48) or start the ice-cream machine. Stir the chilled cream and rum into the custard then pour into the machine and churn until the mix has frozen to the consistency of whipped cream. To store, quickly scrape into plastic freezer boxes and cover with waxed or greaseproof paper and a lid. Finally label, then freeze. When frozen allow about 25–30 minutes in the fridge to soften sufficiently to serve.

Serving
Could be served on a plate flooded with a delicate coffee sauce.

Rose Petal Ice Cream

For this recipe you will need a highly scented rose. It used to be the case that most new hybrid roses looked wonderful but had little or no scent. However, growers now recognise the public demand for both beauty and fragrance and there is now no shortage of wonderfully fragrant varieties available. A selection of roses is in the margin notes.
NOTE: *Please make sure you use untreated roses, i.e. unsprayed roses only.*

INGREDIENTS

	Metric	U.S.	Imperial
Rose heads	3	3	3
Milk	125 ml	½ cup	4 fl oz
Whipping/heavy cream (36 per cent fat)	375 ml	1½ cups	12 fl oz
Egg yolks	2	2	2
Vanilla sugar (see page 36)	100 g	½ cup	3½ oz
Makes about	500 ml	2 cups	16 fl oz

Pull the petals from the 3 roses and check carefully for signs of wildlife; there is often a surprising amount. In a saucepan combine the petals, milk and cream and stirring, bring to just below boiling point. Remove the pan from the heat, cover and leave to infuse. Taste after 10 minutes to see if the flavour is strong enough (how long it will take varies considerably according to the type of rose), then strain to remove the petals. In a heatproof bowl combine the egg yolks and vanilla sugar and beat until they take on a pale colour and lighter consistency. Now gradually beat in the flavoured milk and cream. The bowl can now be placed over a pan of simmering water, or the custard can be returned to the saucepan which is then put on top of a heat-diffuser mat so that it is not in direct contact with the heat. Only if you have an accurate thermometer and/or you are confident that you will not overheat the custard should you put the saucepan over gentle, direct heat. Stir the custard until it reaches 85°C/185°F, or until it has thickened sufficiently to coat the back of a spoon. As soon as the custard reaches this stage plunge the base of the pan into cold water. On no account should the custard be allowed to overheat or boil as the mixture will curdle. (For how to deal with an overheated custard see page 52.) Once cool, the custard can be covered with a circle of lightly buttered greaseproof paper and transferred to the fridge to chill.

When ready, still freeze (see page 48) or start the ice-cream machine. Pour the custard into the machine and churn for about 15 minutes or until the mixture is the consistency of thick cream. Quickly scrape into plastic freezer boxes and cover with a piece of waxed or greaseproof paper and a lid. Finally label, then freeze for a minimum of 1 hour. If frozen solid, allow 20 minutes in the fridge so that the ice cream is soft enough to serve. Serve alone scattered with fresh or crystallised rose petals or with perfectly ripe strawberries.

NOTE: Additional torn rose petals can be added to the ice cream at the last stage of churning. We insist (!) that this ice cream must be served fresh, particularly if fresh rose petals are added at the end of the recipe.

For further excellent advice contact The Royal National Rose Society (see Useful Addresses page 184).

Scented Hybrid Tea Roses: Alec's Red; Blue Moon; Deep Secret; Double Delight; Ena Harkness; Fragrant Cloud; Loving Memory; Papa Meilland; Pristine; Super Star; Velvet Fragrance
Scented Bush Roses: Arthur Bell; Dearest; Elizabeth of Glamis; Escapade; Fragrant Delight; Margaret Merrill; Paul Cherville; Scented Air; Sheila's Perfume; Southampton

Rosemary Sorbet

Delicious and very refreshing but don't attempt this with dried rosemary.

INGREDIENTS

	Metric	U.S.	Imperial
Fresh sprigs of rosemary	5×15 cm	5×6 inches	5×6 inches
Sugar syrup (see page 47)	500 ml	2 cups	16 fl oz
Dry white wine	250 ml	1 cup	8 fl oz
Water	250 ml	1 cup	8 fl oz
Lemon juice	3–4 Tbsp	3–4 Tbsp	3–4 Tbsp
Makes about	1 litre	4 cups	32 fl oz

Rinse and dry the rosemary sprigs before putting them into a small saucepan with the sugar syrup. Bring slowly to the boil then remove the pan from the heat, cover and leave to infuse for a minimum of 30 minutes. Add the remaining ingredients, re-cover and chill in the fridge. The mixture can be left overnight.

When ready, still freeze (see page 48) or start the ice-cream machine and continue until the sorbet is firm enough to serve. Or to store, quickly scrape into plastic freezer containers and cover with a piece of waxed or greaseproof paper and a lid. Finally label, then freeze. Once the sorbet becomes solid it will need about 30 minutes in the fridge before it is soft enough to scoop.

**Mother, may I milk sherbet make?
Yes, my darling daughter;
Order the milk you're told to "take",
But the Sherbet make of water.**

New Orleans rhyme, 1915

In 1915 New Orleans banned any milk sherbet that contained less than 10 per cent butterfat. However, the ordinance apparently excluded frozen water or water ices. It is probably the adoption of this type of ordinance elsewhere that led to sorbets being referred to as sherbets in America.

Rosewater Sorbet

Rosewater, a distillation of red rose petals, has the intense perfumed flavour of its source. It delivers into your mouth the glory of an old-fashioned rose garden in full bloom, but at the same time has a surprising spicy, smoky quality, which is why rose petals are often married with blends of China tea. Be sure to buy triple distilled rosewater or be very disappointed.

INGREDIENTS

	Metric	U.S.	Imperial
Sugar syrup (see page 47)	375 ml	1½ cups	12 fl oz
Water	375 ml	1½ cups	12 fl oz
Rosewater	2 Tbsp	2 Tbsp	2 Tbsp
Juice of lemon, strained	1	1	1
Egg white	1	1	1
Makes about	1.1 litres	4½ cups	36 fl oz

In a large measuring jug combine the sugar syrup, water, rosewater and the lemon juice. Chill in the fridge.

When ready, still freeze (see page 48) or pour into the ice-cream machine and churn for 5 minutes or until it becomes opaque. Using a fork, beat the egg white until loosened and add to the sorbet with the machine still running. Continue until the sorbet is firm enough to serve, or to store, quickly scrape into plastic freezer containers and cover with a piece of waxed paper and a lid. Finally label, then freeze. Once the sorbet becomes solid it will need about 30 minutes in the fridge before it is soft enough to scoop.

SA'ALAB

Throughout the Middle East a traditional ice cream is made of milk, sugar, and some flavouring, but in particular contains the ground root of an orchid – *Orchis mascula* (LINN). It is this ingredient, called sa'alab, that gives the ice cream its name. However, this can be confusing because regional variation and difficulties in translation give rise to quite a number of similar words meaning the same thing e.g. salap, salab, salepi etc.

But the ice cream itself is quite distinctive, having an intense whiteness, a peculiar chewy elasticity and a faintly metallic flavour; all due to the sa'alab. Intrigued by this ice cream, we got more than a little confused when our researches turned up far more permutations on the quantity of sa'alab than it had names. Margaret Shaida, author of *The Legendary Cuisine of Persia* and an expert on Middle Eastern foods, came to our rescue with advice and information that enabled us to start sorting out the anomalies.

Do not attempt to substitute cornflour for sa'alab. It makes a very different type of ice cream. While sa'alab is undeniably a difficult ingredient to find, a few Middle Eastern delicatessens do sell it in the form of a white powder (see Useful Addresses page 184.) The search is worthwhile for the unusual dimension sa'alab gives to the Western idea of ice cream.

Rosewater Sa'alab

INGREDIENTS

	Metric	U.S.	Imperial
Milk	250 ml	1 cup	8 fl oz
Granulated sugar	125 g	½ cup + 2 Tbsp	4½ oz
Sa'alab (see intro)	1 tsp	1 tsp	1 tsp
Rosewater	1 tsp	1 tsp	1 tsp
Makes about	300 ml	1¼ cups	10½ fl oz

Put the milk and sugar and sa'alab into a food processor or blender, and blend in short bursts until the sugar is dissolved. Add the rosewater, 1 tsp or to taste. Chill in the fridge.

When ready, still freeze (see page 48) or start the ice-cream machine, pour in the flavoured milk mixture and churn the sa'alab until ready to serve, about 10 minutes. Serve at once; or to store quickly scrape into plastic freezer boxes, level then cover with waxed or greaseproof paper and a lid. Finally label, then freeze. Once frozen sa'alab takes about 10 minutes in the fridge to soften sufficiently to serve.

Variations

Sa'alab can be made plain (i.e. omitting the rosewater) in which case it is usually served sprinkled with grated bitter chocolate or with chips of frozen clotted cream.

A saffron sa'alab can be made by substituting a pinch of saffron for the rosewater. Soak the saffron in the milk for 30 minutes before starting the recipe.

Saffron Ice Cream

Quite a straightforward ice cream to make but be careful, the saffron flavour is a little tricky to get right. Very little saffron goes a very long way, so a correspondingly minute excess can give a flavour that is downright nasty in a medicinal way. It must also be said that the quality of saffron varies, whether it be in the form of fine red strands (properly the dried stigmas of Crocus sativus) or powder. Since the strands are more readily available, more reliable and slightly cheaper, we normally use these, and for consistency stick to a good quality saffron from around Valencia in Spain. But hair-like strands of saffron are impossible to measure accurately so our advice is to take a modest pinch and proceed with the recipe. Should you think that the flavour is not strong enough, rather than adding more saffron, leave the custard overnight before churning. This will allow the flavour to develop to its maximum.
If you have overdone it in a big way, make up a second batch of unflavoured custard and add it to the first, then churn.

INGREDIENTS

	Metric	U.S.	Imperial
One recipe Rich French Vanilla Ice Cream (see page 51), omitting the vanilla bean and substituting a pinch of saffron strands.			
Makes about	800 ml	3¼ cups	26 fl oz

Follow the method for making Rich French Vanilla Ice Cream (see page 51) up to the stage where the thickened custard is removed from the heat. At this point, add the saffron strands then leave aside to cool, before covering and chilling in the fridge.

Still freeze (see page 48) or churn in an ice-cream machine. After churning the ice cream make sure all the strands of saffron are scraped from the ice-cream paddle and stirred into the ice cream before freezing.

Serving
Serve in a glass with scoops of Honey Ice Cream (see page 100) and Apricot Sorbet (see page 57) so that all the flavours mingle.

Sherry Parfait

See page 49.

Sour Cream Ice Cream with Peanut Brittle

The very slightly sour flavour of the ice cream counterbalances nicely the additional sweetness of the brittle, giving a taste that will seduce even those who hate peanuts.

INGREDIENTS

	Metric	U.S.	Imperial
Milk	250 ml	1 cup	8 fl oz
Vanilla sugar (see page 36)	125 g	½ cup plus 1 Tbsp	4½ oz
Eggs	2	2	2
Sour cream	375 ml	1½ cups	12 fl oz
One recipe Peanut Brittle (see page 163)			
Makes about	1 litre	4 cups	32 fl oz

Using the above quantities of milk, sugar, eggs and sour cream prepare and cook a custard according to the method for making French Vanilla Ice Cream (see page 51). Continue up to the stage when the chilled custard is combined with the sour cream.

When ready, still freeze (see page 48) or start the ice-cream machine and freeze until the ice cream is the consistency of softly whipped cream. While the ice cream is freezing crush the peanut brittle until the pieces are approximately the size of coffee crystals. Then, either sprinkle the brittle into the ice cream as it churns allowing 2 or 3 more revolutions before switching off the machine, or fold into the still-frozen ice cream. Immediately scrape into plastic freezer boxes and cover with waxed or greaseproof paper and a lid. Finally label, then freeze for a minimum of 2 hours until firm enough to serve. Once frozen solid allow about 20 minutes in the fridge to soften sufficiently before serving.

Frozen Stilton Cheese Cream

Stilton cheese seems unlikely to serve as an ice but once they have tasted it, cheese-lovers become addicts to this Victorian delicacy.

INGREDIENTS

	Metric	U.S.	Imperial
Milk	625 ml	2½ cups	20 fl oz
Clove	1	1	1
Stilton cheese	250 g	9 oz	9 oz
White port	4 Tbsp	4 Tbsp	4 Tbsp
Fromage frais/fromage blanc (8 per cent fat)	500 g	2 cups	17½ oz
Makes about	1.3 litres	5½ cups	44 fl oz

Slowly bring the milk and clove to boiling point. Meanwhile discard the rind from the cheese and chop the rest into roughly 1 cm/½ inch cubes. Add to the milk and stir over a gentle heat until completely melted. Remove the pan from the heat, and beat the mixture vigorously for about 30 seconds before adding the port. Then taste and, if necessary, add salt and a little freshly ground black pepper. Cool then chill in the fridge.

When ready, remove the clove, gently beat the fromage frais into the cheese mixture, still freeze (see page 48) or start the ice-cream machine and pour it in.

NOTE: It will probably be necessary to churn this quantity in two separate batches.

Freeze until the mix has frozen to a consistency firm enough to serve; or to store, quickly scrape into plastic freezer boxes and cover with waxed or greaseproof paper and a lid. Finally label, then freeze. Allow about 20–25 minutes in the fridge to soften sufficiently to serve.

Serving
Serve cut into slices as a starter with celery seed biscuits or after a meal with port.

Strawberry Cream Ice
Crème de Fraises

Mrs Marshall in her Book of Ices *(1885) has this ice which is about as near as you are likely to get today to an original nineteenth-century ice cream. In those days all ices were made to be eaten at once or within a couple of hours, as freezers were unknown for longer-term storage. We find that this one is usually all eaten before you can begin to think of storage. It will* store *but is at its best when freshly made.*

INGREDIENTS

	Metric	U.S.	Imperial
Fresh strawberries, fully ripe	450 g	1 lb	1 lb
Vanilla sugar (see page 36)	100 g	½ cup	3½ oz
Whipping/heavy cream (36 per cent fat)	250 ml	1 cup	8 fl oz
Makes about	750 ml	3 cups	24 fl oz

Hull the strawberries then rinse with cold water and dry in a towel or kitchen paper. Transfer the berries to a food processor or blender and add the sugar. Process until reduced to an almost smooth pulp. In a separate bowl beat the cream until it forms soft peaks. Fold in the sweetened strawberry pulp then pour into a large plastic freezer box approx 15×10×7.5 cm/6×4×3 inches then cover with a lid and put into the coldest part of the freezer (at the bottom or in the lower half directly over the freezer coils) for 60–90 minutes, or until the ice cream has started to freeze in a band around the edge. Use a fork to loosen and vigorously mash the frozen ice cream into the softer mixture in the centre. When the mixture is uniform re-cover and return the ice cream to the freezer for a further hour or until softly frozen throughout. At this stage the ice cream can be either beaten again with a fork or whisked using an electric hand beater, or transferred to a food processor or blender. Beat until the ice cream has a uniform creamy consistency. Then re-cover once more and return to the freezer just until it is firm enough to serve; about 30 minutes.

Mrs Marshall's cookery school in London was so successful it was still in operation in the 1930s.

Strawberry Sorbet

A better flavoured sorbet will result from a fully ripened, well flavoured strawberry, so resist imported varieties and use frozen ones when home-grown are out of season. However, the flavour and colour of the sorbet made with frozen berries will be marginally less intense than the fresh. Keen gardeners might like to plan well ahead for a good sorbet and plant varieties such as Royal Sovereign, Aromel and Cambridge Vigour for flavour.

INGREDIENTS

	Metric	U.S.	Imperial
Fresh strawberries	450 g	1 lb	1 lb
Sugar syrup (see page 47)	375 ml	1½ cups	12 fl oz
Juice of lemons, strained	2	2	2
Egg white	1	1	1
Makes about	1.1 litres	4½ cups	36 fl oz

If a seedless sorbet is preferred purée the strawberries, either by rubbing through a sieve, or blending in a machine with a little of the sugar syrup until smooth, then sieve. We prefer to leave the seeds in as it improves the appearance and texture of the sorbet, but it is a matter of personal preference. Blend in the rest of the sugar syrup and add the strained juice of the lemons. Stir thoroughly and taste; the mixture should not be too sweet. Chill in the fridge.

Still freeze (see page 48) or start the ice-cream machine, pour in the liquid and churn for 10 minutes. Using a fork, beat the egg white until loosened and add to the sorbet with the machine still running. Continue until the sorbet is firm enough to serve; or to store, quickly scrape into plastic freezer containers and cover with a piece of waxed or greaseproof paper and a lid. Finally label, then freeze. Once the sorbet becomes solid it will need about 30 minutes in the fridge before it is soft enough to scoop.

Strawberry Spoom

Strawberry spoom is a quick and easy dessert to make when the strawberry season is at its height and a welcome change from strawberries and cream.

INGREDIENTS

	Metric	U.S.	Imperial
Strawberries	225 g	8 oz	8 oz
Sugar syrup (see page 47)	250 ml	1 cup	8 fl oz
Lemon juice	1–2 Tbsp	1–2 Tbsp	1–2 Tbsp
Egg whites	2	2	2
Granulated sugar	70 g	⅓ cup	2½ oz
Makes about	1 litre	4 cups	32 fl oz

Wash, hull and dry the strawberries, liquidise them with the sugar syrup, then strain through a fine nylon sieve to remove any large pips. Add 1 Tbsp of lemon juice, taste and add more lemon, ½ tsp at a time, until the purée is just sweet. Cover and chill thoroughly in the fridge.

In a large grease-free bowl beat the egg whites with a hand-held beater until they form soft peaks, then gradually add the sugar until it is absorbed and the egg whites are in fairly stiff peaks. They need to be stiff enough to incorporate the purée but not so stiff that you cannot fold them into the purée. Fold into the chilled purée, making sure that the purée is completely mixed with the meringue. Then transfer to a plastic freezer box and cover with a piece of greaseproof or waxed paper and a lid. Finally label, then freeze. Eat after about 2 hours, or if frozen solid, allow about 20 minutes in the fridge to soften sufficiently to serve.

STRAWBERRY ICE

4 quarts Strawberries
15 pounds Granulated Sugar
1 ounce Lemon Extract
4 gallons Water
Strawberry-Shade Red Color as required

FIRST:—Place 4 quarts of crushed Strawberries in a stone jar or enamel vessel.

SECOND:—Pour over them 4 gallons Water and 15 pounds of Granulated Sugar.

THIRD:—Add 1 ounce Lemon Extract.

FOURTH:—Mix thoroughly and freeze the same as ice cream.

Strawberry-Shade Red Liquid Color may be added to produce a deep, rich Strawberry Shade.

NOTE:—When using Color, the Ice should be labeled "Artificially Colored."

From *Heller's Guide for Ice Cream Makers*, 1918

Strawberry and Mascarpone Ice Cream

Mascarpone is an Italian cream cheese that is quite simple to make; it can also be bought in tubs from Italian delicatessens and some supermarket chains. Combined with strawberries it makes a magnificently smooth ice cream. This recipe comes from the regrettably now discontinued Cooks *magazine in the U.S.A., with their blessing.*

INGREDIENTS

	Metric	U.S.	Imperial
Strawberries	100 g	2 cups	3½ oz
Milk	250 ml	1 cup	8 fl oz
Egg yolks	4	4	4
Granulated sugar	200 g	1 cup	7 oz
Mascarpone	250 g	1 cup	8¾ oz
Makes about	1 litre	4 cups	32 fl oz

Hull the strawberries then rinse with cold water and dry on a towel or kitchen paper. Use a good processor blender to purée the strawberries, then sieve to remove the seeds. Cover and chill until ready to use.

Bring the milk to boiling point in a non-reactive saucepan. Meanwhile, in a heatproof bowl combine the egg yolks and sugar and beat until they take on a pale yellow colour, with a billowy consistency. Add the hot milk slowly, beating constantly. The bowl can now be placed over a pan of simmering water or the custard can be returned to the saucepan which is then put on top of a heat-diffuser mat so that it is not in direct contact with the heat. Only if you are confident that you will not overheat the custard should you put the saucepan on a gentle direct heat. Stir the custard until it reaches 85°C/185°F or until it has thickened sufficiently to coat the back of a spoon. On no account should the custard be allowed to overheat or boil as the mixture will curdle. (For how to deal with an overheated custard see page 52.)

Remove the pan from the heat and leave to cool for 5 minutes, stirring frequently. Add the mascarpone and stir well until dissolved. Put a piece of lightly buttered greaseproof paper directly on the surface of the custard and press it up against the side of the pan. This will prevent a skin forming while the custard cools. Once cold transfer to the fridge to chill.

When ready, still freeze (see page 48) or start the ice-cream machine, combine the custard and strawberry purée, and pour in the mixture. Leave to churn and freeze until it is the consistency of softly whipped cream. Now quickly scrape into plastic freezer containers and cover with a piece of waxed or greaseproof paper and a lid. Finally label, then freeze. Serve within an hour. If frozen solid it will need about 30 minutes in the fridge before it is soft enough to serve.

HOME-MADE MASCARPONE:

1.25 litres/5 cups/2 pints double cream, 48% fat
Scant ½ tsp tartaric acid
Makes about 750 g/3 cups/1 lb 9 oz

Start the day before. Pour the cream into the top half of a double boiler, or into a bowl placed over a pan of simmering water. Using a thermometer (*this is essential*) heat the cream, stirring occasionally to 80°C/180°F; over or under heating will spell disaster. Remove the pan from the heat and add the tartaric acid. Stir for 30 seconds, remove from the heat and continue to stir for another two minutes, then pour the cream into a cheesecloth-lined colander over a large bowl and allow to drain. Leave in a cool place for not more than 12 hours to drain.

NOTE: Tartaric acid is a vegetable acid used in baking powders and some fizzy drinks and can be bought from any good chemist – *it is not the same as cream of tartar.*

Strawberry Ice Cream Flavoured with Balsamic Vinegar
Gelato Di Fragole All'Aceto Balsamico

If you are staring at this recipe in disbelief, let us assure you at the outset there is no mistake, it does combine strawberries with vinegar and the flavour will out-do that of any strawberry ice cream you have ever tasted. The recipe comes from Entertaining all'Italiana with Anna del Conte, *but we suspect the idea stemmed from her previous book,* Secrets from an Italian Kitchen. *Here Anna describes the rare speciality of Reggio nell' Emilia and Modena, the towns where balsamic vinegar is made. It consists of serving vanilla ice cream with a teaspoon of balsamic vinegar dribbled over each portion. She writes, "The rich dark flavour of the balsamic vinegar cuts into the delicate sweetness of the ice cream and achieves a perfect balance of flavours." It seems to have the same effect in strawberry ice cream – in short, excellent.*

INGREDIENTS

	Metric	U.S.	Imperial
Fresh strawberries	450 g	1 lb	1 lb
Caster/Ultra fine sugar	150 g	¾ cup	5¼ oz
Balsamic vinegar	1 Tbsp	1 Tbsp	1 Tbsp
Whipping/heavy cream (36 per cent fat)	150 ml	½ cup plus 2 Tbsp	5¼ fl oz
Makes about	875 ml	3½ cups	28 fl oz

Wash and hull the strawberries. Dry them thoroughly with kitchen paper then put them in a food processor or blender with the sugar. Set the machine in motion and add the balsamic vinegar through the lid or funnel. Continue to blend until the ingredients have combined to a smooth purée, then pour this into a bowl. Cover and refrigerate for 2–3 hours. The sugar and vinegar will bring out the flavour of the fruit.

When ready, combine the strawberry purée and cream and either still freeze (see page 48) or start the ice-cream machine. Pour the mixture into the machine. Leave to churn until the ice cream has the consistency of softly whipped cream. Quickly scrape into plastic freezer boxes and cover with waxed or greaseproof paper and a lid. Finally label, then freeze. Freeze for 1 hour or until just firm enough to serve; or if frozen solid, allow about 20 minutes in the fridge to soften sufficiently to serve.

Strega Parfait

See page 49.

Beside being variously flavoured, hokey pokey was dreadfully sweet, dreadfully cold, and hard as a brick. Swede turnip, converted into pulp, was known to have formed the base in lieu of more expensive supplies from the cow. Nevertheless, such adulteration is harmless compared to the awful foreign substances, including an enormous number of sewage bacteria even, that have been found to permeate the Italian ice cream, which is often prepared amidst the most loathsome conditions. For twenty years past the Medical Press has been agitating that in order to put a stop to this horrible state of affairs, ice-cream-mongers should be licensed, and the manufacture regulated in the same manner as the milk traffic.

Mrs Marshall,
The Table, 3 August 1901

Green Tea Ice Cream

Japanese shops and specialist tea shops sell green tea packaged as teabags. If loose tea is all that is available, you would need 4 teaspoonsful infused overnight in the milk; the milk will then need straining before making the custard. This ice is an ideal way to finish a Japanese, Chinese or Thai meal.

INGREDIENTS

	Metric	U.S.	Imperial
Milk	300 ml	1¼ cups	10½ fl oz
Green tea teabags	4	4	4
Granulated sugar	100 g	½ cup	3½ oz
Egg yolks	3	3	3
Whipping/heavy cream (36 per cent fat)	250 ml	1 cup	8 fl oz
Makes about	750 ml	3 cups	24 fl oz

Measure the cold milk into a jug and suspend the teabags in it, making sure that they are submerged in the liquid. Cover and refrigerate overnight, stirring once or twice if possible.

The following day, squeeze all the liquid from the teabags back into the milk, discard the bags and bring the milk to just below boiling point. Proceed to make a custard with the flavoured milk, using the above quantities of sugar, egg yolks and cream (though omitting the vanilla bean), following the instructions for French Vanilla Ice Cream (see page 51).

When ready, still freeze (see page 48) or start the ice-cream machine. Pour the chilled mix into the machine and continue to churn until the ice cream is the consistency of softly whipped cream. Quickly scrape into plastic freezer boxes then smooth the surface and cover with waxed or greaseproof paper and a lid. Finally label, then freeze for 2 hours until firm enough to serve. If frozen, the ice cream will need about 20 minutes in the fridge to soften sufficiently to serve.

Earl Grey Tea Sorbet

There is a very straightforward trick we would like to pass on concerning tea infusions. Every recipe we have ever read initially requires boiling water to be poured on to the tea. Ignore this and simply soak the tea in cold water overnight. This method gives a good, rich round flavour with none of the bitter tannin that is immediately released when tea leaves are steeped in boiling water.

NOTE: *Purists can substitute 3 Tbsp of Earl Grey tea leaves for the 4 teabags but we have rarely found anyone who can detect the difference.*

INGREDIENTS

	Metric	U.S.	Imperial
Earl Grey teabags	4	4	4
Water	625 ml	2½ cups	20 fl oz
Sugar syrup (see page 47)	300 ml	1¼ cups	10½ fl oz
Juice of lemon, strained	1	1	1
Egg white	1	1	1
Makes about	1 litre	4 cups	32 fl oz

Add the teabags to the cold water, cover and leave to steep for 24 hours, stirring occasionally. Drain and discard the bags then add the sugar syrup and strained lemon juice. If necessary, chill in the fridge again before making the sorbet.

When ready, still freeze (see page 48) or start the ice-cream machine. Pour in the liquid and churn for 5–10 minutes or until the mixture starts to freeze and look opaque. Using a fork, beat the egg white until loosened and add to the sorbet with the machine still running. Continue until the sorbet is firm enough to serve; or to store, quickly scrape into plastic freezer containers and cover with waxed or greaseproof paper and a lid. Finally label, then freeze. Once the sorbet is frozen allow about 30 minutes in the fridge to soften.

Variations
Russian caravan tea gives a good positive flavour; or try gunpowder green or jasmine tea for a delicate fragrant sorbet.

Tequila Granita

The idea for this sorbet came after we had Margueritas, that were virtually a slush, in a Tex-Mex restaurant in New York. They were delicious. This ice is wonderful after a hot Mexican, Indian or Oriental meal.

INGREDIENTS

	Metric	U.S.	Imperial
Water	625 ml	2½ cups	20 fl oz
Granulated sugar	110 g	½ cup	3¼ oz
Tequila	4 Tbsp	4 Tbsp	4 Tbsp
Cointreau	4 Tbsp	4 Tbsp	4 Tbsp
Juice of lemons, strained	3	3	3
Makes about	1 litre	4 cups	32 fl oz

Bring the water to the boil in a medium saucepan. Stir in the sugar then simmer for 5 minutes. Remove the pan from the heat and stir in the spirits and the strained lemon juice. Cool to room temperature, then chill in the fridge.

For detailed instructions on how to prepare the perfect granita see page 49.

Thyme Granita/Sorbet

See Herb Granitas/Sorbets pages 99 and 100.

It is dangerous to heat, cool, or make a commotion all of a sudden in the body, let it be done which way it may, because everything that is excessive is an enemy to nature.

Hippocrates' fifty-first aphorism, second section, translation by Thomas Masters, *The Ice Book*, Simpkin Marshall, London, 1844

English Toffee Ice Cream

The recipe could not be simpler and the flavour is excellent. The toffee melts more quickly if it is crushed into very small pieces, and we have found that freezing the toffee for 30 minutes makes it more brittle and therefore easier to pound.

INGREDIENTS

	Metric	U.S.	Imperial
Toffee(s), unwrapped	300 g	10½ oz	10½ oz
Milk	250 ml	1 cup	8 fl oz
Whipping/heavy cream (36 per cent fat)	500 ml	2 cups	16 fl oz
Makes about	1 litre	4 cups	32 fl oz

Leaving 50 g/2 oz of toffee in the freezer, crush the remaining toffee and put it in a small saucepan with the milk and half the cream. Heat gently, stirring frequently until the toffee has dissolved. (Using a balloon whisk can speed up the dissolving process a little.)

When the mixture is smooth remove from the heat and cool quickly by sitting the base of the pan in cold water. Once cold, cover and transfer to the fridge to chill.

When ready, still freeze (see page 48) or start the ice-cream machine. Combine the chilled toffee mix with the remaining cream and pour into the machine. Churn for about 20 minutes or until the mixture has the consistency of softly whipped cream. While the ice cream is churning quickly remove the remaining toffee from the freezer and crush it. Sprinkle this directly on to the churning ice cream and allow it to churn for a further 2 or 3 revolutions or sufficient to distribute the toffee chips evenly throughout the ice cream. Stop the machine then quickly scrape the ice cream into plastic freezer boxes. Level the surface and cover with waxed or greaseproof paper and a lid. Finally label, then freeze. Serve after a minimum of 1 hour, or if frozen solid allow about 20 minutes in the fridge to soften sufficiently to serve.

Serving
Serve with baked apple or individual banana and walnut crumbles, or as part of a trilogy of small servings of Crème Fraîche (see page 87) and Chocolate Ice Creams (see page 71).

English Toffee and Rum Ice Cream

INGREDIENTS

	Metric	U.S.	Imperial
One recipe English Toffee Ice Cream (see page 149)			
Dark rum	2–3 Tbsp	2–3 Tbsp	2–3 Tbsp
Makes about	1 litre	4 cups	32 fl oz

Follow the method for making English Toffee Ice Cream (see page 149), to the stage when the chilled mix has been removed from the fridge. Now stir in the remaining cream, then sufficient rum to taste, and continue as directed in the method.

Liquorice Toffee Ice Cream

Not a flavour usually associated with ice cream; nor a colour. If you find it on sale, it is invariably a very daunting black. We found that the simplest method produced a remarkably good flavour, but we drew the line at adding black colouring so our version is a far more subtle battleship grey!

INGREDIENTS

	Metric	U.S.	Imperial
One recipe English Toffee Ice Cream (see page 149) omitting the English toffee and substituting the same weight of liquorice toffees.			
Granulated sugar	2 Tbsp	2 Tbsp	2 Tbsp
Makes about	1 litre	4 cups	32 fl oz

The method is exactly the same as for making English Toffee Ice Cream (see page 149) but dissolve the sugar with all (300 g/10½ oz) of the liquorice toffees in the milk with half the cream at the start of the recipe. No crushed toffee is added to the frozen ice cream.

Tomato Ice Cream – Savoury

This is an ice that is made with mayonnaise using a sunflower oil. It contains very little cream and only one egg and therefore per portion is comparatively low in saturated fats and cholesterol. All too often, this can signal a loss of flavour, but made with well-flavoured, fully ripe tomatoes, it makes a sophisticated ice.

INGREDIENTS

	Metric	U.S.	Imperial
Ripe tomatoes	450 g	1 lb	1 lb
Garlic cloves, chopped	1	1	1
Bay leaves	2	2	2
Tomato purée	1 Tbsp	1 Tbsp	1 Tbsp
Granulated sugar	¼ tsp	¼ tsp	¼ tsp
Freshly ground black pepper			
Mayonnaise			
Egg	1	1	1
Lemon juice	1 Tbsp	1 Tbsp	1 Tbsp
Dijon mustard	¼ tsp	¼ tsp	¼ tsp
Sunflower oil	250 ml	1 cup	8 fl oz
Freshly ground black pepper			
Salt			
Whipping/heavy cream (36 per cent fat), lightly beaten	85 ml	⅓ cup	2¾ fl oz
Makes about	800 ml	3¼ cups	26 fl oz

Wash the tomatoes, quarter and put them in a covered pan with the chopped garlic and bay leaves. Cook gently, covered, stirring frequently, until the tomatoes are reduced to a soft pulp. (Additional water should not be needed if the tomatoes are ripe and they are cooked slowly enough.) Rub the contents of the pan through a sieve. Stir in tomato purée and sugar, then season well with freshly ground black pepper. Cover and chill in the fridge.

To make the mayonnaise, break the egg into a medium-sized mixing bowl. Using an electric hand whisk, beat in the lemon. Then with the machine set at medium speed, whisk in the oil very slowly, a dribbled tablespoonful at a time, until all the oil is added and the mayonnaise forms an emulsion. Add mustard and then salt and pepper to taste. Cover and chill the mayonnaise in the fridge.

When ready, still freeze (see page 48) or switch on the ice-cream machine. Combine the tomato mixture, mayonnaise and lightly beaten cream. Pour into the ice-cream machine and churn for about 10 minutes or until the ice forms soft peaks. Quickly scrape the ice cream into plastic freezer boxes, level the surface and cover with waxed or greaseproof paper and a lid. Finally label, then freeze. Allow about 1 hour in the freezer before eating; if frozen solid allow about 20 minutes in the fridge before serving.

Serving
Serve with cold lemon-dressed seafood, or with a mixed green leaf salad for a light lunch, or with Pea and Mint Savoury Ice Cream (see page 124) as a starter.

Fresh Tomato and Basil Sorbet

Serve as a lunch dish on a hot summer's day with a mixed green salad, or in a chilled red or yellow tomato soup.

INGREDIENTS

	Metric	U.S.	Imperial
Fresh ripe tomatoes	900 g	2 lb	2 lb
Sugar syrup (see page 47)	85 ml	⅓ cup	2¾ fl oz
Fresh basil leaves, chopped	10	10	10
Juice of lemons, strained	4	4	4
Salt and freshly milled black pepper			
Worcestershire sauce	4 drops	4 drops	4 drops
Makes about	750 ml	3 cups	24 fl oz

Skin the tomatoes either by immersing in boiling water for about 1 minute, or by spearing each tomato with a fork and rotating over a gas flame. Quarter, removing the cores, and transfer to a food processor or blender. Blend until smooth then rub through a plastic sieve into a bowl. Stir in the sugar syrup and add the chopped basil leaves. Now add the strained lemon juice then salt, freshly milled black pepper and Worcestershire sauce to taste. Cover and chill in the fridge.

When ready, still freeze (see page 48) or start the ice-cream machine. Pour in the liquid and churn until the sorbet is firm enough to serve; or to store, quickly scrape into plastic freezer containers and cover with waxed or greaseproof paper and a lid. Finally label, then freeze. Once the sorbet is frozen allow about 30 minutes in the fridge to soften before serving.

French Vanilla Ice Cream and Rich French Vanilla Ice Cream

See page 51.

Italian Vanilla Gelato

This is a version of the classic Italian gelato. Usually made entirely with milk, it is therefore less creamy than for example French Vanilla Ice Cream but it is also slightly colder and more icy. (For an explanation of this, see Chapter 9: The Chemistry of Ices page 172.) However, the lower overrun, another characteristic of this ice cream, gives an increased density which has the effect of intensifying the flavour to something that is wholly milk, and is clean, clear and light. A seaside ice cream in every way and many people's idea of what an ice cream should really taste like.

INGREDIENTS

	Metric	U.S.	Imperial
Milk	750 ml	3 cups	24 fl oz
Vanilla bean	1	1	1
Granulated sugar	165 g	¾ cup	6¾ oz
Egg yolks	8	8	8
Makes about	800 ml	3¼ cups	26 fl oz

Using the above ingredients, make, chill and freeze the ice cream according to the instructions for making French Vanilla Ice Cream (see page 51).

NOTE: Because the ice cream is comparatively low in both fat and non-fat milk solids it will take longer to freeze and the consistency of the frozen churned ice cream will not be as thick, almost pourable in fact. This is normal and as it should be (see intro).

Proceed as usual and quickly scrape into plastic freezer boxes and cover with waxed or greaseproof paper and a lid. Finally label, then freeze until firm which will take about 2 hours. Once frozen allow 20 minutes to soften in the fridge before serving.

Mrs Marshall's Vanilla Ice Cream

This comes straight from the pages of Mrs Marshall's Book of Ices (1885) and with her simple directness comes under the heading of "cheap".
It is the ideal sort of ice cream to churn out in quantities for children because you can be sure that nothing in the supermarket can match it for price or integrity of ingredients.

INGREDIENTS

	Metric	U.S.	Imperial
Cornflour	4 Tbsp	–	4 Tbsp
OR			
Cornstarch	–	4 Tbsp	–
Granulated sugar	90 g	½ cup	3¼ oz
Milk	500 ml	2 cups	16 fl oz
Vanilla extract	½ tsp	½ tsp	½ tsp
Makes about	625 ml	2½ cups	20 fl oz

Combine the cornflour and sugar in a bowl. Stir in sufficient of the measured milk to form a thin blend. Bring the rest of the milk to the boil and pour in the cornflour blend in a thin, steady stream, stirring constantly. Return the mixture to the pan and bring to the boil over a moderate heat, stirring constantly. Once the mixture boils adjust the heat to give a gentle simmer and cook for a further 2–3 minutes. Remove the pan from the heat and stir in the vanilla. Lay a piece of greaseproof paper directly on the custard and slightly up the sides of the pan; this is to prevent a skin forming to which this sort of flour-based custard is particularly prone. Leave to cool, then chill in the fridge.

When ready, still freeze (see page 48) or start the ice-cream machine. Strain the custard into a jug and pour into the machine. Churn for about 20 minutes or until the ice cream is firm enough to serve. Or to store, quickly scrape into plastic freezer boxes, smooth the surface flat and cover with waxed or greaseproof paper and a lid. Finally label, then freeze. If frozen solid, allow 20–30 minutes in the fridge to soften sufficiently to serve.

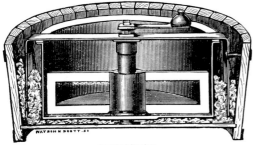

Easy No-Cook Philadelphia Vanilla Ice Cream

This is the easiest type of Philadelphia (or egg-less) ice cream and is particularly suitable for children to make. The recipe for this type of ice cream is reputed to have originated in Philadelphia. Because it contains no egg it melts faster and has the uniform iciness characteristic of the ices of old-fashioned ice-cream sellers.

INGREDIENTS

	Metric	U.S.	Imperial
Vanilla bean	1	1	1
Milk	375 ml	1½ cups	12 fl oz
Caster/Ultra fine sugar	50 g	¼ cup	1¾ oz
Sweetened condensed milk, chilled	125 ml	½ cup	4 fl oz
Whipping/heavy cream (36 per cent fat), chilled	250 ml	1 cup	8 fl oz
Salt	pinch	pinch	pinch
Makes about	1 litre	4 cups	32 fl oz

Split the vanilla bean lengthwise and heat with the milk and sugar, stirring occasionally, to just below boiling point, allow to cool and chill. Remove the bean and scrape out the seeds, adding them to the chilled milk. Cover and chill in the fridge.

When ready, add the chilled condensed milk, cream and salt. Mix together, then still freeze (see page 48) or start the ice-cream machine and pour in the liquid. Leave to churn and freeze for about 20 minutes or until the ice cream has the consistency of very softly whipped cream. Quickly scrape into plastic freezer boxes and cover with waxed or greaseproof paper and a lid. Finally label, then freeze until firm, which will take about 1 hour. Once frozen allow 20 minutes to soften in the fridge before serving.

Soft Scoop Vanilla Ice Cream

This is the home-made equivalent of commercial ice creams that can be served straight from the freezer. Americans will have no problem making this type of ice cream because it depends on a type of sugar available in the U.S.A. where it is known as corn syrup. In Britain it is much easier to use dextrose monohydrate which is cheap and can be bought in powder form from any chemist. The packet will probably read "medicinal glucose" as well as "dextrose monohydrate".

Do not buy the variety that contains vitamin supplements. *(For an explanation of the part sugar plays in the chemistry of ice cream see page 172.)*

INGREDIENTS

	Metric	U.S.	Imperial
Granulated sugar	70 g	⅓ cup	2½ oz
Egg	1	1	1
Milk	300 ml	1¼ cups	10 fl oz
Powdered dextrose monohydrate	3 Tbsp plus 2 tsp	¼ cup	3 Tbsp plus 2 tsp
OR			
Corn syrup	130 ml	½ cup plus 1 Tbsp	4½ fl oz
Whipping/heavy cream (36 per cent fat)	185 ml	¾ cup	6 fl oz
Vanilla extract	2 tsp	2 tsp	2 tsp
Makes about	750 ml	3 cups	24 fl oz

In a large heatproof mixing bowl beat together the sugar and egg. Heat the milk to just below boiling point then pour slowly into the bowl containing the beaten egg and sugar in a thin stream, beating constantly. Position the bowl over a pan of barely simmering water and continue to heat, stirring frequently, until the custard reaches 85°C/ 185°F. Remove from the heat and stir in either the powdered dextrose or the corn syrup. Cover and chill in the fridge.

When ready, stir in the cream and vanilla extract, still freeze (see page 48) or start the ice-cream machine and pour in the custard. Leave to churn for about 15–20 minutes or until the consistency of softly whipped cream. Quickly scrape the ice cream into plastic freezer boxes, smooth the surface flat, cover with waxed or greaseproof paper and a lid. Finally label, then freeze. To serve, remove from the freezer to the worktop. By the time the plates and spoons have been assembled the ice cream will be sufficiently soft to serve.

Well-Behaved Vanilla Ice Cream

An ice cream that contains no eggs and is straightforward and quick to make. The interesting addition is the gelatine which makes the ice cream less prone to melting and more able to keep its shape. The gelatine creates a slightly cooked-milk flavour which is popular because it recalls childhood memories of ice cream.

INGREDIENTS

	Metric	U.S.	Imperial
Water	2 Tbsp	2 Tbsp	2 Tbsp
Powdered gelatine	1 Tbsp	1 Tbsp	1 Tbsp
Milk	500 ml	2 cups	16 fl oz
Granulated sugar	120 g	½ cup plus 1 Tbsp	4¼ oz
Salt	pinch	pinch	pinch
Whipping/heavy cream (36 per cent fat), chilled	500 ml	2 cups	16 fl oz
Vanilla extract	1 Tbsp	1 Tbsp	1 Tbsp
Makes about	1.25 litres	5 cups	40 fl oz

Spoon the water into a medium-sized bowl then sprinkle in the gelatine, whisking constantly. In a saucepan bring the milk to the boil then remove the pan from the heat. Stir in the sugar and the salt, and when the sugar has dissolved pour into the bowl containing the gelatine, stirring all the while. Cover and leave to cool.

Finally add the cream and vanilla. The mixture is now ready to freeze. Still freeze (see page 48) or start the ice-cream machine, pour in the liquid and churn for 20–25 minutes or until the consistency of very soft whipped cream. Quickly scrape into plastic freezer boxes, smooth the surface and cover with waxed or greaseproof paper and a lid. Finally label, then freeze. Serve after about 1 hour; or if frozen hard, allow about 20 minutes in the fridge to soften sufficiently to serve.

Vanilla Yoghurt Ice Cream

INGREDIENTS

	Metric	U.S.	Imperial
Semi-skimmed milk	125 ml	½ cup	4 fl oz
Powdered gelatine	1 tsp	1 tsp	1 tsp
Greek/Russian style yoghurt, room temp.	360 g	1½ cups	12¾ oz
Granulated sugar	150 g	¾ cup	5¼ oz
Vanilla extract	1½ tsp	1½ tsp	1½ tsp
Egg white	1	1	1
Instant dried milk powder	30 g	⅓ cup	1 oz
Water	85 ml	⅓ cup	3 fl oz
Makes about	1 litre	4 cups	32 fl oz

In a small pan bring the milk to boiling point. Remove it from the heat and sprinkle in the gelatine, stirring briskly. Leave it to cool, stirring frequently until the gelatine has completely dissolved. Combine the yoghurt, sugar and vanilla in a bowl. When the gelatine has cooled to the same temperature as the yoghurt combine the two mixtures.

In a separate bowl whisk together the egg white, milk powder and water until the mixture is stiff enough to form soft peaks; fold this into the yoghurt mixture. Still freeze (see page 48) or start the ice-cream machine, pour in the mixture and leave to churn until the ice cream is firm enough to serve. To store, quickly scrape into plastic freezer boxes and cover with greaseproof or waxed paper and a lid. Finally label, then freeze. Once frozen allow 20 minutes to soften in a fridge before serving.

Chinese Walnut Brittle Ice Cream

This recipe is going to raise an eyebrow or two – it is definitely an oddity. How many nut brittles have you come across that contain generous amounts of salt and freshly ground black pepper? But rest assured, the recipe has a perfect pedigree. It comes from the late Jane Grigson's book Good Things, *and when this lady tells you something unusual works, you can bank on it. The magic of the recipe is that, as Jane Grigson wrote, the pepper tastes spicy rather than peppery and leaves one's mouth feeling fresh and clear. Furthermore, when added to ice cream it miraculously keeps these qualities, giving a flavour which is at once rich, yet clean and spicy. A rather adult flavour. Please note, it must be freshly ground black pepper, straight from a peppermill.*

INGREDIENTS

	Metric	U.S.	Imperial
Ice Cream			
Milk	375 ml	1½ cups	12 fl oz
Egg yolks	3	3	3
Vanilla sugar (see page 36)	90 g	½ cup minus 1 Tbsp	3½ oz
Whipping/heavy cream (36 per cent fat)	185 ml	¾ cup	6 fl oz
Brittle			
Granulated sugar	170 g	1 cup minus 3 Tbsp	6 oz
Water	4 Tbsp	4 Tbsp	4 Tbsp
Salt	1 tsp	1 tsp	1 tsp
Walnut pieces	115 g	1 cup	4 oz
Freshly ground black pepper		see method	
Makes about	1 litre	4 cups	32 fl oz

Follow the method for making French Vanilla Ice Cream (see page 51, omitting the vanilla bean and substituting vanilla sugar). Once the custard has cooled, cover and chill in the fridge.

To make the brittle: put the sugar and water in a heavy pan and heat gently, stirring occasionally until the sugar has completely dissolved. Now turn up the heat and boil briskly until the syrup reaches the soft ball stage, 112–115°C/233–240°F. Add the salt and walnuts and continue cooking to the hard crack stage, 148–154°C/298–309°F, turning the pepper mill 20–25 times over the pan between stirs. Quickly scrape the mixture from the pan on to a greased baking tray and pat the nuts flat with the back of a spoon. Leave to cool and harden. Tap to break the brittle into pieces then pound several pieces at a time in a pestle and mortar until reduced to about the same size as coarse salt crystals. Transfer to a screw-top jar until ready to use.

When the custard is sufficiently chilled, either still freeze (see page 48) or start the ice-cream machine. Pour it into the machine and continue to churn until the ice cream is the consistency of softly whipped cream. Quickly scrape into plastic freezer boxes, sprinkling in 150 g/1 cup/5¼ oz of the crushed brittle as you go. Finally, give the ice cream 1 or 2 stirs to distribute the brittle evenly then smooth the surface and cover with waxed or greaseproof paper and a lid. Finally label, then freeze. Serve after about 2 hours, or, if left to freeze hard, the ice cream will need about 20 minutes in the fridge to soften sufficiently to serve.

Whisky and Honey Parfait

Having had Atholl Brose and loved it, we were convinced that the same principle could be used to make an ice cream. How wrong could we be? All our efforts produced different versions of frozen porridge. In the end we were forced to turn the idea on its head and come up with a superlatively flavoured whisky and honey parfait which can be put into a container that has been lightly spread with butter and coated with lightly toasted pinhead or rolled oatmeal.

INGREDIENTS

	Metric	U.S.	Imperial
Honey, clear	125 ml	½ cup	4 fl oz
Water	85 ml	⅓ cup	3 fl oz
Egg yolks	5	5	5
Whipping/heavy cream (36 per cent fat)	250 ml	1 cup	8 fl oz
Whisky	4 Tbsp	4 Tbsp	4 Tbsp
Makes about	1 litre	4 cups	32 fl oz

Combine the honey with the water and warm very gently until the honey is completely dissolved. The syrup should be between 30 and 40°C/86–104°F (around blood heat). Now follow very carefully the instructions for making a parfait (see page 50).

COUPE JACQUES
Fill a champagne glass or ice cup with equal quantities of lemon ice and strawberry ice, add one spoon fresh fruits steeped in kirsch in the middle. Decorate with crystallised cherries and halved almonds. Sprinkle a few drops of kirsch on top.

The type of "ice" is never specified in any reference to this coupe, but try it with lemon sorbet and strawberry ice cream.

Mulled Wine Sorbet

This recipe came about through a suggestion from Delia Smith. We devised this recipe for her book Delia Smith's Christmas.

INGREDIENTS

	Metric	U.S.	Imperial
Orange	1	1	1
Lemons	1½	1½	1½
Red wine	250 ml	1 cup	8 fl oz
Cloves	3	3	3
Cinnamon stick	5 cm	2 inch	2 inch
Grated nutmeg	pinch	pinch	pinch
Ruby port	2 Tbsp	2 Tbsp	2 Tbsp
Sugar syrup (see page 47)	250 ml	1 cup	8 fl oz
Egg white	1	1	1
Makes about	750 ml	3 cups	24 fl oz

Thoroughly scrub then dry the orange and lemons. Use a potato peeler to remove three 2.5×1 cm/1×½ inch strips from the orange and one of the lemons. Cut these across very finely to give hair-like strips. Squeeze the juice from the orange and 1½ lemons. Combine the wine, spices, strips of zest and strained orange and lemon juice in a saucepan. Bring to the boil, simmer for 1 minute, then remove the pan from the heat. Stir in the port and sugar syrup, cover and leave to cool, then chill in the fridge.

When ready, still freeze (see page 48) or start the ice-cream machine. Pour in the liquid and churn for about 8 minutes. Using a fork, beat the egg white until loosened and add to the sorbet with the machine still running. Continue until the sorbet is firm enough to serve. Or to store, quickly scrape into plastic freezer containers and cover with waxed or greaseproof paper and a lid. Finally label, then freeze. Once the sorbet becomes solid it will need about 30 minutes in the fridge before it is soft enough to scoop.

Muscat Sorbet

The success of this sorbet will depend on the flavour and quality of the dessert wine used. As long as the wine fits this bill anything from a muscat to a home-made elderflower will do.

INGREDIENTS

	Metric	U.S.	Imperial
Dessert wine	375 ml	1½ cups	12 fl oz
Sugar syrup (see page 47)	250 ml	1 cup	8 fl oz
Water	250 ml	1 cup	8 fl oz
Juice of lemon, strained	1	1	1
Egg white	1	1	1
Makes about	1 litre	4 cups	32 fl oz

To the measured wine, add the sugar syrup, water and strained juice of the lemon. Cover and chill in the fridge.

When ready, still freeze (see page 48) or start the ice-cream machine. Pour in the liquid and churn for about 5–10 minutes, or until it starts to become opaque. Using a fork, beat the egg white until loosened and add to the sorbet with the machine still running. Continue until the sorbet is firm enough to serve; or to store, quickly scrape into plastic freezer boxes and cover with waxed or greaseproof paper and a lid. Finally label, then freeze. Once the sorbet becomes solid it will need about 20 minutes in the fridge before it is soft enough to scoop.

Zabaglione Parfait.

See page 49.

**Little Boy Blue, go blow your horn,
There's ice cream aplenty as sure as you're born;
Go call in the children – I want them to share
In our wonderful luncheon of rich, frozen fare.**

The Soda Fountain, May 1915

CHAPTER 7

Biscuits and Sauces for Ice Cream

Biscuits

Ice-Cream Wafers

SUITABLE FOR OVEN-BAKED OR MACHINE-MADE
CONES

This recipe makes a plain, very thin, light, crisp biscuit, suitable to accompany all manner of sweet ices. When oven-baked they can be curled in the manner of tuiles, but these biscuits are not quite malleable enough to take kindly to shaping into cigarettes. However, should you become the proud possessor of an electric ice-cream cone (or pizelle) maker (very similar to an electric waffle iron, see page 42) we think you will find this recipe preferable to any supplied by the manufacturers of these machines.

INGREDIENTS

	Metric	U.S.	Imperial
Icing sugar	150 g	1 cup	5¼ oz
Unsalted butter (at room temperature)	65 g	⅓ cup	2¼ oz
Egg whites (140 ml)	4	4	4
Plain/All purpose flour, sifted	175 g	1¼ cups plus ½ Tbsp	6¼ oz
Cornflour OR	1 tsp	–	1 tsp
Cornstarch	–	1 tsp	–
Sesame or poppy seeds (optional)	3–4 Tbsp	3–4 Tbsp	3–4 Tbsp

If oven-baking the wafers, preheat the oven to 190°C/ 375°F/Gas Mark 5. Use non-stick baking trays, otherwise line with silicone baking paper greased sparingly with tasteless oil.

To prepare the mix, sift the icing sugar into a bowl, then use your hands to rub in the butter. Once no free sugar remains, you can use a hand-beater or an electric beater to beat the mix until paler in colour and lighter in texture. Now add the egg whites a little at a time, beating until smooth between each addition. Finally, combine the flour and cornflour, sift in the bowl then fold in until the mixture is smooth.

To oven bake

Use a palette knife to spread the mix thinly into 10 cm/ 4 inch circles on the (prepared) baking trays.

NOTE: This mixture does not spread much during baking. The biscuits can be left plain, or sprinkled with sesame or poppy seeds before baking, if liked. Bake in the centre of the oven for 6–8 minutes. Remove immediately from the tray using a palette knife and either curl (see directions for forming tuiles page 161) or leave to cool lying flat on a wire rack.

To use an electric cone-maker

Leave the machine to heat until it reaches the correct temperature. It might be necessary to lightly oil the cooking surfaces before the first wafer is baked but not thereafter. Put 1 Tbsp of mix in the centre of the base plate, bring down the top lid and use the clip to clamp the base and top handles firmly shut. If a little too much mix has been used, some of it will quickly flow out around the edge, but by the second or third attempt you will be able to gauge almost exactly the amount required just to cover

There is a man that sells ice cream
In little curley waffles
He always says "To me, it seems
Your appetite is awful"

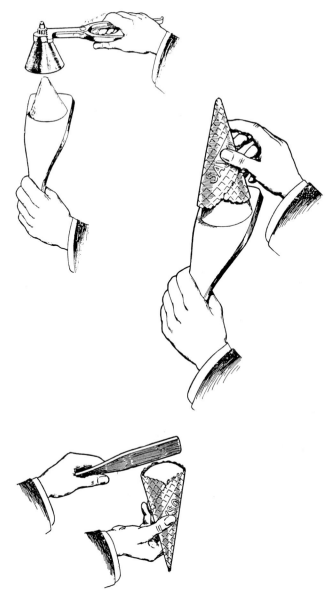

Filling an ice cream cone.

the base plate and no more. Cook until uniformly golden brown, usually about 90 seconds. You can lift the lid to see how the cooking is progressing – it will not break the wafer.

As soon as it is sufficiently browned remove the wafer and with a clean cloth to protect your hands, form it into a cone. You can do this "free-hand" or more readily using a wooden cone-shaped form (see Useful Addresses page 184). Make sure the wafer cone is sufficiently cooled and firm enough to hold its shape before leaving to cool on a wire rack. Eat the same day.

NOTE: Once you know the exact quantity of mix the machine will take, it is possible to obtain a sesame or poppy seed-edged cone by sprinkling the perimeter of the base plate with seeds, then spooning the mix into the centre; cook and roll in the same way.

It's my dream
To eat ice cream
and keep my shirt clean,
and it's known
that a cone
is safer
than a wafer.

Norman Hollands

Almond Wafer Biscuits

This recipe produces a very crisp, thin biscuit (or cookie) with a subtle almond texture and flavour – nothing like the wafers associated with commercial ices. We decided to make it our basic wafer biscuit – as many ices combine beautifully with this flavour. It can be made into four shapes; two to accompany ice cream, and two to contain it. Whichever shape you opt for, a flexible palette knife and an abundant supply of non-stick silicone paper are a must.

Then you need to close the kitchen door and concentrate, because this type of biscuit needs precision, speed and accuracy, starting with the biscuit mix. Measure this as accurately as possible because a teaspoonful here or there can make the difference between success and failure. Once you get accustomed to the way the mix bakes in your oven (accurate timing will give a consistent result), the next critical point is gauging the cooling and degree of flexibility of the biscuits. Don't panic and rush to remove the biscuit from the baking tray the instant it comes out of the oven. Hold on for 30 seconds or so (exactly how long depends on the thickness of your baking tray and therefore how much it retains the heat), then quickly roll, press or drape the biscuits into the shape of your choice. If it is too hot, the biscuit will be very fragile and tear easily. If it gets too cool, it will become too crisp or brittle to roll. One last point: the shaped biscuits take a surprising time to become crisp after baking; they need time to cool, and then some, before they are fully crisp. Stored in an airtight container at this stage, they will keep for up to 1 week.

INGREDIENTS

	Metric	U.S.	Imperial
Butter	3 Tbsp	3 Tbsp	3 Tbsp
Egg whites	2	2	2
(Or 65ml)		(Or 4 Tbsp + 1 tsp)	(Or 4 Tbsp + 1 tsp)
Castor sugar	85g	½ cup – 1 Tbsp	3 oz
Plain/All purpose flour	3 Tbsp	3 Tbsp	3 Tbsp
Cornflour	1 Tbsp	–	1 Tbsp
Or			
Cornstarch	–	1 Tbsp	–
Ground almonds	4 Tbsp	4 Tbsp	4 Tbsp
Almond extract	a few drops	a few drops	a few drops
Makes about	36	36	36

Position the oven shelf centrally and preheat to 220°C/425°F/Gas Mark 7. Line 2 baking trays with non-stick silicone paper and grease the paper with a solid piece of

A 1937 advertisement.

butter. (Melted butter will not coat this type of paper as evenly as solid butter does, and treated in this way the biscuits lift off in the cleanest possible way.)

Melt the 3 Tbsp of butter in a small saucepan and leave to cool. Sift together the flour and cornflour and combine with the ground almonds.

If using a food processor

Combine the egg whites and sugar in the bowl and process for about 10 seconds. Add the combined flour, cornflour and ground almonds. Replace the lid, set the machine in motion and pour in the cooled butter in a thin stream via the funnel. Stop and scrape down the base and sides of the bowl; add the almond extract, blend briefly once more, then the mix is ready to use.

If making by hand

Whisk the egg whites until they form soft peaks then gradually whisk in the sugar. Now fold in alternate amounts of the combined flour, cornflour and almonds, then the cooled butter, in about 3 steps until all have been incorporated into a smooth mix. Lastly stir in a few drops of almond essence, and the mix is ready to use.

TO SERVE WITH ICE CREAM

Almond tuiles

These curved wafer biscuits are formed by bending the hot biscuit around the curve of a rolling pin, giving the characteristic shape of Provençal roof tiles, hence the name. Have ready a rolling pin (the thinner type is better for these biscuits; it does not need greasing) and about 4 Tbsp of flaked almonds. Allowing about 3 biscuits per tray drop scant dessertspoons of mix, spaced well apart, on to the prepared trays. Use a palette knife or the back of a spoon to spread out the batter evenly and very thinly into rounds about 9–10 cm/3½–4 inches in diameter. Sprinkle with the flaked almonds then bake for 5–7 minutes. When ready the biscuits will have a clearly defined, golden-brown outer rim while the centre remains a very pale yellow.

Remove from the oven and allow to cool for a few seconds. (Here, if you move quickly, the second tray can be put into the oven to bake and a timer set.) Now, using the palette knife, quickly remove the biscuits from the tray to the rolling pin, keeping them nut side up. If you protect your hand with a clean cloth, the biscuits can be gently squeezed to the shape of the rolling pin. Leave to cool for a few minutes then transfer to a wire rack so you are ready for the next batch. Prepare the third batch of biscuits for baking in exactly the same way but give the baking tray time to cool before lining with paper, greasing and spreading the batter.

Cigarettes

Make the biscuits as for the tuiles, but omit sprinkling with flaked almonds before baking. On removal from the oven roll them into thin cylinders around the handle of a wooden spoon. Leave to set for 1–2 minutes before withdrawing the spoon handle. Transfer the biscuits to a wire rack until crisp.

TO CONTAIN ICE CREAM

Cornets or cones

Make the biscuits as for tuiles, omitting the flaked almonds and using a little more mix; spread the mix out to rounds 14–15 cm/5½–6 inches in diameter. On removal from the oven form into cone shapes. It is just possible to do this "free-hand" but it is much easier to roll them around a wooden form (see Useful Addresses page 184). NOTE: Sadly, cream-horn moulds produce a cone too small for most purposes. You should aim to produce a cone that has a top diameter comparable to that of the average ice-cream scoop, about 5 cm/2 inches.

Tulipes

Make the biscuit as for the cornets, spreading the mix out in circles of about 15 cm/6 inches before baking. Have ready an upturned glass with a base about 5 cm/2 inches in diameter. On removal from the oven, place the hot biscuit centrally on the glass; then, with your hands protected with a cloth, press the biscuit gently down the sides of the glass to form a frilled edge, cup-like container. Some recipes may suggest forming tulipes over an orange but a glass gives a flatter base and therefore a more stable container when served on a plate.

I sit in the dark, I am all alone.
Enter a child and an ice cream cone.

A parent is easily beguiled
By sight of this coniferous child

The friendly embers warmer gleam,
The cone begins to drip ice cream.

Cones are composed of many a vitamin.
My lap is not the place to bitamin.

Although my raiment is not chinchilla,
I flinch to see it become vanilla.

Coniferous child, when vanilla melts
I'd rather it melted somewhere else.

Exit child with remains of cone.
I sit in the dusk. I am all alone,

Muttering spells like an angry Druid,
Alone, in the dusk, with the cleaning fluid.

Ogden Nash *c.* 1942,
"Family Reunion", *Verses from 1929 On*

Brandy Snap Biscuits

A successful biscuit to serve with ices. Although the usual cylindrical shape of Brandy Snaps is not particularly appropriate to serve with ices, if left as a flat biscuit, or curved in the manner of tuiles (see previous recipe), or formed into cornets or tulipes to contain ice cream, the brandy snap recipe works well. The ginger flavour is not obtrusive, and works particularly well with ices such as pear or melon, or the ginger can be left out, if you prefer.

Please read the introduction to the preceding recipe for Almond Wafer Biscuits as those guidelines also apply to the making and baking of Brandy Snap Biscuits.

INGREDIENTS

	Metric	U.S.	Imperial
Golden syrup	115 g	⅓ cup	4 oz
Demerara sugar	115 g	⅔ cup plus 2 tsp	4 oz
Butter	115 g	½ cup (1 stick)	4 oz
Plain/All purpose flour	115 g	¾ cup plus 2 Tbsp	4 oz
Ground ginger OR	1 tsp	1 tsp	1 tsp
Lemon rind	1 tsp	1 tsp	1 tsp
Lemon juice OR	1 tsp	1 tsp	1 tsp
Brandy	1 tsp	1 tsp	1 tsp

Position the oven shelf centrally and preheat the oven to 160°C/325°F/Gas Mark 3. Line 2 baking trays as directed for Almond Wafer Biscuits (see page 160).

In a heavy saucepan combine the syrup, sugar and butter and heat gently, stirring, until the butter has melted and the sugar dissolved. Remove from the heat and leave to cool slightly before sifting in the flour, the ginger or lemon rind and the lemon juice or brandy.

Drop teaspoons of mixture on to the prepared baking sheets, spacing them at least 7.5 cm/3 inches apart. Bake for about 8 minutes or until the mixture has spread out to a very thin brown bubbly topped disc, slightly darker brown around the edge. Remove from the oven, and leave to cool for a few seconds. Have a palette knife to hand, then as soon as the biscuits are firm enough to remove from the tray without damage, but still very flexible, proceed to form them into the shape of your choice.

NOTE: the remaining uncooked mix will get firmer as it gets colder. Indeed, it gets to the stage where the mix can be formed into small balls by hand and patted on to the baking tray. These will spread thinly with the heat of the oven and the resulting biscuits will be exactly the same as the first.

Flat biscuits
These can be used to decorate or accompany coupes of ice cream and can be as small or large as you wish; simply adjust the amount of mix to give the size of biscuit you choose and, once baked, transfer to a wire rack to cool.

Curved biscuits
Follow the directions given for forming Almond Tuiles (see page 161).

Cornets and tulipes
Follow the instructions given under Almond Wafer Biscuits (see page 160).

NOTE: We do not recommend shaping this mix into cigarettes as this produces a biscuit that is hard to bite.

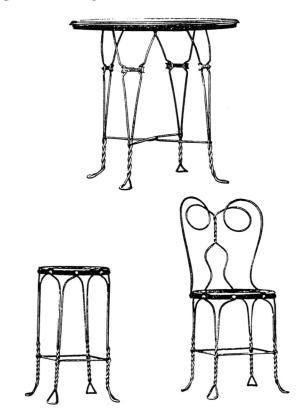

American wire furniture, popular in ice-cream bars *c.* 1930.

Allspice Biscuits

This biscuit recipe was a happy discovery some years ago in Nathalie Hambro's book Particular Delights; *we have been churning them out ever since. They are thinnish, black, very crisp, spiced biscuits, light years away from anything you will find in a packet. The allspice, cocoa-pepperiness goes well with chocolate, nut (particularly walnut) and coffee ices.*

INGREDIENTS

	Metric	U.S.	Imperial
Plain/All purpose flour	225 g	2 cups minus 2 Tbsp	8 oz
Baking powder	1 tsp	1 tsp	1 tsp
Ground allspice berries	1 tsp	1 tsp	1 tsp
Freshly ground black pepper	½ tsp	½ tsp	½ tsp
Cinnamon	½ tsp	½ tsp	½ tsp
Cocoa powder	85 g	1 cup minus 2 Tbsp	3 oz
Butter (at room temperature)	170 g	¾ cup	6 oz
Granulated sugar	225 g	1⅛ cups	8 oz
Vanilla extract	1½ tsp	1½ tsp	1½ tsp
Egg	1	1	1
Makes about	48	48	48

Sift together the first 6 ingredients and set aside. In a large mixing bowl, beat the butter, sugar and vanilla extract until pale and light. Whisk the egg briefly then add in stages to the butter mix beating well between each addition. Fold in the sieved dry ingredients, stirring just sufficiently to form a dough. Have ready a sheet of silicone paper measuring about 40×20 cm/16×8 inches. Shape the dough into an even sausage, about 30 cm/12 inches in length, and roll up in the paper. Slide on to a baking tray to prevent it distorting or breaking, then transfer to the fridge to chill until firm; about 3 hours.

When ready, preheat the oven to 190°C/375°F/Gas Mark 5. Use either non-stick baking trays or line with silicone paper; moisten a piece of kitchen paper with tasteless oil and wipe over both tray or paper. Use a sharp knife to cut the dough into 5 mm/¼ inch thick slices. Arrange a little apart on the baking trays to allow for some expansion during baking.

Bake for 10–12 minutes, changing the trays around in the oven halfway if the biscuits seem to be baking unevenly. The biscuits are done when they resist the imprint of a finger. Be careful not to overbake them; because they are nearly black, you need to look at them carefully to detect signs of overbaking. Use a spatula to transfer the biscuits to a wire rack to cool.

Nut and Seed Pralines/Brittles

If you ever taste home-made and commercial peanut and sesame seed brittles, side by side, it is quite startling to find how much better the home-made product is.
Caramel is comparatively simple to make **but you must take great care when making it**, *bearing in mind that it reaches the same sort of temperatures as oil does when deep-frying. Also, the sugar caramelises (darkens) rapidly, so do not leave the pan once you have started to heat the sugar, but give it your undivided attention from start to finish.*

INGREDIENTS

	Metric	U.S.	Imperial
To granulated sugar	100 g	scant ½ cup	3½ oz
add **one** of the following nuts or seeds			
1. Whole unblanched almonds, toasted	100 g	generous ¾ cup	3½ oz
2. Sesame seeds	55 g	⅓ cup plus 1 Tbsp	2 oz
3. Walnut pieces	85 g	¾ cup	3 oz
4. Shelled, skinned, roasted peanuts	100 g	heaped ½ cup	3½ oz
5. Skinned, chopped hazelnuts, toasted	50 g	⅓ cup	1¾ oz
Some tasteless oil			

Select a good solid baking tray and wipe over with a pad of kitchen paper moistened with a tasteless oil.

Have the nuts or seeds of your choice ready, toasted and still warm, or warm in the oven; this stops them clumping together when they are stirred into the caramel.

Put the sugar into a 14–15 cm/5½–6 inch diameter saucepan. Cook over a heat slightly less than moderate, leaving the sugar undisturbed until there is a clearly visible edge of liquefied sugar just beginning to tinge brown. Now stir slowly as the sugar liquefies and colours. As soon as the syrup is clear and a honey colour, stir in the warmed nuts and continue to stir until the colour is a deep golden brown similar to the darker colour of some liquid honeys. **Taking great care**, immediately pour the mixture on to the baking tray; the large nuts might need spreading out a little. Leave the mixture to cool and harden.

We find it best to break the made praline or brittle into rough pieces then store them in a screw-top jar in the fridge. The pieces can then be crushed to whatever size is preferred for a particular purpose. It will keep for several weeks in the fridge, really until it is sticky, but can be frozen for about a year – only be careful to avoid any moisture coming into direct contact with the mixture as it will start to dissolve.

To crush the sugar/nut mix we prefer using an old-fashioned pestle and mortar as it gives you most control over the degree of fineness. Using a food processor works reasonably well if you want a fine powder, but beware of overprocessing or you might end up with a sticky paste.

NOTE: Clean the pan by soaking in water.

Ice cream postage stamps.

Sauces

Butterscotch Sauce

Can be served hot or cold and will keep happily for up to three weeks in the fridge in a screw-top jar. As the sauce cools it will thicken, so served straight from the fridge it is usually preferable to thin it with a little water, or if you are going for bust, cream.

INGREDIENTS

	Metric	U.S.	Imperial
Soft brown sugar	75 g	½ cup packed	2¾ oz
Granulated sugar	50 g	4 Tbsp	4 Tbsp
Unsalted butter	50 g	4 Tbsp	4 Tbsp
Golden syrup	150 g	½ cup	5¼ oz
Whipping/heavy cream (36 per cent fat)	125 ml	½ cup	4 fl oz
Vanilla extract	¼ tsp	¼ tsp	¼ tsp
Makes about	500 ml	2 cups	16 fl oz

Combine the first 4 ingredients together in a saucepan and cook over a very low heat until the ingredients have melted and most of the sugar dissolved. Raise the heat a little to bring the mixture to a gentle boil and leave to cook in this manner, uncovered, for 5 minutes. Remove the pan from the heat and stir in the cream and vanilla extract. The sauce is now ready to serve.

The Ice Cream Cone is the only ecologically sound package known. It is the perfect package.

United States Health Education and Welfare Official, quoted on the T.V. show "60 Minutes", 1969

Chocolate Fudge Sauce

This can rightly be described as all-purpose.
As a sauce it can be served hot or cold, but it also has the advantage of remaining the same consistency as an ice cream when frozen and so makes an excellent ripple in vanilla, banana, chestnut, coffee or pear ice creams.

INGREDIENTS

	Metric	U.S.	Imperial
Soft brown sugar	50 g	⅓ cup packed	1¾ oz
Granulated sugar	25 g	2 Tbsp	2 Tbsp
Unsalted butter	50 g	4 Tbsp	4 Tbsp
Golden syrup	150 g	½ cup	5¼ oz
Cocoa powder★	1 Tbsp	1 Tbsp	1 Tbsp
Whipping/heavy cream (36 per cent fat)	185 ml	¾ cup	6 fl oz
Plain/semisweet chocolate, chopped★★	50 g	⅓ cup	1¾ oz
Vanilla extract	¼ tsp	¼ tsp	¼ tsp
Makes about	400 ml	1⅔ cups	14 fl oz

★ See Ingredients page 35.
★★ See Ingredients page 34.

Combine the first 4 ingredients together in a saucepan, and add the sieved cocoa powder. Cook over a very low heat until the ingredients have melted and most of the sugar dissolved. Raise the heat a little to bring the mixture to a gentle boil and leave to cook in this manner, uncovered, for 5 minutes. Remove the pan from the heat and stir in the cream, then the chopped chocolate and vanilla. When the chocolate has melted return the pan to the heat, bring to the boil and boil gently for 1 minute, whisking steadily. The sauce will now be smooth. Allow to cool a little before using hot, or serve at room temperature or chilled. The sauce will keep in the fridge in a screw-top jar for up to 3 weeks. As the sauce cools it will thicken, so served straight from the fridge it will probably need thinning with a little additional cream.

RIPPLES

If you intend using Chocolate Fudge Sauce in this way, work to a basic formula of 125 ml/½ cup/4 fl oz of (room temperature) sauce to 1 litre/4 cups/32 fl oz of freshly made ice cream.

We recommend using a rectangular plastic freezer box about 1½ times the capacity needed, as this will give enough space to fold the 2 mixes together without loosing any overboard.

Quickly spread half the freshly churned ice cream in a layer covering the base of the box, then blob small spoons of half the sauce on top to give an erratic layer; don't attempt to spread it. Repeat the layering with the remaining ice cream and sauce then use a large spoon to turn the mix over from top to bottom of the box about 3 times. This should only haphazardly combine the 2 mixtures leaving clear seams of fudge sauce patterned throughout the ice cream. Cover and freeze in the usual way.

Light Lemon and Sultana Sauce

The simplest sauces seem to work best with ice cream. This one has a clean, clear and slightly sharp flavour that counterbalances richness. It goes particularly well with apple and pear ice creams.

INGREDIENTS

	Metric	U.S.	Imperial
Lemon	1	1	1
Cornflour	1 Tbsp	–	1 Tbsp
OR			
Cornstarch	–	1 Tbsp	–
Granulated sugar	110 g	½ cup plus ½ Tbsp	4 oz
Water	250 ml	1 cup	8 fl oz
Sultanas	50 g	–	1¾ oz
OR			
Golden raisins	–	⅓ cup	–
Makes about	375 ml	1½ cups	12 fl oz

Wash and dry the lemon. Remove the zest, preferably using a lemon zester, or finely grate into a small saucepan. Mix with the cornflour and sugar; then using a small whisk, gradually blend in the water. Bring to the boil over a moderate heat, stirring. Boil gently for 2–3 minutes then remove the pan from the heat. Add the strained juice of the lemon and the sultanas. Serve, warm or cold. Use within a day.

Rose Pouchong Tea Syrup

Other types of teas can be used, jasmine, gunpowder, green,
Japanese green tea, all the oolongs and pouchongs; just choose
a flavour that marries best with the sorbet or ice to be served.
For example, we suggest:
Red bean with green tea syrup.
Mango sorbet with jasmine tea syrup.
The trick is not to overheat the tea and have it release its full
complement of tannin; warming and prolonged soaking gives
the flavour without the bitterness, to produce a sauce that is
subtly sharp with smoke and flower overtones.

INGREDIENTS

	Metric	U.S.	Imperial
Sugar syrup (see page 47)	250 ml	1 cup	8 fl oz
Rose pouchong tea	2 Tbsp	2 Tbsp	2 Tbsp
Lemon or lime juice	¼–½ tsp	¼–½ tsp	¼–½ tsp
Orange flower water	¼–½ tsp	¼–½ tsp	¼–½ tsp
Makes about	250 ml	1 cup	8 fl oz

Pour the syrup into a small saucepan and add the tea
leaves. Heat just until the syrup is hand-hot – then
remove from the heat.

(If you have a microwave, pour the syrup into a
microwave-safe jug, add the leaves and microwave for 1
minute on full power.)

Once the syrup has cooled, cover it and chill overnight
in the fridge. The following day strain the liquid through
a fine sieve or tea strainer, pressing the leaves firmly to
extract the maximum flavour. Stir in the lemon or lime
juice and orange flower water. The syrup is then ready to
serve.

NOTE: When using teas other than rose pouchong omit
the orange flower water.

An example of an elaborate modern mould, made in non-
toxic metal from a vast range still being manufactured by
Letang in France. Total capacity approximately two and a
half litres.

This selection of bombes is taken from *Ma Cuisine* by
Auguste Escoffier, Flamerion & Cie, Paris, 1934, and
Cooking à la Ritz by Louis Diat, who was the Chef at the Ritz
Carlton, New York, published by *Restaurant Trade Journal*,
London, *c.* 1930. It will give some idea of the wide variety of
types of bombes that exist. In fact the name of the bombe can
frequently describe completely different combinations of ices
in any one bombe.

There seems to be no definitive guide or list, but *Herrings
Dictionary of Classical and Modern Cookery*, originally *Lexicon
der Kuche*, has 147 different combinations and *Repertoire de la
Cuisine* has 126. Although many of these are common to
both lists, each has a number of unique ones. (See Useful
Addresses page 184).

Name	Lining, ice cream	Centre
Aida	Strawberry	Kirsch and maraschino
African	Chocolate	Praline
Alsacienne	Pistachio	Chocolate
Bordelaise	Pistachio	Apricot
Camargo	Peach	Kirsch
Chinese	Vanilla	Tea containing diced sponge cake in rum
Duchesse	Orange sorbet	Kirsch
Favorite	Chestnut	Apricot
Florida	Tangerine	Curaçao
Olympia	Peach	Brandy flavoured peach, with peaches soaked in brandy
Richelieu	Raspberry sorbet	Anisette
Sarah Bernhardt	Strawberry	Caramel
Suzette	Vanilla	Chartreuse
Tosca	Praline	Chocolate

CHAPTER 8

Bombes and Moulded Ices

Whatever you have ever read about moulded ices or bombes, treat with a great deal of suspicion. An ice that eventually emerges as a sorry-looking melting mass, with a granite hard core that resists even a hot knife, we would judge as having not "worked". Using this as our criterion, we believe that the majority of recipes have not been tested, because with the knowledge we now have, we know they would never work. Since this type of dessert takes time and trouble and uses expensive ingredients, it is something you would probably only do for special occasions; all the more reason to look for guaranteed results.

Moulding ices is not straightforward. You have to overcome several inbuilt design problems to achieve a respectable-looking turned-out mould which is a combination of different ices and flavourings, and which you can readily cut to serve.

The first thing to consider is the mould. **If you have any antique ice cream bombes or metal moulds we strongly recommend that these are kept solely to decorate your kitchen and not put to any practical use. The metals may well be toxic.**

However, before rushing out to buy expensive new moulds pause and consider if you are likely to get sufficient use out of them to justify the expense. One of the most successful moulds is a simple plastic pudding basin. It conducts hot and cold temperatures quickly and is flexible. This flexibility is important because it allows the bowl to be squeezed gently to deform the shape slightly, pulling the bowl out of contact with the frozen ice cream. This allows air up into the base of the mould and releases the air lock which deposits the ice neatly on to the plate. The ice can then be decorated with all manner of cream, fruit or chocolate to disguise the humble origin of the shape or it can be smoothed with a knife to modify the angle of the base.

If you consider it worth the outlay, then of the types that are available (see Equipment page 38) we would recommend you choose one of the following:

1. *Tin-lined copper bombe*
This has a screw in the rounded top that is removed to release the air lock when turning out the ice. Expensive. (See illustration page 168.)

2. *Aluminium bombe*
Similar to the shape above, but with a flatter top and no screw to release the air lock; but the metal is soft enough to be flexible so the mould can be gently squeezed to release the ice in the same manner as the plastic bowl described above. Cheap.

3. *Tall, thin, conical, sugar-loaf shaped mould, in stainless steel*
Because of the greater weight of ice in the base, this shape turns out best of all the moulds, but when cut and served makes oddly shaped individual portions. Very expensive.

As a general guide we would advise you to stick to as plain a mould as possible. Decorated moulds require careful filling to avoid air locks or pockets and they are not so easy to turn out. Since the very nature of ice cream is to melt, some blurring of the detail is inevitable and often the result is disappointing.

Much more elaborate hinged moulds are available, particularly in France (see Useful Addresses page 184). If the hinged mould is large enough to serve upwards of six portions make sure that the mould has been made in more than two sections so that the ice can be turned out easily.

Avoid large moulds in two hinged pieces which open like a book and are a tall shape that must be served upright, e.g., a large strawberry. Opening the mould is easy; extracting the ice undamaged from the remaining half of the mould is very tricky.

We do not recommend using glass or pottery for moulding ices. Even if they are suitable for freezing, they have no flexibility and hold the heat, which causes an unnecessary amount of melting to the outside of the ice.

NOTE: There seems to be some confusion between chocolate and ice-cream moulds. The difference is very simple; ice-cream moulds are always sealed with either a lid or a base. Chocolate moulds are usually in two halves held together with clips and are open-ended in order that melted chocolate can readily be poured in and out to build up sufficient layers to make a casting.

Ice Trophy à la Brittanique, Fred T. Vine, 1890

For the filling the aim is to achieve a uniform consistency, soft enough to eat but firm enough to serve. This is only achieved by using one type of ice or ice cream for the lining and another for the centre. The lining can be either an ice cream or a sorbet.

The core must be an ice that contains air trapped either in beaten egg or cream, and/or alcohol. Air displaces water, giving a softer ice; alcohol lowers the temperature at which the mix will freeze and so remains, by comparison, softer than the outer layer.

It is impossible to make a successful bombe/mould of one type of ice cream because it cannot be thawed evenly throughout. But there are two exceptions:–

1. Moulds that are small enough to serve as individual portions are small enough to thaw uniformly.
2. Large moulds are successful if the ice cream is made, the mould filled and frozen for no more than 2 hours. At this stage the outside is frozen hard enough to successfully unmould the ice and the centre has not had sufficient time to be fully hardened. So just 10–20 minutes in the fridge will soften the outside sufficiently for the entire bombe to cut nicely when served.

When moulds were in their heyday in the nineteenth century that is how moulded ices and bombes would have been made. The ice caves in which the bombe/moulds were frozen would have achieved temperatures similar to a modern freezer but would not have been capable of sustaining these temperatures for long periods without the frequent addition of quantities of salt and ice.

Mrs Marshall's classic bombe shapes, unaltered since 1894.

The best quality elaborate pewter moulds for iced bombes. Each mould was in three or more parts to make removal of the frozen pudding less difficult. Francatelli, 1894.

It is arguable that the modern freezer is the bane of good ice-cream making as it takes ices down to temperatures that are really low.

Since moulds come in all shapes and sizes be prepared for some recipes to be in excess of what is needed to fill a mould. Sometimes it is either impractical or mathematically impossible to scale down recipes to get the exact amount. It is much simpler to make up a full recipe and store any excess.

ASSEMBLING BOMBES

To make bombes you need patience as it takes a lot of time to get each ice to the right consistency for each stage. For the classic style of bombe, in two or more layers, start making at least a day in advance.

Always chill the mould for at least 30 minutes in the freezer, before putting the lining (outside) ice into the bombe mould. It is important to have the lining ice cream at a frozen consistency where it can be pushed into position and stay there. After a brief freezing, about 30 minutes, it will probably need some adjustment and repair work to smooth it out and make sure that it is an even thickness.

Freeze the outside layer until firm, then put in the centre, making sure that it is firmly packed and that there are no air pockets.

Leave a small gap at the top of the mould for expansion as ices expand about 4 per cent during freezing. Cover with a round of freezer-layering tissue or waxed or greaseproof paper, put on the lid and freeze for a minimum of 2 hours or overnight.

To turn out the bombe/mould we have found that dipping into a bowl full of warm water is the best method. (Hot water melts the surface of the ice too much; cold water simply freezes on the exterior of the container and hot towels are difficult to handle and are awkward to arrange so that the whole surface of the mould gets an even heat.)

So, taking it directly from the freezer, plunge the mould up to its neck in warm water (35°C/95°F) for 10 seconds, unscrew, and dry the mould with a cloth. Remove the lid and peel off the lining paper. Invert on to a chilled plate or dish and gently squeeze the mould if plastic or aluminium to release the air lock, unscrew the plug if copper, and the ice should come cleanly away from the mould.

If any repairing is needed this is done now (we recommend the back of a melamine spoon) and the iced bombe returned to the freezer just long enough to re-freeze the surface, about 30 minutes or until needed. Perfectly turned-out ices (e.g. stainless steel cones) and the repaired versions, should be put into the fridge for 10–20 minutes to soften sufficiently for serving. You can always try a trial cut to make sure the inside is softened sufficiently, and repair the cut with a melamine spoon or the blade of a knife dipped in warm water before you serve the bombe.

If you are going to decorate the bombe we prefer a decoration which gives the diner some clue as to the contents of the bombe.

BOMBE RECIPES

The list of classic bombes gives an idea of how to match harmonising flavours. All sorts of permutations are possible using the ices in this book, provided you stick to the rules we suggest.

However, making a classic-style bombe is a fairly

lengthy process, and the result is rich. Below are some suggestions for bombes/moulds more quickly made of lighter types of ices – perhaps more suited to today's needs.

Strawberry Sorbet and Framboise Ice-Cream Ring

Using the Easy No-Cook Philadelphia Vanilla Ice Cream cuts down some of the work and adding the framboise marries it very successfully with the light, fresh-tasting Strawberry Sorbet. Using a ring mould means that it can be assembled in one go. The ring makes a very attractive summer ice cream if the centre is filled with summer soft fruits and served with a red berry sauce.
Using these basic ideas many other combinations are possible using other no-cook ice creams and sorbets in the book.

INGREDIENTS

One recipe Easy No-Cook Philadelphia Vanilla Ice
    Cream (see page 153)
Framboise liqueur 2½–3 Tbsp
One recipe Strawberry or Raspberry Sorbet (see pages
    145 and 136)

You will need a 1.75 litre/7¼ cup/60 fl oz ring mould.

Make the ice cream according to the recipe (see page 153), reducing the amount of vanilla to ½ tsp and stirring in the framboise liqueur just before churning. Transfer to the fridge to harden sufficiently to use; not more than 2 hours.

Make up the sorbet (see page 145 or 136) and refrigerate until firm enough to scoop. Thirty minutes before you estimate the ices will be ready to assemble, put the ring mould in the freezer.

When ready, fill the mould with alternate large spoonfuls of sorbet and ice cream, pressing each addition firmly up against the preceding ice, not forgetting the base and sides of the mould. Cover with freezer-layering tissue and freeze.

Unmould according to instructions, turning out on to a well chilled plate. Immediately fill the centre with a combination of prepared summer fruits and decorate with fresh leaves, and return to the fridge for about 20 minutes to soften sufficiently. Serve with a red berry sauce.

Blackberry Spoom and Sorbet Bombe

This bombe uses a single basic sorbet mix, half of which is used as a sorbet for the lining, the other half combined with meringue to make a spoom to form the soft inner core. Very light, very fresh-tasting, utterly delicious, it contains no cream at all.

INGREDIENTS

	Metric	U.S.	Imperial
One recipe Blackberry Sorbet (see page 63)			
Egg white	1	1	1
Granulated sugar	65 g	¼ cup plus 1 Tbsp	2¼ oz

You will need a bombe mould of approximately 1½ litres/6 cups/50 fl oz capacity. Make the sorbet mixture and divide the liquid mix in two. Make the first part into a sorbet and line a bombe mould with it, making sure the walls are of an even thickness. Freeze till solid.

In a medium-sized grease-free bowl beat the egg white with a hand-held electric beater until it forms soft peaks, then gradually add the sugar and continue beating until it forms stiff peaks. Take the second half of the sorbet mix and fold the liquid into the meringue, a little at a time, making sure that the purée is completely mixed with the meringue. Pour into the centre of the bombe and freeze.

To turn out follow the instructions above (see page 169).

Neapolitan ice spoon, waffle irons and ice spatula with
pewter freezing pot and pail.

Christmas Cake Ice Cream with Brandy Parfait

After the heaviness of a Christmas dinner this bombe is a welcome relief from Christmas pudding.
The two recipes combined make 2.2 litres/9 cups/72 fl oz so you can make two bombes, using plastic pudding basins as moulds to echo the traditional Christmas pudding basin shape.

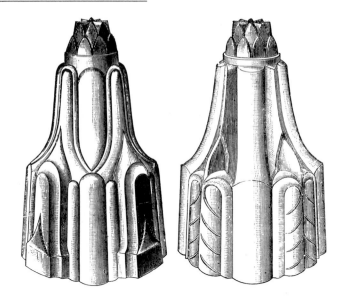

INGREDIENTS

One recipe Christmas Cake Ice Cream (see page 79)
One recipe Brandy Parfait (see page 49)

Make the Christmas Cake Ice Cream according to the recipe and freeze for about 1–2 hours until it is the right consistency to line a bombe mould. Even if you are using plastic moulds it is a good idea to chill them for 30 minutes in the freezer. Line the moulds and freeze. Check after about 1 hour in the freezer and neaten, if necessary. While they are freezing, make the parfait and when it is ready pour into the centre of the moulds. Cover with freezer-layering tissue or waxed or greaseproof paper and freeze overnight. To turn out follow the instructions above (see page 169).

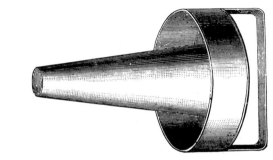

Cover and pipe for above moulds.

French Silver Gilt Ice-Cream servers, *c.* 1860. In the latter part of the 19th century when the making of ice cream became more popular in the homes of the well-to-do, manufacturers exploited this market with all manner of expensive china, glass and cutlery. These servers are just one example of an extraordinary range of cutlery devoted to the service of ice cream.

CHAPTER 9

Chemistry of Ices

Most books on ices contain a fairly respectable collection of recipes. Few, if any, tackle the physics and chemistry of making ices, especially books for the domestic market, because it is such a complex subject. Had the information in this chapter been readily available to us at the outset a lot of time and ingredients would not have been wasted in unsuccessful experiments.

This part of the book is for serious makers of ices, to help them understand the limits to which it is necessary to work when making up new recipes, how to evaluate recipes for all manner of ice creams and sorbets, anticipate their qualities (good, bad or indifferent) and if necessary how to correct an imbalance of ingredients. All this, of course, subject to personal taste – a most important proviso.

Serious commercial ice-cream makers should refer to Arbuckle, Rothwell and Preti (see Bibliography page 186) and the ice-cream courses run in Britain and America (see Useful Addresses page 184).

Ices have two common ingredients: water and air.

They then divide neatly into milk-based, cream-based and sugar-syrup based ices.

All ices, sweet and savoury, are a mixture of:

Water (on its own or in milk)
Air
and flavouring

With the possible addition of some of the following:

Sugars or sweeteners (e.g. honey, natural sugars in fruit etc.)
Fats, milk or non-milk based (e.g. vegetable oil)
Milk solids, non-fat (i.e. lactose, protein and minerals)
Egg yolks or whites or both

Champion Hand Ice Machine, 1890.

And in the case of commercial ices:

> *Stabilisers and*
> *Emulsifiers (other than eggs)*
> *and colourings*

In order to give a clear explanation of the physics and chemistry, it is necessary to deal with the two types of ices separately, as milk-based ices have very different characteristics from water-based ices.

Milk-Based Ices

Milk-based ices contain ice crystals, fat globules, air cells, all dispersed in a liquid (water) which contains sugar, milk protein and minerals. The ingredients are stabilised in a foam by the freezing of varying percentages of the liquid.

NOTE: At no point does all the liquid ever freeze.

All these constituents have a direct bearing on the resulting milk-based ice. So the recipe that is used and the manner in which all the ingredients are combined (e.g., cooked, churned, frozen and thawed) will give the ice its particular character.

WATER

On its own water freezes into hard ice, but when it is churned and frozen in combination with the other ingredients, this straightforward process is modified in several crucial ways.

At around $-8.3°C/17°F$, some 67 per cent of the water has formed ice crystals, depending on the recipe. These ice crystals should be as small as possible in order to make a smooth ice cream.

Rapid freezing ensures a burst of growth of many small seed crystals simultaneously throughout the mix, inhibiting the growth of large ones; the action of churning disperses the crystals evenly throughout the mix, keeping them moving and preventing them from fusing together. Hence, a still frozen ice cream, although beaten once or twice during freezing, will still contain large ice crystals, giving it a coarser texture and a colder taste than the churned version.

AIR

The incorporation of air into ice cream is the second most important influence on the texture of ice cream in that it separates the ice crystals and fat globules and holds them in a foam suspension.

In commercial ice cream, manufacturers can double the original volume of their product by the introduction of compressed air during churning. This considerable commercial advantage has unfortunately distorted the public perception of what ice cream should be. Home-made churned ice cream, which is unlikely to expand much beyond 25 per cent during making, is appreciably denser than the commercial product.

SUGAR

Sugar is required in all ices:
1. To give the required sweetness.
2. To build up the body and viscosity and give smoothness to the texture of the ice. Because it contributes body to ice cream, dissolved sugar is referred to as a *solid* in the formulation of balanced ice-cream mixes.
3. To influence the freezing point. In an ice-cream mix the sugar will be dissolved in the water of either eggs or milk and/or cream. Introducing sugar increases the density of the mix and depresses the freezing point, which means that it will require a lower temperature to make the water solidify into ice.

Once the ice cream mixture starts to freeze, small ice crystals of almost pure water start to form. Therefore the remaining sugar solution becomes even more concentrated (denser) and the freezing point is lowered still further.

The lower the temperature gets, the more ice crystals form, and the more concentrated the sugar solution becomes. However, it gets to a point where the sugar concentration is so high that, startling as it may seem, there will always be some liquid in an ice cream. This is what makes some ice creams scoopable at sub-zero temperatures.

FAT

Fats are the most expensive ingredients in ice cream, and air is the cheapest. For this reason they are the two most frequently varied ingredients; cheap manufactured ice cream having little fat and a lot of air, and premium a lot of fat and little air.

In home-made ice cream the fat comes mostly from milk and cream and is present in the form of globules which inhibit the growth of larger ice crystals by keeping the small ice crystals apart. The amount of fat in ice cream dictates the richness of the finished ice cream and its lubricating effect causes a smooth sensation in the mouth.

MILK

Whole milk consists of water, fat and M.S.N.F. (milk solids non-fat) in the following proportions.

Water		87 per cent
Milk fat or		
Butterfat		4 per cent
M.S.N.F.		
Lactose	5 per cent	
Protein	3 per cent	
Minerals	1 per cent	9 per cent
		100 per cent

THE COMPOSITION OF OTHER TYPES OF MILK AND CREAM AND BUTTER

	Fat per cent	M.S.N.F. per cent	Sugar per cent	Total solids per cent	Water per cent
WHOLE MILK	4	8.8	—	12.8	87.2
MILK POWDER					
full cream	27	70	—	97	3
skim	—	97	—	97	3
EVAPORATED					
MILK	9	22	—	31	69
SWEETENED CONDENSED					
whole milk	9	22	44	75	25
skim milk	—	26	44	70	30
WHIPPING					
CREAM	38	5.4	—	43.4	56.6
UNSALTED					
BUTTER	84	—	—	84	16

THE MINIMUM PERCENTAGE OF FAT IN MILKS AND CREAMS FOR U.K. AND U.S.

	U.K. Milk fat per cent	U.S. Milk fat per cent
Skim milk	1.6–1.7	0.5
Low fat	—	0.5–2
Whole milk	4	3.25–4
Half and half	—	at least 10
Half cream	13	—
Light cream	—	18
Single cream	19	—
Whipping cream	**35**	30
Heavy cream	—	**36**
Double cream	48	—
Clotted cream	55	check package

NOTE: Almost all milk in the U.S.A. is homogenised.

ICE CREAM

The secret of sweet ice-cream making is having a correct balance of ingredients:

1. Between fat and sugar.

2. Between total solids and water.

There are a number of opinions about this. However, these are the areas within which acceptable ice creams can be made that can be stored.

It is possible to make ices outside these proportions provided they are eaten within hours of their making. However, they will frequently deteriorate in quality if stored and defrosted.

The fat/sugar ratio should ideally be within these proportions to ensure there is enough sugar to overcome or balance the fattiness of the mix.

It may be necessary to add more sugar in certain cases of particularly sour fruits.

Fat should not be less than 5 per cent or more than 20 per cent. At much below 5 per cent it will be a sherbet. If it is more than 20 per cent, there is a danger of the ice cream becoming very dense and chewy.

Sugar should not be less than 12 per cent and not really more than 20 per cent.

1. THE FAT/SUGAR BALANCE

fat per cent	sugar per cent	
6	12.0	
7	12.5	
8	13.0	normal
9	13.5	commercial
10	14.0	ice cream
11	14.5	range
12	15.0	
13	15.5	
14	16.0	
15	16.5	
16	17.0	
17	17.5	
18	18.0	
19	18.5	
20	19.0	

NOTE: Commercial ice creams are normally within the 6–12 per cent fat range.

2. THE TS (TOTAL SOLIDS) TO WATER BALANCE

This ensures among other things adequate smoothness and body.

Too much water = large ice crystals = insipid taste and no body.

Too little water = sandiness due to the crystallisation of the lactose.

Solids include sugar, fat, and M.S.N.F. (q.v.) plus any solids in fruit etc. that has been added to the ice cream.

M.S.N.F. will absorb in the region of six times their own weight of water in a mix. This is important as excess M.S.N.F. will create lactose crystallisation in storage, and too low a percentage could lead to iciness in storage due to all of the water not having been absorbed.

THE FORMULA FOR CALCULATING THE PERCENTAGE OF M.S.N.F. NEEDED

$$\text{M.S.N.F. per cent} = \frac{100 - (\text{percentage of all solids other than M.S.N.F.})}{7}$$

So for a mixture with 8 per cent fat and 13 per cent sugar:

$$\text{M.S.N.F.} = \frac{100 - (8+13)}{7} = \frac{100 - 21}{7} = 11.3 \text{ per cent}$$

M.S.N.F. should be 11.3 per cent

For commercial ices, according to Preti in *Il Gelato Artigianale Italiano*, the percentages by weight of the ingredients in ice cream should be within the following:

Sugar	14–20 per cent
Fat	6–14 per cent
M.S.N.F.	6–11 per cent

For quality ice creams the figures should be within the following:-

Sugar	16–18 per cent
Fat	8–11 per cent
M.S.N.F.	9–10 per cent

Ice creams below 30 per cent in **total** solids are likely to be icy in texture.

In order to calculate the various percentages and make up ice-cream recipes, we find the following chart simplifies the calculations.

Typical clothing worn by Soda jerks, *c.* 1900.

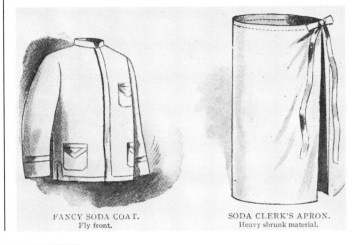

FANCY SODA COAT.
Fly front.

SODA CLERK'S APRON.
Heavy shrunk material.

CALCULATIONS

All calculations are done in weights *not* volumes

	Weight	Fat	M.S.N.F.	Sugar	Other solids
Sugar					
Milk★		4 per cent	8.8 per cent		
Cream★		38 per cent	5.4 per cent		
Egg yolk 20 g each		33 per cent			17 per cent
Egg white 40 g each					14 per cent
Flavour★★					
Total weight		Total fat	Total M.S.N.F.	Total sugar	Total other solids
Percentage of total weight		Fat per cent	M.S.N.F. per cent	Sugar per cent	Other solids per cent

Fat + M.S.N.F. + Sugar + Other solids = Total solids   per cent

Notes

  ★ Milk and cream percentages are *minimum* legal figures. It is for this reason we have taken the cream (whipping U.K.; heavy U.S.A.) fat percentage at 38 per cent as in analysis it always comes out a few percentage points above the legal minimum. Ice-cream manufacturers check each delivery and calculate the mix on the basis of the result. (For other creams and lactic products, see chart on page 35.)

  ★★ See chart on page 178 for fruit and vegetables solid and sugar percentages. For other ingredients see page 34.

SAMPLE CALCULATION

This calculation is based on Rich French Vanilla Ice Cream, see page 51.

All calculations are done in weights *not* volumes

	Weight	Fat	M.S.N.F.	Sugar	Other solids
Sugar	90 g			90 g	
Milk★	375 g	15 g 4 per cent	33 g 8.8 per cent		
Cream★	175 g	70 g 38 per cent	10 g 5.4 per cent		
Egg yolk 20 g each ×5	100 g	33 g 33 per cent			17 g 17 per cent
Egg white 40 g each					14 per cent
Flavour★★					
Total weight	740 g	Total fat 118 g	Total M.S.N.F. 43 g	Total sugar 90 g	Total other solids 17 g
Percentage of total weight		Fat per cent 15.9	M.S.N.F. per cent 5.8	Sugar per cent 12.2	Other solids per cent 2.3

Fat + M.S.N.F. + Sugar + Other solids = Total solids 35.6 per cent

Cold Dog advertisement (*c.* 1926).

Water-based ices

SUGAR SYRUP

In order to simplify the making of sorbets and granitas, almost all the recipes in this book are made with a **simple syrup**.

SIMPLE SYRUP

Simple syrup is best made in quantity and kept in a fridge. However, these tables will enable you to make small quantities.

METRIC

1,000 ml water	+	1,000 g sugar	= 1,600 ml syrup
750		750	= 1,200 ml
625		625	= 1,000 ml
500		500	= 800 ml
375		375	= 600 ml
✗ 250		250	= 400 ml ✗
125		125	= 200 ml

U.S.A.

34 fl oz water	+	40 fl oz sugar	= 54 fl oz syrup
OR			
4 cups		5 cups	= 6⅔ cups
3		3¾	= 4¾ cups
2½		3⅝	= 4 cups
2		2½	= 3¼ cups
1½		2⅜	= 2⅓ cups
1¼		1⅞	= 2 cups
1		1¼	= 1½ cups
½		⅝	= ¾ cups

For more advanced sorbet and granita making we advise the purchase of a saccharometer or hydrometer (see Equipment page 42). Try to get one calibrated in Baumé as they are much easier to read and work with. If it is calibrated in decimal scale there is a conversion table (see right).

The lower the density of the liquid the lower the instrument is in the liquid. The higher the density, i.e. the more sugar that is dissolved, the "thicker" or denser the liquid, and therefore the higher the instrument will rise out of the liquid.

TABLE FOR CONVERTING DECIMAL SCALE TO DEGREES BAUMÉ

If you find that the saccharometer is measured in density rather than degrees Baumé, you can convert them.

Decimal scale	Degrees Baumé	Decimal scale	Degrees Baumé
1.28	32	1.14	18
1.27	31	1.13	17
1.26	30	1.12	16
1.25	29	1.12	15
1.24	28	1.11	14
1.23	27	1.10	13
1.22	26	1.09	12
1.21	25	1.08	11
1.20	24	1.07	10
1.19	23	1.06	9
1.18	22	1.05	8
1.17	21	1.05	7
1.16	20	1.04	6
1.15	19	1.04	5

NOTE: You can find a holder for the saccharometer (an éprouvette) made in tin or stainless steel in specialist kitchenware shops (see page 43).

THE EFFECT OF ADDING WATER TO THE STANDARD SUGAR SYRUP

METRIC

250 ml sugar syrup		= 28° Baumé
250 ml	+ 250 ml water	= 16°
250 ml	+ 500 ml	11°
250 ml	+ 750 ml	8°
250 ml	+ 1 litre	6°
250 ml	+ 1.25 litres	5°

U.S.A.

1 cup sugar syrup		= 28° Baumé
1	+ 1 cup water	= 16°
1	+ 2	11°
1	+ 3	8°
1	+ 4	6°
1	+ 5	5°

NOTE: See the formula page 47 for making standard quantities of sugar syrup.

Please read Equipment (page 42) concerning saccharometers/hydrometers for an explanation of how these instruments work and why they are necessary for making sorbets and granitas.

SORBETS AND GRANITAS

Sorbets should be within the following density readings:

Without alcohol	17–20° Baumé
With alcohol	14–17° Baumé

Granitas should be around the 9° Baumé in order to produce a granita that is truly grainy. With alcohol added, around 8° Baumé is the best.

NOTE: Care must be taken as the amount of fibrous material in some fruits that is needed to get a reasonable flavour can seriously distort the Baumé reading or make it impossible to read.

"DOLLY MADISON'S SURPRISE"
Ice Frozen Desserts

THE COMPOSITION OF FRUIT AND VEGETABLES

	PERCENTAGES BY WEIGHT				
	Water	Sugar	Other solids	Total solids (Sugar + other solids)	
Apple	85	11	4	15	
Apricot	85	10	5	15	
Avocado	68	1	31	32	(Fat 24)
Banana	74	19	7	26	
Blackberry	85	9	6	15	
Blackcurrant	81	10	9	19	
Blueberry	77	20	3	23	
Carambola (Star fruit)	91	4	5	9	
Cherry (Morello)	85	11	4	15	
Cherry (Sweet)	83	13	4	17	
Clementine	87	10	3	13	
Coconut	45	5	50	55	(Fat 36.5)
Cranberry	87	8	5	13	
Currant	16	66	18	84	
Date (dried)	20	65	15	80	
Elderberry	81	7	12	19	
Fig	80	13	7	20	
Fig (dried)	25	54	21	75	
Gooseberry	87	10	3	13	
Grape	81	16	3	19	
Grapefruit	89	9	2	11	
Greengage	81	14	5	19	
Guava	81	7	12	19	
Jackfruit	73	15	12	27	
Kiwi	84	10	6	16	
Lemon	90	3	7	10	
Lime	91	2	7	9	
Lychee	82	17	1	18	
Mandarin	87	10	3	13	
Mango	82	13	5	18	
Medlar	87	4	9	13	
Musk Melon	87	12	1	13	
Nectarine	88	9	3	12	

(left) This serves to underline how mistakes become accepted mythology. Dolly Madison, or her servants, definitely made ice cream in the White House from 1809 to 1817, but not in an ice-cream machine which was not invented until 1846.

Orange	86	10	4	14
Papaya				
(Paw Paw)	88	2	10	12
Passion fruit	77	13	10	23
Peach	88	9	3	12
Pear	84	10	6	16
Pepper	91	3	6	9
Persimmon	81	16	3	19
Pineapple	85	13	2	15
Plum	84	12	4	16
Prune	24	55	31	86
Pumpkin	91	3	6	9
Quince	83	8	9	17
Raspberry	84	6	10	16
Redcurrant	85	8	7	15
Rhubarb	94	2	4	6
Strawberry	90	6	4	10
Tomato	94	3	3	6

Source: Food Composition and Nutrition Tables 1986/7, *Wissenschaftliche Verlagsgruppe MBH*, Stuttgart

Note the physical strength required to transport this weight of ice on a man's back down a mountainside. Their only aid seems to have been a sheepskin to insulate their backs. Then we saw the postmark of 1908 and were surprised that this was going on so comparatively recently.

CHAPTER 10

Tasting Ice Cream and Ices

". . . smell and taste form a single sense, of which the mouth
is the laboratory and the nose is the chimney; or, to speak more exactly, of
which one serves for the tasting of actual bodies and the other for the
savourings of their gases."

JEAN BRILLAT-SAVARIN, *The Physiology of Taste*, 1825.
Translated by M. F. K. Fisher.

"What is a good ice cream?"

"What are the qualities you look for in an ice cream?"

These are the two questions we are most commonly asked and yet books on ices, other than those written for the industry, ignore this most important feature, which is how to assess quality. Since our book is concerned with the production of quality ice cream, this chapter describes the guidelines that we used to judge whether a recipe was good enough to be included.

More importantly this chapter is particularly addressed to the hapless British who within living memory have no heritage of quality ice cream and little or no knowledge of how good ice cream should taste.

Part of the explanation must be that almost a whole generation was deprived of ice cream during and for some years after the Second World War. (Food rationing did not cease until 1954.) This, coupled with the British tolerance of poor-quality food, has enabled manufacturers to take advantage of the situation and sell us ice cream which, as Jane Grigson said, is "largely air and fakery".

It is a curious fact that childhood memories of ice cream, whether recalled accurately or not, remain the basis for adult judgements on taste. Obviously the British start off at a disadvantage compared with other nations.

But what also have to be taken into account at this stage are the differing national characteristics of ice cream. For example, the Americans will prefer ice cream that is sweeter, richer and softer than the Italians, who would look for a milkier, dense and colder ice, whereas the French would want a rich, very smooth ice cream with more sophisticated flavour.

However, the rise of the multi-national ice-cream companies is blurring these distinctions. For example, in Italy, a wide range of restaurants offer a dessert menu comprising an identical range of ice creams, all from identical freezers supplied by the company who make the desserts. We hope this monotonous diet will begin to pall, and in order to win back jaded diners restaurateurs will have their chefs produce their own ices again. Some of the lost characteristics and qualities of differing flavours and textures will happily be restored.

The problems of tasting are compounded by the fact that the image of ice cream promoted in magazines, books and advertisements is of rock-hard, frozen scoops of ice; never shown melting, which is the ideal state for tasting. Frozen hard, even the best ices are nearly inedible, and quite flavourless as the taste buds are anaesthetised at this temperature.

Ice cream should ideally be eaten between -15 to $-8°C/4$ to 18°F. The ideal temperature according to Arbuckle (*Ice Cream AVI*, Westport, Conn, 1986) is $-13°C/8°F$.

Sorbets and sherbets should be eaten below $-13°C/8°F$ and granitas when they are ready, straight from the freezer.

So, given the ice served at the correct temperature, how do we judge an ice cream? There are five criteria.

1. APPEARANCE

The colour of the ice cream should be appropriate to the flavour. Any whole fruit, nuts etc, that have been added to the ice cream should be evenly distributed. There should be no ice crystals on the surface and no evidence of shrinkage from the sides of the container.

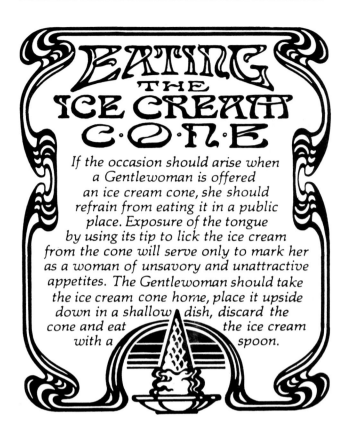

EATING THE ICE CREAM C·O·N·E

If the occasion should arise when a Gentlewoman is offered an ice cream cone, she should refrain from eating it in a public place. Exposure of the tongue by using its tip to lick the ice cream from the cone will serve only to mark her as a woman of unsavory and unattractive appetites. The Gentlewoman should take the ice cream cone home, place it upside down in a shallow dish, discard the cone and eat the ice cream with a spoon.

2. BODY

We consider the body of the ice cream to be everything you can detect with the eye before tasting. As it is scooped from the container to a plate, note the resistance of the ice cream. If it is too firm to scoop it will be uncomfortable to eat and too cold to taste. The body of the ice cream should not be waxy, gummy, crumbly, soggy or fluffy.

3. TEXTURE

Taste a sample; the initial texture should be smooth. Push it with the tongue on to the roof of the mouth. If it is rough but rapidly clears as the ice cream melts in the mouth the ice crystals are too large. If however a sandy roughness persists it is due to lactose crystallisation, caused by too much M.S.N.F. (see page 30).

4. FLAVOUR

Is the flavour appropriate to the mix? Is it too elusive or too overpowering? Flavour should be identifiable for what it is, and the ice cream should not be so rich that it swamps the flavour, nor the flavour so rich that you cannot eat more than one or two spoonfuls.

Sweetness is the element which most commonly offends; it is highly subjective, and in our experience it is the flavour that people comment on first. Since sugar is one of the cheapest ingredients in commercial ice cream, it is the one that is most likely to be overdone. Beware oversweetness killing the freshness of flavour, especially in fruit-based ice creams.

The flavour should not stop when the ice is swallowed. Does it leave a pleasant aftertaste? There should be neither cooked-milk flavour, nor any metallic or rancid flavours detectable in the ice cream.

5. MELT

The ice cream should melt to a creamy liquid. It should not remain like shaving foam, or separate, or curdle.

Appendices

Appendix 1

MILK AND CREAM FAT CONTENTS AND SUBSTITUTES

	U.S.		U.K.
Milk	3.35 per cent (whole)		4 (full cream)
Half and half	10.5 per cent		
		Light	12 per cent
Light	18 per cent	Single	18 per cent
Whipping U.S.A.	30 per cent		
Heavy	36 per cent	Whipping	36 per cent
		Double	48 per cent
		Clotted	55 per cent

Substitutes

To make *U.S. Heavy* or *U.K. Whipping*, use 3 parts U.K. double cream to 1 part whole milk.

Appendix 2

CRUSHED ICE AND SALT RATIOS FOR MAKING AND HARDENING ICES

Freezer size	Making			Hardening		
	Ice	Salt		Ice	Salt	
		Rock	Table cups			Rock	Table cups★★
2 qt★ (1.9 L)	10 lb	2	1⅓	5 lb	2	1⅓
4 qt★ (3.8 L)	15 lb	3	2	5 lb	3	2
6 qt★ (5.7 L)	20 lb	3½	2½	5 lb	3½	2½

★ U.S. quart = 32 fl oz
★★ U.S. cup = 250 ml

Appendix 3

VOLUME

Metric		Imperial		U.S.		
ml	litres	fl oz	pint	cup	fl oz	pint
25	.025					
30		1.0		⅛		
50		1.75				
62		2.0		¼		
75		2.5				
85.24		3.0		⅓		
100	.100	3.5				
125	.125	4.0		½	4.0	¼
142		5.0	¼			
150		5.25				
155		5.5				
170		6.0				
185		6.0		¾		
200		7.0				
220		7.5				
250	.250	8		1	8.0	½
255		9.0				
285		10	½			
500	.500	16.0		2	16.0	1
570		20	1.0			
1,000	1.0	32	1 pt 12 oz	4	32.0	2
1,115	1.10	40.0	2	5	40	2½

MISCELLANEOUS CONVERSIONS

Spoons to millilitres

One U.S. cup	Teaspoon	= 5 ml
	Tablespoon	= 15 ml
	48 teaspoons	= 250 ml
	or 16 tablespoons	
	or 8 fl oz	

Fractions of cups to ml to tablespoons

⅛ cup = 31.25 ml = 2 tablespoonfuls
¼ cup = 62.5 ml = 4 tablespoonfuls
⅜ cup = 93.75 ml = 6 tablespoonfuls = ¼ cup *plus* 2 Tbsp
½ cup = 125 ml = 8 tablespoonfuls
⅝ cup = 156.25 ml = 10 tablespoonfuls = ½ cup *plus* 2 Tbsp
¾ cup = 187.5 ml = 12 tablespoonfuls
⅞ cup = 218.75 ml = 14 tablespoonfuls = 1 cup *minus* 2 Tbsp
1 cup = 250 ml = 16 tablespoonfuls = 1 cup

...une trop grande quantité de liqueur ferait rater infailliblement la glace

ALCOHOL IN ICES

There is a considerable temptation to go on adding alcohol to an ice until the mixture tastes right but, because alcohol depresses the freezing point, adding more than a certain amount can result in a mix that never freezes.

Below are both the guidelines given as a simple rule of thumb and, for the enthusiastic mathematician, the formula on which they are based.

First check the freezer temperature (see page 47) to ensure that it is able to achieve a low enough temperature to freeze ices with the alcohol content you choose.

Depending on the alcohol used and the type of 'ice', the following rules apply in a 1 litre, 4 cup, 32 fl oz mix:

Spirits (40 per cent alcohol by volume) reduce the freezing point by
in sorbets: approx 0.6°C (1.1°F) per 15ml/1 Tablespoon added
in ice creams and parfaits: approx 1.0°C (1.8°F) per 15ml/1 Tablespoon added

Fortified wines, sherry and port (20 per cent alcohol by volume) reduce the freezing point by
in sorbets: approx 0.3°C (0.6°F) per 15ml/1 Tablespoon added
in ice creams and parfaits: approx 0.6°C (1.2°F) per 15ml/1 Tablespoon added

Wines (10 per cent alcohol by volume) reduce the freezing point by
in sorbets: approx 0.2°C (0.3°F) per 15ml/1 Tablespoon added
in ice creams and parfaits: approx 0.3°C (0.6°F) per 15ml/1 Tablespoon added

The mathematically minded may like to calculate it themselves:

$$dT = \frac{1860.C}{M(100-C)}$$

where C = % concentration
M = molecular weight
Molecular weight of EtOH = 46

For example:

1% EtOH in water $\quad dT = \frac{1860.1}{46.99} = 0.40°C$

1% EtOH in 35% solids mix. $\quad dT = \frac{1860.1}{46.65} = 0.62°C$

Explicit de coquina que est optima medicina.

"Here ends [the work] on cookery, which is the best medicine."

Quotation at end of second section,
The Forme of Cury, 1381

Useful Addresses

EQUIPMENT GENERAL
MAIL ORDER
Lakeland Plastics
Alexandra Buildings,
Windermere, Cumbria
LA23 1BQ.
Tel. 0153-948-8100.
Fax. 0153-948-8300.
Ice-cream machines, plastic
freezer boxes – all sizes – lolly
moulds, bowls, spatulas, simple
bombe moulds, whisks, freezer
boxes and bags, ice mats and ice
packs and most of the equipment
difficult to find elsewhere. Fast
and efficient mail order,
catalogue on request.

Nisbets
Kelso House, Waterloo Street,
Old Market, Bristol BS2 0PH.
Tel. 0117-955-5843
Fax. 0117-955-0036
Ice-carving tools and moulds.
Fridge and freezer
thermometers, excellent whisks,
ice-cream scoops/dippers.
Professional ice-cream machines,
from about £800.
General equipment for the
catering trade. Catalogue on
request.

U.S.A.
Williams Sonoma
P.O. Box 7456,
San Francisco CA 94120.
Tel. 415-421-7900
Tel. 1-800-541-2233
Pizelle makers and ice-cream
making equipment. Mail order
in U.S.A. only.

Digital thermometers
Nisbets
(see above)

**Rubber spoon-shaped
spatulas**
Rubbermaid is available from
Nisbets (above) and from
Divertimenti, London.
Tel 0171-935-0689
Mail order available on request.

U.S.A.
Rubbermaid, Winchester,
Virginia 22601
Tel. 703 667 8700.

Kulfi moulds
Popat Store
138 and 158 Ealing Road,
Wembley, Middlesex. HA0 4PH
Tel. 0181-902-4182 or
0181-903-6397.
Kulfi moulds in metal and
plastic. The only place we have
seen the stands to hold kulfi
moulds whilst they are in the
freezer. Personal shoppers only.

Moulds are also available from
other good Indian supply shops.

Silver leaf
Also referred to as Vark. Take
care that it is silver leaf and that
it is edible. Some is aluminium
leaf for the picture framing
world! You are safe buying it
from The Curry Club which
only sells silver leaf. 6 sheets
from around £4.

The Curry Club
39 Staffordshire Street,
Peckham,
London SE15 5TL
Tel. 0171-639-3456
Fax. 0171-639-3752

Cone-maker shapes
Mail order details from:
Randal and Juli Marr,
Magdalene House Designs,
Magdalene House,
Langthorne, Bedale,
North Yorkshire DL8 1PQ
Tel. 0167-742-4332

Ice-cream equipment
FRANCE
E. Dehillerin (ask for Frank)
18–20 Rue Coquilliere,
Paris 75001, France.
Tel. (1) 42 36 53 13.
    (1) 45-08-86-83
Excellent range of elaborate ice-
cream moulds and bombes, and
ice-cream moulds in stainless
steel; cone shaped and
Neapolitan rectangular for hokey
pokey. Saccrometers and
eprouvettes. Mail order,
catalogue on request.

Melamine spoons
Leifheit
4, Eastman Road,
Acton, London W3 7QS.
Tel. 0181-749-7211.

U.S.A.
Polder
200 Central Avenue,
Hartsdale, New York 10530.
Tel. 914-683-3733.
Melamine spoons in shapes that
work.

Ice-cream machines
Gaggia
Crown House,
Milecross Road,
Halifax, West Yorkshire
HX1 4HN.
Tel. 0142-223-0295
Contact for nearest stockist.

Magimix
Magimix (U.K.) Ltd.,
115a High Street,

Godalming,
Surrey GU7 1AQ.
Tel. 048-342-7411.
Contact for nearest stockist.

U.S.A.
Norland Aluminum Products
Minneapolis, MN 55416.
Tel. (612) 920 2888.
Contact for nearest stockist.

White Mountain Freezer Inc.
Lincoln Avenue Extension,
P.O. Box 459,
Winchendon, Mass. 01475.
Tel. 508-297-0015.
Fax. 508-297-0041.
Ice and salt hand and electric
freezers with stainless steel cans
and wooden buckets, from 2
quart USA to 5 gallon USA.
To order direct call in USA on
Tel. 1-800-343-0065.

SUPPLIES
Milk powder
Nido Full Cream Milk Powder
Dietetics department,
Nestlé U.K. Ltd.,
St Georges House,
Croydon CR9 1NR.
Tel. 0181-667-5111.
Available from most Middle
Eastern shops or will supply
directly, mail order.

Scented geraniums
National Pelargonium
Collection
Fibrex Nurseries,
Honeybourne Road,
Pebworth, nr Stratford on Avon
CV37 8XT.
Tel. 0178-972-0788, for opening
hours and travel directions.

**Flavoured teas for sorbets
and ices**
Algerian Coffee Stores
52 Old Compton Street,
London W1V 6PB.
Tel. 0171-437-2480.

Sa'alab or salap
Turkish Food Centre,
Ridley Road,
London E8 2NZ.
Tel. 0171-249-4872.

Elderflower Cordial
Belvoir Fruit Farms,
Belvoir, Grantham, Lincs.
Tel. 0147-687-0286 for nearest
stockist.

Vanilla
J Sainsbury Special Selection
Lakeland Plastics (see under
equipment)
Dean and Deluca, USA
(see under mail order)

ASSOCIATIONS AND
GROUPS
Ice Cream Alliance
92 Gray's Inn Road,
London WC1X 8AH.
Tel. 0171-405-0712.
U.K. Independent Trade
Association.

U.S.A.
Ice Screamers
P.O. Box 465
Warrington P.A. 18976.
Bi-monthly newsletter and
association for collectors of all
items associated with ice cream
and ice-cream parlours.

International Ice Cream
Association
888 Sixteenth Street, N.W.,
Washington, D.C. 20006.
Tel. 202-296-4250.

ICE-CREAM COURSES
Courses range from one week to
many months, contact:-
Ed Marks
Ice Screamers
2733 Lititz Pike
P.O. Box 5487
Lancaster P.A. 17601

U.K.
Reading University

U.S.A.
Maryland University

BOOKSHOPS
Books for Cooks
4 Blenheim Crescent
London W11 1NN
Tel. 0171-221-1992
    0171-221-8102
Fax. 0171-221-1517

U.S.A.
Kitchen Arts and Letters
1435 Lexington Avenue
(between 93 and 94th St)
New York
NY 10128
Tel. 212-876-5550.
Fax. 212-876-3584

MAIL ORDER
In U.S.A. any locally
unobtainable ingredients can be
obtained by mail order from:-
Dean and Deluca
560 Broadway, New York,
N.Y. 10012.
Tel. 212-431-1691 or
    800-221-7714

There are many combinations and ways of making soda fountain dishes. *The Dispensers Formulary* or *Soda Water Guide*, published in 1915 by *The Soda Fountain* magazine, had over 3,000 recipes for soda fountains and was considered to be the Bible of soda fountains.

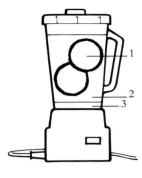

MILK SHAKE

1. 2 scoops ice cream
2. 20 oz milk, full cream
3. 1 Tbsp malted milk powder (optional for malted milk shake)
4. Liquidise for about 30 seconds or until smooth and thick.

BANANA SPLIT

1. Ripe banana, split lengthwise
2. 3 scoops ice cream assorted flavours
3. ½ oz each of three toppings, one on each ice cream: 4. Whipped cream; 5. Crushed nuts; 6. Cherries

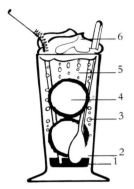

ICE CREAM SODA

1. 1½ oz syrup or fruit in syrup
2. 1 soda spoon ice cream, whipped cream or flavoured cream
3. Soda or carbonated water to ¾ full
4. 2 scoops ice cream
5. More of 3 to fill glass
6. Whipped cream

Serve with straw and soda spoon.

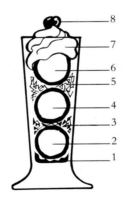

SUNDAE

1. ½ oz of syrup or crushed fruit
2. 2 scoops ice cream
3. 1 oz of syrup or crushed fruit
4. Nuts, crushed
5. Whipped cream
6. Cherry

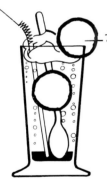

or

7. Balance a scoop of ice cream on the rim of the glass.

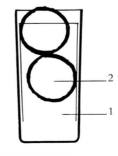

KNICKERBOCKER GLORY

An English adaptation of the Knickerbocker Sundae which originated in New York.

1. ½ oz chocolate syrup
2. Scoop of vanilla ice cream
3. ½ oz crushed raspberry
4. Scoop of ice cream
5. ½ oz crushed pineapple
6. Scoop of ice cream
7. Whipped cream
8. Brandied or glacé cherry

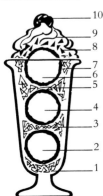

AMERICAN PARFAIT

1. Soda spoon of syrup or crushed fruit
2. 1 scoop ice cream
3. Soda spoon of syrup or crushed fruit
4. 1 scoop ice cream
5. Soda spoon of syrup or crushed fruit
6. 1 scoop ice cream
7. Soda spoon of syrup or crushed fruit
8. Soda spoon of crushed nuts or nuts in syrup
9. Whipped cream
10. Cherry

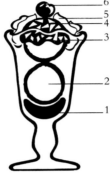

FLOAT

see page 27
1. Milk Shake or Soda
2. Scoops of Ice Cream

Selected Bibliography

Ministry of Agriculture and Fisheries, *Food Standards Report on Cream*, H.M.S.O., London (1982)

Anderson, *The Complete Book of Homemade Ice Cream*, Barton, New York (1973)

Frandsen/Arbuckle, *Ice Cream and Related Products*, AVI Westport, Connecticut (1961)

Arbuckle, *Ice Cream* 4th Edition, AVI Westport, Connecticut (1986)

Wendell Arbuckle, *Ice Cream Recipes and Formulas*, General Print, Maryland (1987)

Arbuckle, *Ice Cream Store Handbook*, Arbuckle & Co, Maryland (1983)

Arbuckle, *The Little Ice Cream Book*, Arbuckle & Co, Maryland (1981)

Walter Bachman, *Swiss Bakery and Confectionery*, Maclaren, London (1949)

Max Baer, *The Preparation and Processing of Ice Cream Mix*, Olsen, Milwaukee (1927)

Filippo Baldini, *De' Sorbetti*, Arnaldo Forni Editore, Naples (1784)

Gretel Beer, *Ice Cream Dishes*, Herbert Jenkins, London (1952)

Boeglin, *Sundaes, Ice & Cream Sodas, How to Make,* Jenkins, London (1927)

Bonauguri & Mairi, *Tecnica del Fredo*, Hoepli, Milan (1977)

Capeder, *I Gelati*, Falbri, Milan (1983)

Collett, *Ice Creams*, Black, London (1979)

Colpi, *The Italian Factor*, Mainstream, Edinburgh (1991)

J. Stevens Cox, *Ice Cream in Queen Victoria's Reign*, The Toucan Press, Guernsey C.I. (1970)

Society of Dairy Technology, *Ice Cream*, London (1981)

Dallison/Cartez, *Glaces Dessing/Tolera*, Paris (1982)

Daly Brothers, *What Every Ice Cream Dealer Should Know*, New York (1914)

de Gouy, *Ice Cream and Ice Cream Desserts*, Dover, New York (1938)

Paul Dickson, *The Great American Ice Book*, Atheneum, New York (1972)

J. & C. Dueker, *The Old-Fashioned Homemade Ice Cream Cook Book*, Bobbs-Merrill, Indianapolis (1974)

G. Dumont-Lespine, *Entrements et boissons glacés*, Max Glottschalk, Paris

Edwards/Croft, *The Great Ice Cream Book*, Absolute, Bath (1984)

Monica Ellis, *Ice and Ice Houses Through the Ages*, Southampton University (1982)

Farbi, *I Gelati*, Farbi, Milan (1989)

Leonard R. M. Feltham, *The Making of Ice Cream* 1st edition, Heywood, London (1934)

Leonard R. M. Feltham, *Service for Soda Fountains*, Heywood, London (1936)

Walter W. Fisk, *The Book of Ice Cream*, Macmillan, New York (1924)

C. E. Francatelli, *The Royal Confectioner*, Chapman and Hall, London (1874)

Glass Circle No 5, Various Antique Collectors Club, London (1986)

Fernanda Gosetti, *Il Gelato*, Fabbri Editori, Milan (1985)

Harvey and Hill, *Milk Products*, Lewis, London (1937)

Hayne, *Ice-Cream Making on a Small Scale*, McLaren, London (*c.* 1920)

Hayward-Tyler, *Aerated Water Machinery*, Chester-Master, Gloucester (1893)

Heller's Guide for Ice Cream Makers, B. Heller & Co., Chicago (1918)

Phyllis Hobson, *Making Ice Cream, Ices and Sherbets*, Garden Way, Vermont (1977)

Bernice Hurst, *The Homemade Book of Ice Cream*, Apple Press, London (1934)

Ice Cream Industry Year Book 1958–59, Benn, London

Felicity Kinross, *Coffee and Ices*, London (1991)

Klein, *The Joy of Ice Cream*, Barron Woodbury, New York (1985)

Simon I. Leon, *Candy and ice cream making (Encyclopaedia of)*, Chemical Pub., New York (1959)

Mrs A. B. Marshall, *The Book of Ices* (4th edition), Marshall's, London (1885)

Mrs A. B. Marshall, *The Book of Ices*, Marshall's, London (1926)

Mrs A. B. Marshall, *Fancy Ices*, Marshall's, London (1894)

Mrs A. B. Marshall, *Marshall's Catalogue of Moulds*, Marshall's, London (*c.* 1880)

P. Michael, *Ices and Soda Fountain Drinks*, Maclaren & Sons, London (*c.* 1925)

Ojakangas, *Great Old-Fashioned American Desserts*, Dutton, New York (1987)

Ralph Pomeroy, *The Ice Cream Connection*, Paddington Press, London (1926)

Folco Portinari, *Voglia di Gelato*, Idealibri, Milan (1987)

S. Beaty Pownall, *The "Queen" Cookery Books ICES*, Horace Cox, London (1899)

G. Preti, *Il Gelato Artigianale Italiano*, Hoepli, Milan (1985)

Quinn, *Old-fashioned Homemade Ice Cream*, Dover, New York (1984)

Robert G. Reid, *Ice Cream Plant and Manufacture*, A. J. Rayment, London (1924)

J. Rothwell, *Ice Cream Making*, Reading University (1985)

C. Herman Senn, *Luncheon and Dinner Sweets including the Art of Ice Making*, Ward Lock & Co., London (*c.* 1920)

Seranne, *Complete Book of Desserts*, Faber Cook Book Club, London (1967)

Wayne Smith, *Ice Cream Dippers*, Walkersville, Maryland (1986)

Soda Fountain, *The Dispensers Formulary or Soda Water Guide*, Haynes, New York (1915)

Marco del Soldo, *Manual Practico del Gelatiere*, De Vecchi, Milan (1986)

Spiller, *Wild About Ice Cream*, Barrons, New York (1985)

Jim Tarantino, *Sorbets*, Crossing Press, Freedom, California (1988)

William Terrington, *Cooling Cups and Dainty Drinks*, Routledge, London (1869)

Fred T. Vine, *Ices, Plain and Decorated*, British Baker & Confectioner, London (1890)

Fred T. Vine, *Ices for Shop Sale*, British Baker & Confectioner, London (1910)

Wheaton, *Victorian Ice Cream and Ices*, MOMA/Scribners, New York (1984)

Gaylord Willis, *Old Uncle Gaylord's Ice Cream Book*, Brandon, San Francisco (1975)

Indexes

RECIPES

Where not specified the recipe is for an ice cream.

The Authors

ROBIN WEIR

Is a Director of a product development and marketing company, has had a lifelong interest in food and is an enthusiastic amateur cook. He has recently published *The Compleat Mustard* (written in association with Rosamond Man) and is Adviser to a major supermarket chain.

CAROLINE LIDDELL

Is a professional food writer and has taught at Prue Leith's school. She has worked with several well known cookery presenters; recently she assisted the Roux Brothers on both their television series, *At Home with the Roux Brothers*, and the accompanying book. Her other previous books include *The Wholefood Cookery Book* and *The New Baking*.